Brazil in British and Irish Archives

Brazil
in British and Irish Archives

SECOND EDITION

Oliver Marshall

Centre for Brazilian Studies
University of Oxford

Oliver Marshall is a Research Associate at the Centre for Brazilian Studies, University of Oxford. His publications include English, Irish and Irish-American Pioneer Settlers in Nineteenth-Century Brazil *(Oxford, 2005).*

ISBN 0-9544070-8-3

© Centre for Brazilian Studies, 2007

First edition, 2002
Second edition, 2007

Designed by Meg Palmer, Third Column
Printed by Lightning Source

Contents

Foreword

The Centre for Brazilian Studies, established in 1997, is a University of Oxford centre of advanced study and research. One of its principal aims has been to promote a greater knowledge and understanding of Brazil – its culture, society, politics, economy, ecology, international relations and, not least, its history – through a programme of lectures, seminars, workshops and conferences, research projects, and publications. The Centre publishes working papers, research papers and monographs. *Brazil in British and Irish Archives* (2002), a guide to the rich and diverse manuscript collections, public and private, relating to Brazil in British and Irish archives, libraries and museums, was the first book of reference published by the Centre. It has been updated and expanded for this second edition.

The guide ranges from the 16th to the 20th century but, not surprisingly, is particularly strong on the 19th and early 20th centuries when Britain was the pre-eminent political and economic power and also had significant social, cultural and intellectual influence in Brazil. It will be of great value to researchers in the UK, Brazil and elsewhere on many aspects of Brazilian history but especially relations between Brazil and Britain. The publication of a guide to archives with material on Brazil throughout the UK is also in keeping with the Oxford Centre's national responsibilities in the field of Brazilian Studies.

I am most grateful to Regina Weinberg, Executive Director, and other members of the Board of Directors of Vitae – Apoio à Cultura, Educação e Promoção Social in São Paulo for generously agreeing to fund both the initial research and the publication of the first edition of this important guide. This second edition draws on the additional research carried out for the publication of the book in Portuguese translation *Brasil nos arquivos britânicos e irlandeses: Guia das fontes* (2007), financed by the Brazilian Ministry of Culture as part of its 'Projeto Resgate Barão do Rio Branco' coordinated by Dra Esther Caldas Bertoletti.

The research for both the original guide and the Portuguese edition/ second edition in English was carried out with imagination and persistence by Oliver Marshall, one of the Centre's Research Associates.

Leslie Bethell
Director
Centre for Brazilian Studies
University of Oxford

Introduction

In 1807–8 the Portuguese royal family and court was transferred under British naval escort to Rio de Janeiro ahead of Napoleon's armies advancing on Lisbon. This event drastically altered the way in which Brazil related to the rest of the world. Suddenly Brazil found itself open to direct foreign trade and investment, and Britain immediately established itself as the country's main trading partner, exerting enormous economic and political influence.

One enduring legacy of the close relationship that was to develop between Britain and Brazil is the existence in the British Isles of a wealth of archival holdings relating to Brazil. This is the first guide devoted to this rich resource. *Brazil in British and Irish Archives* is not an inventory of manuscripts of Brazilian interest – an impossible task given the size of many of the collections – but instead sets out to assist researchers in identifying potential sources, with individual repositories listed place-by-place.

The collections that are listed and described in the guide are extremely varied, offering unique insights into many topics of importance in the history of Brazil. The transfer of the Portuguese royal family to Brazil, mediation leading to Brazilian independence, regional rebellions and conflicts with neighbouring countries, the suppression of the slave trade, the construction of railways and the development of the coffee trade and also of banking are just a few examples of topics for which important manuscript sources are held in Britain. And although archival material illustrating Brazil's so-called 'British century' – the 19th century – naturally represents a very substantial proportion of the guide's entries, there is also much more besides. Scattered between several archives, for example, are important items documenting English and Irish attempts in the 17th century to establish settlements or trading posts along the Amazon – a part of South America that was also to attract the interest of British explorers, missionaries, investors, naturalists and anthropologists in the 19th century. Also of some significance are letters and other reports dating from the 17th and 18th centuries presenting views of competing European interests in the northeast, south and elsewhere in Brazil.

Nor are the archives lacking in 20th-century material relating to Brazil. Although Britain gradually lost its pre-eminent economic position in Brazil to the United States, major financial interests – such as railways, public utility companies, manufacturing industries and banking – were retained well into that century. While British archival holdings relating to these topics can sometimes be disappointing, frequently collections are found to feature very useful material. British archival holdings for the 20th century also testify to keen interest within the Foreign Office and other British government departments in Brazilian internal political developments and Brazilian external relations. In the 1930s and 1940s, for example, Brazilian attitudes to fascism in Italy and national socialism in Germany were carefully observed by British diplomats. There were negotiations regarding Brazil as a possible home for refugees fleeing Europe before, during and after World War II.

For most of the centuries covered by the archival material described in the guide, Britain was a global power with a vast empire. This dimension is addressed by many manuscript holdings, with documents found on diverse topics ranging from the fate of an obscure Brazilian pirate marooned in the far-off Maldive Islands, to the cod trade from Newfoundland to northern Brazil, to the long-lasting frontier dispute involving British Guiana, to the suppression of the Atlantic slave trade, as already mentioned. All these subjects – and many more besides – can be explored in British archives.

The archival repositories described in the guide vary enormously. Some are major national collections containing a great deal of material of Brazilian interest on a diverse range of topics, often spanning centuries. In such cases, the guide presents general descriptions of the Brazil-related holdings, with examples of representative or exceptionally notable individual documents or files given by way of illustration. The entry for the National Archives is the most obvious case in point, its vast holdings representing by far the richest source of Brazil-related archival material in Britain. The importance of the National Archives' collections is reflected in the number of pages in the guide that are devoted to describing the various archives that have been deposited there – a far greater proportion of the guide than is given to any other single repository. On the other extreme, an entry for a town or county record office may include the listing of the repository's entire Brazil-related holdings. For such archives, holdings of Brazilian interest will comprise a very small proportion of the personal papers of a particular diplomat, politician, naval officer or business, often amounting to no more than a few isolated documents. While such disparity among collections may at times appear odd, it was felt important to include all those repositories where manuscripts relating to Brazil have been identified, if only to enable users to deduce from an archive's entry that the range of material one might have expected or hoped to find is not in fact held.

Although considerable efforts were made to ensure that as wide a range of archival holdings as possible is described in the guide – public records, business records, private papers of individual politicians, naval officers, explorers and travellers – there clearly remain gaps. These occur mainly where records have either not been kept or have been destroyed or where they have otherwise disappeared. For example, searches revealed a surprising lack of correspondence or other papers relating to Irish-based religious societies who sent missionaries to Brazil. And while the records of British businesses that had dealings with Brazil – as importers of Brazilian produce, as exporters of British manufactures or as direct or indirect investors – provide the basis of many of the archival listings, collections can be disappointing or, for many key businesses, non-existent. Railway records, for example, are at best patchy and for many companies virtually or completely non-existent. The same appears to be so for construction industries, whose legacies endure in many parts of Brazil. For example, the Scottish architectural ironworks designer and producer Walter MacFarlane & Co., also known as the Saracen Foundry, exported to Brazil numerous pre-fabricated buildings. Although some of these buildings survive intact, such as the public market in Manaus and, most notable of all, Fortaleza's Teatro José de Alencar, the business records and original architectural drawings have not been so fortunate. All that survive are catalogues and other sales publications.[1]

Even business archives that were known to have been held privately in Britain are not necessarily secure. In frustration, for example, one can point to the apparent disappearance of the papers of the Rio de Janeiro Flour Mills and Granaries Ltd (usually referred to as Rio Flour) and its associated company, Frumentum Shipping Company, after they had been consulted by historians.[2] For some collections the situation is worse still, in that their Brazil-related papers have vanished before being

---

1   These are held by Heritage Engineering [www.heritageengineering.com] which purchased the MacFarlane name and specialises in the reproduction and renovation of architectural iron structures.

2   Peter Walne, ed (1973), *A Guide to Manuscript Sources for the History of Latin America and the Caribbean in the British Isles* (London), pp. 473 and 489; and Richard Graham (1966), 'A British industry in Brazil: Rio Flour Mills, 1886–1920', *Business History*, 8/1, pp. 13–38. Fortunately, some of Rio Flour's papers were microfilmed, with copies held by the University of Texas at Austin's Benson Library.

explored by historians. The records of the formerly Croydon-based woodbrokers Churchill & Sim Ltd included some intriguing reports and correspondence dated 1811–14 concerning consignments of brazilwood being shipped from Brazil to England and shipments of general merchandise being sent out from England and destined for Rio de Janeiro merchants. With the liquidation of Churchill & Sim Ltd in the 1990s, the records appear, for the time being at least, to have been lost, although hopefully they remain in a solicitor's vault or other secure location, ready to be rediscovered in years to come.[3]

Fortunately, however, many business archives – and other privately held collections – have been deposited in secure repositories, such as the Guildhall and University College libraries (for business records) or the British Library or local record offices (for political papers). In a few cases important Brazil-related collections have been transferred to university libraries in the United States or elsewhere abroad. For example, the records accumulated in the London headquarters of the St John d'El Rey Mining Company (an exceptionally well-organised and complete business history collection) are held by the Benson Library of the University of Texas at Austin, supplementing the operational records that remain in the company offices in Nova Lima, Minas Gerais.[4] Similarly for diplomatic papers, the important Brazil-related correspondence of Sir Charles Stuart, Baron de Rothsay (1779–1845) is in the Lilly Library of the University of Indiana, Bloomington. Included amongst the over 1,500 documents is correspondence from many influential British, Brazilian and Portuguese political and military figures, especially concerning Stuart's mediation efforts leading to Portugal's recognition of Brazilian independence in 1825.[5] Of more recent creation, Amnesty International's International Secretariat has transferred its archive to the International Institute of Social History in Amsterdam. Covering the period 1961–97, the records include much material relating to Brazil, most notably the files concerning political prisoners during the period of the military dictatorship (1964–85).[6]

---

3   Walne, pp. 457–58. The National Register of Archives (see p. 229) holds a catalogue of the papers (*NRA 22594 Churchill*) which, while intriguing in the description, offers no clues to their current location.
4   William Callaghan (1979), 'Gold mining on the Brazilian frontier: the Archives of the St John d'El Rey Mining Company', *The Library Chronicle of the University of Texas*, 11, pp. 27–32. The mine is now owned by Mineração Morro Velho, a wholly owned subsidiary of South Africa's AngloGold Company.
5   For a full description of the holdings, see under '*Stuart MSS*' at www.indiana.edu/~liblilly/.
6   For information on the Amnesty International archive, see www.iisg.nl/archives.

Despite these various shortcomings, there is no doubt that manuscript holdings in Britain and Ireland are a rich resource for the study of many areas of Brazilian history. Producing this guide has confirmed that fact, and it is hoped that the guide conveys some of the wealth and diversity of this resource.

October 2002

*　　　*　　　*

The publication of *Brazil in British and Irish Archives* in Portuguese provided an opportunity to produce a revised and expanded English-language edition of the guide. On a most basic level, over the past five years there have been changes to names of institutions (none more important than that of the Public Record Office, now the National Archives), new addresses and opening hours, all of which have been added to the guide. Far more significant, however, is the fact that this new edition includes more institutions as well as additional archival collections in repositories that were previously listed. Repositories that are entirely new to the guide are the British Postal Museum & Archive (postal history), the Wiener Library (the Holocaust and German Jewish refugees), the Birmingham Archdiocesan Archives and the Cornwall Record Office (migration), the Gloucestershire Archives (naval history), the Caernarfon Record Office and Guernsey's Island Archives Service and the Priaulx Library (shipping and trade) and Bolton Archive and Local Studies Service (the textile industry). While of course the material within these collections that is described varies considerably in significance, all offer valuable insights into Brazilian history generally, and the Brazilian–British relationship in particular.

As well as these entirely 'new' collections, included are descriptions of additional material 'discovered' in archival repositories that were included in the original edition of the guide. Of particular note are Cambridge University Library's holdings of the archives of the British and Foreign Bible Society and, in complete contrast, the archives of Vickers, one of Britain's most important shipbuilders and manufacturers of armaments. Other significant additions to the guide include Brazilian consular archives and also records concerning coal exports that are held in the Glamorgan Record Office; company records that are held by the Dundee City Archive and Record Centre that concern jute sales to, and rope manufacturing in, São Paulo; documents held by the National Archives of Scotland concerning Scottish emigrants and merchants in Brazil; naval records in the National Library of Scotland; additional papers of a coffee merchant in London's Guildhall Library; and records held by the Lancashire Record Office of a manufacturer of looms and related equipment.

Despite the guide's expansion, there naturally remain omissions, some of which were discussed in the guide's earlier introduction (see pp. xiii–xiv). A mysterious absence from this is any archival holdings of the Vestey Group, a British corporation that, since the late 19th century, has had a significant presence in ranching and commercial agriculture in Rio Grande do Sul, São Paulo and elsewhere in Brazil. Although efforts were made to identify Vestey material for inclusion in this edition, no collections were found. If the company has created and maintained an archive, it seems that any holdings are beyond the reach of researchers.

Considerable efforts were also made to locate archives relating to missionaries from Ireland in Brazil, long the most significant point of contact between the two countries. Although, to this day, religious orders have dispatched Irish priests and nuns to Brazil, records are either non-existent, closed to researchers or hidden away, uncatalogued, amidst wider diocesan holdings.

But even if these and the other highlighted 'missing' archives never emerge, other collections of importance surely will be made available. Thanks to constant advances of the Internet and the catalogues of individual libraries, museums and record offices, many of which are linked via electronic networks (see pp. 250–52), identifying relevant archival holdings is becoming evermore straightforward. It seems certain that Brazil-related resources in British and Irish archives will continue to emerge.

October 2007

*   *   *

ACKNOWLEDGEMENTS

I would like to express my thanks to Professor Leslie Bethell, Director of the Centre for Brazilian Studies, Oxford, whose idea it was to produce a guide to resources relating to Brazil held by British archives, libraries and other institutions. Over a period of months, the scope of the project changed as it became apparent that the most useful guide would focus exclusively on Brazil-related manuscript and other archival holdings. The project was generously funded by the Vitae foundation, without whose support archival research and the production of the first edition of the guide, *Brazil in British and Irish Archives*, would not have been possible. Research for the second edition was made possible thanks to funding from the Brazilian Ministry of Culture to produce a separate Portuguese edition of the guide.

In researching this guide, archivists and librarians throughout Britain and Ireland have been extremely helpful, responding to general appeals for uncovering Brazil-related material and replying to specific telephone and written queries. I tried personally to visit as many repositories as possible and I am very grateful for the on-the-spot assistance that I received from librarians and archivists, who produced seemingly endless boxes or files of documents that I had requested and who frequently suggested other collections that might be worth investigating.

Apart from Professor Bethell who offered many suggestions and comments, I must also thank the historians Malcolm Deas, Marshall C. Eakin, Richard Graham, Colin Lewis and João Roberto Martins. All either responded to my queries regarding the location of a particular collection (or collections) of papers or provided more general advice concerning Brazil-related archival holdings in Britain and Ireland. As always, Alan Biggins, Librarian at the Hispanic & Luso-Brazilian Council (Canning House), was exceptionally encouraging and provided many helpful suggestions.

In Oxford, I am grateful to Margaret Hancox, Julie Smith, Ailsa Thom and Kate Candy, administrators of the Centre for Brazilian Studies, for their support during each stage leading to, and including, the actual production of the guide.

Several other individuals were involved at the production stage: Meg Palmer, the designer, came up with many solutions regarding the presentation of the text; Margaret Doyle was an extremely helpful copy-editor; and Henry Stedman was a very accurate proofreader.

Oliver Marshall
London
October 2002 and November 2007

LOCATION OF ARCHIVES

SHETLAND

Lerwick

SCOTLAND

Aberdeen

Dundee

Glasgow   Edinburgh

NORTHERN
IRELAND

Belfast

Durham

Northallerton

Preston   Bradford   Hull

Bolton   Leeds

Liverpool   Manchester
Leigh

Dublin

EIRE

Caernarfon

Nottingham

Stafford   Norwich

Wolverhampton
Aberystwyth   Birmingham

Dudley   Coventry   Cambridge

Warwick

WALES   Aylesbury

Chelmsford

Gloucester   Hatfield

Cardiff   Oxford   London

Chippenham   ENGLAND

Southampton

Dorchester   Chichester

Exeter   Portsmouth

Truro

Porthcurno

GUERNSEY

St Peter
Port

ABERDEEN

UNIVERSITY OF ABERDEEN LIBRARY

Special Collections & Archives
King's College
Aberdeen AB24 3SW

www.abdn.ac.uk/diss/historic/

Tel: (01224) 272 598 • **Fax:** (01224) 273 891
E-mail: speclib@abdn.ac.uk

Open: Mon–Fri 9.30am–4.30pm.
Closed: Public holidays and over Christmas and New Year.
Admission: Advance notice preferred.

Introduction:

The Special Collections & Archives section of the University of Aberdeen Library holds the university's own archives, records of local families, estates, institutions and businesses as well as a number of manuscript collections covering wider Scottish, British and international interests.

Collections:

Only one University of Aberdeen Library manuscript collection with Brazil-related content has been identified.

> *AU MS 851 to 853; AU MS 2988/1 to 3* – **James W.H. Trail**
> *English*
> Of particular Brazil-related importance in this collection of the papers of James William Helenus Trail (1851–1919), professor of botany at the University of Aberdeen, are the three journal volumes relating to an expedition to the Brazilian Amazon. The account covers the Atlantic voyage to Pará (Belém) and Trail's extensive travels within the Amazon between September 1873 and March 1875, commenting on the topography, flora and fauna that he encountered. Other material includes a catalogue of plants collected during the expedition and a copy of a paper read by Trail at various meetings, entitled 'Notes by a naturalist in the valley of the Amazon'.

ABERYSTWYTH

NATIONAL LIBRARY OF WALES / LLYFRGELL GENEDLAETHOL CYMRU

www.llgc.org.uk

Department of Manuscripts
Aberystwyth SY23 3BU

Tel: (01970) 632 800 • **Fax:** (01970) 632 983
E-mail: holi@llgc.org.uk

Open: Mon–Fri 9.30am–6pm, Sat 9.30am–5pm.
Closed: Public holidays and first full week of October.
Admission: Proof of identity required.

Introduction:

The National Library of Wales is the largest research library in Wales and a legal deposit library of British and Irish publications. The manuscript holdings of the National Library mainly relate to the history and culture of Wales. Where material concerning overseas countries is held, the creator or recipient of the documents usually has a close link with Wales.

Collections:

Brazil-related manuscript holdings identifiable in the National Library of Wales are almost always small in number and found scattered within much broader collections. Most of the library's manuscript holdings are listed online at www.llgc.org.uk:81/index.htm (select the 'manuscripts: schedules' database), although many of the catalogue entries are not detailed enough to be helpful in a Brazil-related keyword search.

Bute Papers: Frederick Grigg
English
Brazil-related letters appear within the personal correspondence and papers of John, 2nd Marquis of Bute (1804–55). Most of the relevant items concern the appointment of Frederick Grigg in 1830 as commissioner of arbitration at Rio de Janeiro, under the United Commission established under the treaties for the prevention of the slave trade [*April–Aug 1830 – L11/26, 33, 42 et seq.*]. Other Grigg correspondence includes a March 1838 report on the state of Brazil, including the election of a new regent (and hostility from

Rio Grande do Sul and Bahia to the government), and the continued importation of African slaves [*L15/40*]. There are also letters and papers from Grigg on his work in Rio de Janeiro, including refuting allegations laid before the British Parliament in 1838 that the Mixed Commission had received slaves hired out by the Brazilian government [*L16/136*].

Penralley Papers: George Augustus Bowring
English
The papers accumulated by the James and Williams families of Penralley, Rhaeadr, Radonshire include several late 18th- and early 19th-century series of letters, usually sent while their writers served in the Navy, with brief mentions of Brazil. Only the letters of George Augustus Bowring (1825–55) include detailed discussions of Brazil. Born in England, Bowring spent most of his childhood in Oporto, Portugal (1833–44) from where in 1844 he moved to Brazil, living mainly in Aracati (in the province of Ceará), but also in the city of Pará (Belém). In 1849 Bowring returned to England. The eight Brazilian letters [*L1244–L1251*] describe Aracati and Pará, discuss business affairs (including Bowring's deliberations on becoming a Catholic for reasons of personal advancement) and marriage prospects in Britain.

Powis Papers: Robert Clive
English
In March 1743, Robert Clive (1725–74) – the future Robert, Lord Clive, proconsul of India – set sail for India as a 17-year-old East India Company clerk. Clive's ship, the *Winchester*, followed the normal route, sailing between West Africa and Brazil, with the intention of picking up the southeast trade winds for the passage around the Cape of Good Hope. In September 1743 the *Winchester* called at Pernambuco (Recife) for repairs, remaining there until February 1744. Documents [in Box VII of the collection] include *Winchester*'s log and several letters from Clive to his father, describing the Atlantic crossing and providing some detailed impressions of the city of Pernambuco and its hinterland.

Dr Joan Richards Letters
English
A volume [*Misc. Vol. 333*] of extracts of letters (1965–66) from Joan Richards to her father in Aberystwyth, recounting experiences as a missionary amongst the Waurá tribe of the Xingú in Mato

Grosso. Richards' work included preparing a translation of the New Testament into the Waurá language.

Welsh in South America
Welsh (some English and Spanish)
In 1850 a Welsh agricultural settlement scheme was launched in Rio Grande do Sul, an effort that gradually collapsed. Some of the survivors moved south to Patagonia, where they joined other Welsh immigrants who had arrived in 1865, with whom they shared their Brazilian pioneering experience. Although the National Library of Wales has important manuscript holdings relating to Welsh emigration, including much on Patagonia, very little material exists on the Rio Grande do Sul settlement attempt. Apart from reports, diaries, letters, articles, poetry, etc. concerning Patagonian experiences, a few documents – including the following – offer at least passing mentions to the Brazilian colonisation attempts:

- *MS. 6242E* – Letter (in English) outlining briefly the story of Welsh emigration (c. 1851) to Rio Grande do Sul, Oct 1895.

- *MS. 16827C* – Notebook (in Welsh) of Edward Thomas of Foel, Llangadfan, of his travels in Patagonia and Brazil, 1886–93.

- *MS. 18175B* – Extracts (in Welsh) from the diaries and letters of T. Benbow Phillips, a particularly important source for the history of Welsh settlement in Brazil.

Note: Smaller manuscript holdings relating to the Welsh in South America are held by the Library of the University of Wales, Bangor [www.bangor.ac.uk/archives], although Brazil-related content has not been identified.

AYLESBURY

CENTRE FOR BUCKINGHAMSHIRE STUDIES

County Hall
Walton Street
Aylesbury HP20 1UU

www.buckscc.gov.uk/archives

Tel: (01296) 382 587 • **Fax:** (01296) 382 771
E-mail: archives@buckscc.gov.uk

Open: Mon–Thurs 9am–5.15pm, Fri 9am–3.45pm.
Closed: Public holidays.
Admission: Appointment advisable.

Introduction:

The Centre for Buckinghamshire Studies documents the history of the county and people of Buckinghamshire. Material relating to foreign countries is usually held only if the creator of a manuscript has a link with Buckinghamshire.

Collections:

It appears that only one collection held by the Buckinghamshire Records and Local Studies Service features a document relating to Brazil.

D 22/40/7 – Reed Family Papers: Personal papers of Rev. G.V. Reed (1816–86)
English
This 1852 journal recounts a voyage from Liverpool to Valparaiso via Madeira and Brazil on the Pacific Steam Navigation Company ship *Quito*. The journal was written by someone identified only as 'a lady' in the Rev. Reed's household. Included are descriptions of Pernambuco and Rio de Janeiro.

BELFAST

PUBLIC RECORD OFFICE OF NORTHERN IRELAND

www.proni.nics.gov.uk

66 Balmoral Avenue
Belfast BT9 6NY

Tel: (028) 9025 5905 • **Fax:** (028) 9025 5999
E-mail: proni@dcalni.gov.uk

Open: Mon–Fri 9.15am–4.45pm (Thurs 9.15am–8.45pm).
Closed: Public holidays and two weeks over late November and early December.
Admission: Proof of identity required.

Introduction:

The Public Record Office of Northern Ireland (PRONI) is the official repository for public records in Northern Ireland. Although it was established in 1923, the earliest document that is held by PRONI dates from 1219. Archival holdings include not only records of government departments and courts of law but also items deposited by private individuals, churches, and social and sporting institutions. Particularly important are the business archives, believed to be the largest holdings of their kind in the United Kingdom.

Collections:

The relatively few Brazil-related items that have been identified as held by PRONI are scattered within several very large collections. Apart from a few isolated items, the most likely sources of Brazil-related documents will be the business archives. Examples of the isolated items include an account of the 1835 siege of Pará [*D669*]; some 1809–14 correspondence of Staples, McNeile & Co., dealers in provisions, hides and tallow, from Rio de Janeiro [*D1567*]; an 1817–21 diary of Lieut. A.C. Dawson on board the HMS *Tigris* and the HMS *Spartan* describing visits to the West Indies and Brazil; and material within the papers of Viscount Castlereagh (see p. 7).

Robert Stewart, Viscount Castlereagh, 2nd Marquess of Londonderry Papers
English

The private papers of Robert Stewart, Viscount Castlereagh (1769–1822) mainly consist of letters from British political figures, although many concern Britain's foreign relations. Although Castlereagh served as foreign secretary between 1812 and 1822, there appears to be little correspondence directly relating to Brazil during this period (though many letters cover Portuguese affairs for the years 1807–9, some of which have a bearing on Brazil). Although there is a catalogue to the papers it is not indexed, with the only information provided for most items being the date and author. Examples of the few Brazil-related documents in the collection are:

- *D3030/2598* – Draft memorandum on the transfer of the Portuguese government to Brazil, Feb ?1808.

- *D3030/3377* – Letter discussing the possibility of placing the princess of the Brazils at the head of the regency of Spain, 30 Aug 1812.

- *D3030/5330* – Letter referring to alarming accounts of insurrection in Brazil, 14 May 1817.

Textile industry records
English

PRONI holds many archives of companies associated with Northern Ireland's once important textile (notably linen) industry. Although exports were vital for this sector, few documents relating to business dealings with Brazil have so far been identified. Note should be taken of the following collections:

- *D1193/OF/3 – Broadway Damask Co. Ltd* – Foreign order book noting the sale and shipment of bleached damask, etc., to Brazil, 1919–29.

- *MIC/142 – R & J Workman* – The collection includes ledgers outlining Brazilian sales of the muslin and sewed work that the company manufactured and provides details of voyages to Rio de Janeiro, 1825–45.

BIRMINGHAM

BIRMINGHAM ARCHDIOCESAN ARCHIVES

Cathedral House **www.birminghamdiocese.org.uk**
St Chad's Queensway
Birmingham B4 6EU

Tel: (0121) 230 6252 • **Fax:** (0121) 230 6279
E-mail: archives@rc-birmingham.org

Open: Mon–Fri 9am–5pm.
Closed: Public holidays.
Admission: Appointments essential.

Introduction:

The Birmingham Archdiocesan Archives is the repository for the records created centrally and by individual parishes of the Roman Catholic Church in the West Midlands.

Collections:

Apart from some very limited correspondence relating to investments in companies with Brazilian interests, it is believed that only one collection in the Archives features Brazil-related material.

> *P303/6/2 – **The Rev. G. Montgomery's Register (31 Aug 1867–4 July 1868)***
> *English*
> In 1868 over three hundred Irish Catholics left Wednesbury,
> a town in the industrial 'Black Country', north of Birmingham,
> to join an agricultural colony in Santa Catarina. The group was
> organised by George Montgomery, Wednesbury's parish priest,
> who believed that Brazil, as a Catholic and largely agricultural
> country, would offer English and Irish Catholics both spiritual and
> material prospects far superior to those in either England or the
> United States. *The Rev. G. Montgomery's Register* was an
> occasional newsheet in which Montgomery discussed local
> economic conditions and described his plans and hopes for the
> creation of agricultural colonies in Brazil for poor English and
> Irish Catholics.

UNIVERSITY OF BIRMINGHAM LIBRARY
Special Collections   **www.is.bham.ac.uk/specialcoll**
Edgbaston
Birmingham B15 2TT

Tel: (0121) 414 5838 • **Fax:** (0121) 471 4691
E-mail: special-collections@bham.ac.uk

Open: Mon–Fri 9am–5pm.
Closed: Public holidays, Christmas through New Year and one
week in July.
Admission: Letter of recommendation from a colleague or supervisor
required on first visit. If consulting the Eden Papers, a
letter in advance is required outlining the precise nature
and purpose of the research being undertaken and the
documents that will be consulted. The archivist will then
seek permission from the Eden family for the papers to
be consulted.

Introduction:

The University of Birmingham's Special Collections are based on the
19th-century amalgamation of medicine- and science-based printed
works. The collections now comprise some 60,000 rare and early printed
books published since 1471 and around two million manuscripts.
Principal amongst these are the archives of the Young Men's Christian
Association (YMCA) and the Church Missionary Society (CMS) and
the private and semi-private papers of Neville Chamberlain (best known
as prime minister from 1937 to 1940) and Anthony Eden (see p. 11).

Collections:

There appears to be very little Brazil-related material held by the University of Birmingham's library. Especially noticeable is the lack of Brazil
content amongst records of Birmingham-centred businesses that might
have exported machine tools or other metallurgical items to South America.
Even the political and missionary archival collections, in which Brazil-
related documents might be expected to be found, yield very little.
Although there is an online archive catalogue, not all collections are
included: while the CMS and Chamberlain papers are listed on the online
catalogue, only a printed handlist is available for the Eden papers.

Note: Although Brazil-related material has not so far been identified amongst the business history collections of the Birmingham City Archives [www.birmingham.gov.uk], there are at least some documents concerning local exports to Brazil that are held nearby in Dudley at the Black Country Living Museum (see p. 42).

Church Missionary Society
English

The Church Missionary Society (CMS) was established in 1799 with the intention of spreading the Gospel worldwide. Working alongside the established Anglican Church, CMS missionaries were active in many parts of the world, including East and South Asia, Africa and the British West Indies. The collection consists of detailed records of each mission, including missionaries' letters and diaries. Brazil-related material appears to be found exclusively amongst the records of the British Guiana missions, an area where there was considerable CMS activity in the mid-19th century. The collection includes some 1830s and 1840s records of CMS missions in the Brazil–British Guiana border region around Pirará, such as letters concerning alleged cross-border incursions by Brazilians (1843) and various journals, most notably one detailing an 1838 expedition to the southern border with Sir Robert H. Schomburgk (see also under British Library, p. 106 and Royal Geographic Society, p. 192).

Eden Papers
English

Included amongst the extensive deposits of private papers of Anthony Eden (1899–1977), whose political career culminated in the prime ministership (1955–57), are documents accumulated while foreign secretary (1936–38, 1940–45 and 1951–55). Very few items of correspondence relate to Brazil – limited to a few short letters discussing Brazilian views of the political situation in France and Italy in 1943 and brief mentions of Brazilian military operations in North Africa and Italy. Microfilm copies of the Foreign Office related documents are held by the National Archives (see p. 152).

BOLTON

BOLTON ARCHIVE AND LOCAL STUDIES SERVICE

www.bolton.gov.uk

Bolton Central Library
Le Mans Crescent
Bolton BL1 1SE

Tel: (01204) 332 185 • **Fax:** (01204) 332 225
E-mail: archives.library@bolton.gov.uk

Open: Mon 9am–5.30pm, Tues–Fri 9am–5.30pm,
Sat 9am–5pm.
Closed: Public holidays.
Admission: Appointment not required.

Introduction:

The Bolton Archive and Local Studies Service documents the history of Bolton Metropolitan Borough. Material relating to other countries is held when there is a connection with Bolton.

Collections:

During the 19th century, Bolton emerged as one of England's most important cotton textile and thread manufacturing town. Foreign trade was vital for Bolton's economy, both in terms of the import of raw materials and the export of textiles. Although the Bolton Archive holds the records of numerous local businesses, documents relating to Brazil have been identified in only one collection.

ZHD – *Richard Harwood & Son, Ltd*
English
Richard Harwood went into business as a cotton spinner in about 1850 with several large-scale mills being developed over the subsequent fifty years. Most records relate to the 20th century, following the establishment of Richard Harwood & Son in 1898. There are complete financial records covering the 1920s and 1930s including:

- *ZHD/248 & 249* – Sales order books listing customers in Brazil, 1923–33.

- *ZHD/251* – Sales order books listing customers in Brazil and other South American countries, 1937–42.

- *ZHD/280* – Letters from J.P. Cardim, São Paulo, concerning representatives in Brazil, 1932.

BRADFORD

BRADFORD DISTRICT ARCHIVE

(West Yorkshire Archive Service)
Bradford Central Library
15 Canal Road
Bradford BD1 4AT

www.archives.wyjs.org.uk

Tel: (01274) 731 931 • **Fax:** (01274) 734 013
E-mail: bradford@wyjs.org.uk

Open: Mon, Tues, Thurs, Fri 9.30am–1pm and 2–5pm.
Closed: Public holidays.
Admission: Appointment required.

Introduction:

The Bradford District Archive, a constituent archive of the West York-shire Archive Service (see also under Leeds District Archive, p. 77), is a local authority archives office, its primary purpose being to collect, preserve, catalogue and make available to the public local records of the district it serves. These records include archives of the local authority itself, schools, churches, businesses, solicitors, families, estates and individuals as well as maps, photographs and ephemera.

Collections:

Only one Brazil-related collection has been identified as being held by the Bradford District Archive. The collection provides a unique local view of one of the largely disastrous South American emigration schemes that were frequently promoted in England during the 19th century.

BBD 1/1/115 – 1 box – **Bradford Borough Council Town Clerk: Papers of the Brazilian Emigrants Relief Committee**
English
In 1891 several hundred people were recruited in Bradford for work in São Paulo. Some of the emigrants were natives of Yorkshire but many – if not most – were recent immigrants to Bradford, mostly Eastern European Jews. It is not entirely clear what attracted the emigrants to the Brazilian scheme – whether

they believed that they were going out as labourers on coffee
plantations, to establish their own small farms or to work in
textile factories, as most had done in Bradford. The collection
of papers (1891–92) includes records of the relief committee,
lists of members of the committee, reports on the condition of the
distressed emigrants in Brazil and correspondence with British
government emigration officials and diplomats in both London
and Brazil.

CAERNARFON

CAERNARFON RECORD OFFICE / ARCHIFDY CAERNARFON

www.gwynedd.gov.uk

Swyddfa'r Cyngor
CAERNARFON
LL55 1SH

Tel: (01286) 679 095 • **Fax:** (01286) 679 637
E-mail: archives.caernarfon@gwynedd.gov.uk

Open: Tues–Fri 9.30am–12.30pm and 1.30–5pm
(Wed 1.30–7pm).
Closed: Mondays and public holidays.
Admission: Proof of identity and a permanent address required.

Introduction:

The Caernarfon Record Office documents the history of the Welsh town of Caernarfon and villages in the former county of Caernarfonshire. Documents concerning other parts of Wales or abroad are held if the originator has some relation to Caernarfonshire.

Collections:

Coastal Caernarfon had a significant maritime tradition with, during the 19th century, apprentice seamen from the port of Porthmadog frequently progressing to find work on larger vessels based in Liverpool, Swansea or Cardiff. The few documents relating to Brazil that have been identified as being held by the Caernarfon Record Office relate to merchant shipping.

XM 2460 – Papers of Captain Robert Griffiths
English
Robert Griffiths (b. 1855/6) was a master mariner from the fishing village of Aberdaron, on the Lleyn Peninsular. In 1893 he became the captain of *Beeswing*, a large steel barque, remaining with the vessel until around 1910. The *Beeswing* was the only vessel of the Beeswing Sailing Ship Co. Ltd, a merchant shipping company established in Porthmadog in 1892, remaining active until 1910.

It would appear that during these years the *Beeswing* undertook several voyages to South America, transporting coal from south Wales to Brazil and Argentina.

The following documents feature information on aspects of the *Beeswing*'s 1893–94 voyage to South America:

- *XM 2460 / 8 – Statements of Accounts 1893–1907*. Financial accounts relating to the second voyage of the *Beeswing* from Eastham via Cardiff to Rio de Janeiro and back from La Plata (Argentina) to Hull on 22 Nov 1893 to 3 Nov 1894.

- *XM 2460 /3 2: Miscellaneous – Public Protest*. Documents referring to an official protest made by W.G. Abbot, British consul general in Rio de Janeiro, and Captain Griffiths, against the Brazilian Coaling Co. Ltd., the Brazilian Government and others relating to delays and expenses incurred between 28 Dec 1893 and 13 March 1894 when the *Beeswing* was fired on by warships commanded by anti-government insurgents.

*XM 3137 – **Captain John Owen and the voyage of the Republic to Brazil***

English

Miscellaneous documents relating to the voyage to Brazil in 1893–94 of the *Republic*, a barque owned by the Republic Ship Co.. John Owen, the master of the *Republic*, suffered from yellow fever and "congestion of the brain" while in Rio de Janeiro; documents issued by local doctors describe his medical condition and treatment. Included in this collection is a detailed statement of accounts concerning the voyage.

CAMBRIDGE

CAMBRIDGE UNIVERSITY LIBRARY
Department of Manuscripts
West Road
Cambridge CB3 9DR

www.lib.cam.ac.uk/MSS

Tel: (01223) 333 143 • **Fax:** (01223) 333 160
E-mail: mss@lib.cam.ac.uk

Open: Mon–Fri 9am–7pm, Sat 9am–5pm.
Closed: Public holidays and one week in September.
Admission: Letter of introduction (preferably academic) and proof of identity required. To access the collections, contact the Admissions Office by telephone (01223 333084) or e-mail admissions@ula.cam.ac.uk to make an appointment to apply for a Reader's Ticket.

Introduction:

The first formal library of the University of Cambridge was created in the second decade of the 15th century. The library has been a legal deposit copyright library for Britain and Ireland since 1709. The library has developed one of Britain's most extensive collections of Brazil-related printed material. Brazil-related acquisitions have featured in a systematic manner only since 1966 but there are considerable holdings from prior to that year.

Collections:

There has never been a systematic search of the library's Brazilian holdings of books, maps and manuscripts, in part due to cataloguing limitations. It appears that holdings of Brazil-related manuscripts are extremely limited, particularly compared to the material relating to former Spanish American territories. Where relevant manuscripts are identifiable from the various printed catalogues and handlists, they are almost always small in number and scope and are found scattered within much broader collections. The 'Janus' electronic catalogue (http://janus.lib.cam.ac.uk) provides access to catalogues of a growing proportion of the archives held by Cambridge University Library as well as the libraries of the university's constituent colleges. The work is in progress, with new catalogues being added regularly.

*BSAX – **British and Foreign Bible Society***
English (some German)
The British and Foreign Bible Society was founded in London in
1804 with the aim of supplying Bibles and Scriptures without
comment, on a worldwide basis, in local languages and at
affordable prices. The principal archival series are the minutes of
committees, correspondence, registers and financial records, and
deposited papers. In addition, the Society's published annual
reports and magazines are also held, containing a wealth of
information. Basic searches of the Society's archives can be
conducted via the Janus catalogue (see p. 18) and by using the
search term "Brazil" one can identify the names of individual
correspondents, places and dates.

Relating to Brazil, it is material within the Agents Books and
the foreign correspondence that is especially valuable. With the
oldest Brazilian documents appearing to date from 1818, the
contents are extremely varied in terms of subject matter, detail and
place. Some letters and reports merely highlight basic accounting
topics but detailed descriptions of Protestant communities
(Brazilian as well as British, German and other foreign) and their
treatment by the national and local authorities are important
subjects. Most of the authors of the reports and letters are British
and German missionaries but there are also merchants and
agricultral settlers who felt it was their duty to spead the gospel in
"papist" Brazil. An especially significant correspondent was the
Scottish Presbyterian missionary Robert Reid Kalley (1809–88),
with at least 38 letters from Madeira and Rio de Janeiro being held.

*DAR 1 to 265 – **Charles Darwin Papers***
English
Although there are extensive holdings of letters, notebooks and
other papers of the naturalist Charles Darwin (1809–82), very few
examples of Brazil-related material are represented in the collection.
After graduating from the University of Cambridge in 1832, Darwin
was recommended to Robert FitzRoy (see p. 20), commander of
the HMS *Beagle*, as a naturalist to sail on a circumnavigation
voyage being planned by FitzRoy. The voyage lasted from 1832 to
1836. On his return to England, Darwin published, with great
success, the book *Journal of Researches [....] during the Voyage of
HMS Beagle*, and he went on to produce his most important book,
On the Origin of Species by means of Natural Selection (1859).

The Darwin collection is considerable, including his library
(with personal annotations in many of the volumes), correspondence
and notebooks relating to the voyage of the *Beagle* and to the
publication of Darwin's work. Apart from highly specialised
manuscripts concerning palaeontology, specific Brazil-related
material is extremely limited. There are few Brazilian references
even in the lists of *Beagle* specimens and the diaries of
observations on zoology and geology of places visited.

Regularly updated handlists to the collection are available.
For correspondence to and from Darwin (detailing published and
unpublished letters), search the *Online Calendar of the
Correspondence of Charles Darwin* [www.lib.cam.ac.uk/
Departments/Darwin/]. Several 1832 letters offering descriptions
of Rio de Janeiro and the Brazilian forest are listed.

Add. 8853 – Robert FitzRoy Papers
English
Robert FitzRoy (1805–65) was a hydrographer and meteorologist
who served in the Royal Navy, eventually rising to the rank of
vice-admiral. In 1827 FitzRoy sailed to South America on the
HMS *Thetis*, and in 1828 he received his first command, on the
HMS *Beagle*, to survey the Patagonian coastline. Between 1832
and 1836 FitzRoy continued his surveying work in Patagonia, as
well as other parts of South America, circumnavigating the world.
On board the *Beagle* during this second voyage was the young
naturalist Charles Darwin (see p. 19).

The collection consists of letters (1816–52) from FitzRoy,
including many written during his first mission to South America
(1827–28). Detailed accounts of FitzRoy's stay in Brazil are given,
including descriptions of travelling by land and sea from Rio de
Janeiro to the town of São Paulo, Santos, and the island of Santa
Catarina. In letters from Montevideo, FitzRoy also comments on
the war between the forces of newly independent Brazil and
Argentina, describing it as 'a lazy proceeding quite worthy of the
Portuguese'. No letters survive describing the Brazilian portion of
FitzRoy's travels with Darwin on the *Beagle*.

Add. 7348 and 7450 – Ludlow Papers: Charles B. Mansfield
English
Charles B. Mansfield (1819–55) was a chemist and author of
Paraguay, Brazil and the Plate (Cambridge, 1856). This collection

consists of six letters, dated 1852, written during his journey in South America and relating his impressions of Brazil, amongst other places.

Add. 9303 / 17 to 21 – Sir Graham Moore
English

As commander in the Royal Navy, Sir Graham Moore (1764–1843) commanded the HMS *Marlborough*, one of the British ships that escorted the Portuguese royal family to Brazil in 1807–8 in advance of Napoleon's invading armies. Three volumes of Moore's diaries (1784–1843) include an important and detailed account of the transfer of the royal family to Bahia and Rio de Janeiro.

MS 9278 – George Ramsay, 12th Earl of Dalhousie
English

George Ramsay (1806–80) joined the British Navy in 1820, reaching the rank of rear-admiral in 1862 and vice-admiral in 1869. Ramsay was commander-in-chief of the South America Station between 1866 and 1869, and he personally commanded the HMS *Narcissus*. Two private journals are held covering Ramsay's South American command: Volume I covers 8 June 1866 to 3 May 1868, and Volume II covers 4 May 1868 to 31 May 1869. The journal entries are especially valuable for Ramsay's observations regarding both the military and political aspects of the Paraguayan War (the War of the Triple Alliance) and descriptions of leading military and political figures, but they also discuss other South American naval capacities and other issues. Diary entries are for Brazilian ports (especially Rio de Janeiro) as well as Buenos Aires and along the Paraná River. Although they are important documents and in excellent condition, the script is extremely difficult to decipher.

Vickers Archive
English

This collection of papers, photographic negatives and film charts the rise and post-war metamorphosis of what was once one of the largest armaments companies in the world. The bulk of this collection covers the period 1870–1970, and together with the records of Vickers also includes records of the company's former rivals Armstrong Whitworth of Newcastle, taken over in 1928 (see also under 'National Maritime Museum', p. 173). The archives are described in L.A. Ritchie, *The Shipbuilding Industry: A Guide to Historical Records* (Manchester, 1992).

Although the collections certainly feature some material relating to the Brazilian Navy, cataloguing is imprecise. Items include photographic prints of vessels supplied to, or originally ordered for, Brazil, and lists of ships built at the Vickers and Armstrong Whitworth yards, usually with brief specifications of the vessels, including ships supplied to Brazil (*Vickers Documents 589, 811, 818*). There are also references to business with the Brazilian government in the minute books of the various Vickers companies. There are few correspondence files relating specifically to business with Brazil, although there is one file listing financial information concerning armament contracts with Brazil covering 1925–37 (*Vickers Document 533*).

CHURCHILL ARCHIVES CENTRE

Churchill College
Cambridge CB3 0DS

www.chu.cam.ac.uk/archives/

Tel: (01223) 336 087 • **Fax:** (01223) 336 135
E-mail: archives@chu.cam.ac.uk

Open: Mon–Fri 9am–5pm.
Closed: Public holidays.
Admission: By appointment only. Contact in advance, preferably in writing, giving details of research subject. Two forms of identification required, one of which confirms the address of the researcher.

Introduction:

The Churchill Archives Centre is the home of the papers of Sir Winston Churchill and more than 570 other collections of personal papers and archives documenting the history of the Churchill era and beyond. The centre holds the papers of politicians, scientists, public servants, diplomats, soldiers, sailors and airmen, with the Churchill Papers forming the basis of the collection.

A recent acquisition is the collection of Margaret Thatcher's personal and political papers. It awaits to be seen whether any Brazil-related content is included in this recent acquisition.

Collections:

The catalogues for most collections are searchable online. The Churchill Papers are particularly well catalogued, and the online search facility is available at the archive's website. Online catalogue searches of other papers are possible via http://janus.lib.cam.ac.uk. In addition to the Churchill Papers (see below), transcripts of oral history interviews with British former diplomats reveal some references and discussions relating to Brazil.

Churchill Papers
English

The Churchill Papers consist of the original documents sent, received or composed by Sir Winston Churchill (1874–1965) during the course of his long and active life. Best known as wartime prime minister and minister of defence (1940–45), Churchill also served as prime minister between 1951 and 1955. He held several ministerial positions, including home secretary (1910–11), first lord of the admiralty (1911–15 and 1939–40), secretary of state for war and air (1919–21) and chancellor of the exchequer (1924–29).

The papers contain everything from Churchill's childhood letters and school reports to his final writings. They include his personal correspondence with friends and family and his official exchanges with kings, presidents, politicians and military leaders. Some of the most memorable phrases of the 20th century are preserved in his own drafts and speaking notes for the famous wartime speeches. The Churchill Papers comprise an estimated one million individual documents.

Most of the Brazil-related documents are notes responding to invitations, birthday greetings or similar brief memos. Correspondence concerns many subjects, from discussions relating to Brazilian participation in World War II to the supply of Brazilian cigars. Examples of Brazil-related items in the collection are:

- *CHAR 13/29/216* – Minute (1914) from Churchill, first lord of the admiralty, on the supply of rifles from Brazil.

- *CHAR 20/112/102* – Telegram (11 June 1943) from President Roosevelt to Churchill stating that he agrees with his proposal to approach Prime Minister Salazar of Portugal on the lines which he suggested and explaining his idea to replace Portuguese troops in the Azores with Brazilians.

- *CHAR 20/140A/71–2* – Report (14 July 1944) from Dr Leslie Burgin [Liberal Nationalist MP] to Anthony Eden on his visit to Brazil, commenting on: the political and economic conditions; his success in informing Brazil of Great Britain's experiences in the front line; and the relations between Britain and Brazil.

- *CHAR 20/170/80* – Telegram (24 Aug 1944) from Churchill to the president of Brazil expressing his admiration for the character and bearing of the soldiers in the Brazilian Expeditionary Force, whom he had recently inspected in Italy.

CARDIFF

GLAMORGAN RECORD OFFICE / ARCHIFDY MORGANNWG

www.glamro.gov.uk

Glamorgan Building
King Edward VII Avenue
Cathays Park
Cardiff CF10 3NE

Tel: (029) 2078 0282 • **Fax:** (029) 2078 0284
E-mail: GlamRO@cardiff.ac.uk

Open:	Tues–Thurs 9.30am–5pm, Fri 9.30am–4.30pm, Wed to 7pm by appointment.
Closed:	Mondays, public holidays (and usually the day after).
Admission:	Visitors are advised to book a place in the searchrooms.

Introduction:

The Glamorgan Record Office documents the history of the county and people of Glamorgan in south Wales. Material relating to foreign countries is usually held only if the creator of a manuscript has a link with Glamorgan.

Collections:

Despite the importance of the port of Cardiff and significant 19th- and early 20th-century trading ties with South America, very few items featuring Brazilian content have been identified amongst the holdings of the Glamorgan Record Office. Additional material relating to Brazil's commercial links with Wales can be found under 'Caernarfon', pp. 16–17.

DFBO – Sir Brooke Boothby Papers
English
Brooke Boothby (1856–1913) was a British career diplomat who served as secretary of legation in Rio de Janeiro, 1898 to 1901. Although the collection is quite extensive, records relating to the time Boothby was in Brazil are absent.

D175 – Brazilian Consulate, Cardiff
Portuguese
The Brazilian consulate in Cardiff was established in the 1870s, largely as a consequence of the city's port and the significant coal trade between south Wales and Brazil. This collection consists of two volumes of the consulate's financial and administrative records covering the years 1939–45 and 1959–61.

DER – Evans and Reid Coal Company Ltd
English
Evans and Reid Coal Company was established in 1890, its main business being the export of coal and the import of wooden pit props. The Company developed a network of foreign agents as well as branch offices in England. The South America-related material includes account books detailing exports to Brazil and general files covering the debts of Seixas Brothers & Co., a failed Brazilian trading company.

George Benvenuto Buckley Mathew Papers
English
George Benvenuto Buckley Mathew (1807–79) was a British career diplomat who served in many parts of Latin America, holding the post of British minister in Rio de Janeiro between 1867 and 1879. Despite his long residency in Rio de Janeiro, Brazil-related records within the collection are limited to entries in a one-volume diary [*D/D MW 181*] that covers an 1866 tour of Central and South America. (See also under Liverpool Record Office, p. 84.)

CHELMSFORD

ESSEX RECORD OFFICE

Wharf Road
Chelmsford CM2 6YT

www.essexcc.gov.uk/heritage/ero/

Tel: (01245) 244 644 • **Fax:** (01245) 244 655
E-mail: ero.enquiry@essexcc.gov.uk

Open: Mon 9am–8.30pm, Tues–Thurs 9am–5pm,
              Fri–Sat 9am–4pm.
Closed: Public holidays.
Admission: Advanced contact advised to ensure that the material to
              be consulted is on-site. Proof of identity and address
              required.

Introduction:

The Essex Record Office documents the history of the county and people
of Essex. Collections held include local government records and papers
of local churches, schools, businesses, clubs and societies, and families.
Material relating to foreign countries is usually held only if the creator
of a manuscript has a link with Essex.

Collections:

Only two collections have been identified in the Essex Record Office
that include Brazil-related content. The electronic catalogue may be
searched via the internet, although access can be gained using a PC only.

Barnard Letters

English
Amongst the extensive 19th-century correspondence of members of
the local Barnard family is a single letter [*D/DQ14/95*] dated June
1817 from G.W. Barnard in Rio de Janeiro to his brother, Charles.
The letter includes details of the voyage to Brazil and a description
of Rio de Janeiro, a city that Barnard dislikes.

Paroissien Papers
English

Born in Braintree, Essex, James Paroissien (1785–1827) was one of thousands of men who travelled to the Banda Oriental (Uruguay) seeking employment at the time of the British occupation (1806–7). With the evacuation of Montevideo, Paroissien relocated to Brazil, spending several weeks on the island of Santa Catarina from September 1807 before arriving in Rio de Janeiro in January 1808. Towards the end of that year Paroissien left Brazil for Buenos Aires and spent the remainder of his life as a mercenary in Chile, Peru and Bolivia.

The collection consists of extensive fragments of a journal kept by Paroissien for most of his life, letters to his family in Essex and accounts books. Brazil-related journal entries and letters are quite extensive. Included are detailed descriptions of the island of Santa Catarina and its small capital, Desterro, to which Paroissien considered moving in 1808 to establish himself as a merchant. Especially interesting are Paroissien's observations of Rio de Janeiro society, its population having suddenly exploded due to the very recent arrival of the Portuguese royal family and thousands of courtiers. While in Brazil, Paroissien responded to the Prince Regent's apparent fondness for butter by accepting a position to establish a dairy at a royal estate at Santa Cruz, to the southwest of Rio de Janeiro. Included are several accounts of Paroissien's experiences at the estate.

After Paroissien moved to Spanish America, he only once returned to Brazil. Journal entries cover his 1822 visit to Rio de Janeiro and refer to changes that have taken place to the fabric of the city over the intervening years.

CHICHESTER

WEST SUSSEX RECORD OFFICE

Sherburne House

www.westsussex.gov.uk/cs/ro/Home.htm

3 Orchard Street
Chichester

Correspondence address:
West Sussex Record Office
c/o County Hall
Chichester PO19 1RN

Tel: (01243) 753 600 • **Fax:** (01243) 533 959
E-mail: records.office@westsussex.gov.uk

Open: Mon–Fri 9.15am–4.45pm, Sat 9.15am–12.30pm and
1.30–4.30pm.
Closed: Public holidays and one week in early December.
Admission: Appointment advisable.

Introduction:

The West Sussex Record Office documents the history of the county and people of West Sussex. Collections held include local government records and papers of local churches, schools, businesses, clubs and societies, and families. Material relating to foreign countries is usually held only if the creator of a manuscript has a link with West Sussex.

Collections:

Only one collection in the West Sussex Record Office has been identified as featuring some Brazil-related content.

Papers of Claude Henry Mason Buckle
English
Having joined the British Navy in 1817, Claude Buckle (1803–94) rose to the rank of admiral. Brazil-related items in the collection are diaries kept by Buckle while serving off the west coast of Africa, engaged in the suppression of the Atlantic slave trade. Of particular interest are the following:

- *BUCKLE/474* – Feb–Aug 1849 – Diary kept on board the HMS *Centaur* while serving as flag captain. Buckle records the proceedings of the vessel in search of slave-trading ships. Included is an account of the capture of the Brazilian slaver *Sirena*, accounts of excursions on the African mainland burning villages thought to encourage the slave trade, and of routine on board the *Centaur*.

- *BUCKLE/475* – Aug 1849–Jan 1850 – Continuation of the previous diary (see above). Describes the capture of the Brazilian slaver the *Veloz* and attacks on coastal villages to recover an English merchant schooner captured by Brazilian or Portuguese pirates.

- *BUCKLE/477* – Nov 1850–Jan 1851 – Diary kept on board the steamship HMS *Cyclops*, returning to England from Ascension Island where Buckle had taken ill. Refers to the capture of a Brazilian brig by the *Cyclops* and contains extracts from Admiralty Orders relating to the procedure for seizing slave ships.

CHIPPENHAM

WILTSHIRE AND SWINDON RECORD OFFICE

Wiltshire and Swindon History Centre
Cocklebury Road
Chippenham
Wiltshire SN15 3QN

www.wiltshire.gov.uk/ archives

Tel: (01249) 705500 • **Fax:** (01249) 705527
E-mail: wsro@wiltshire.gov.uk

Open: Mon–Fri 9.15am–5pm (Wed 9am–7.45pm).
Closed: Public holidays and two weeks in late January.
Admission: Appointment advised and proof of identity required.

Introduction:

The Wiltshire and Swindon Record Office documents the history of the county of Wiltshire and the town of Swindon. Other material is usually held only if there is a link with Wiltshire.

Collections:

It appears that only three Wiltshire and Swindon Record Office collections feature limited Brazil-related material.

*WRO 540/275 – **Charles Phipps Diary and Letters, 1867–68***
English
This collection includes a more than one-hundred-page diary of Charles Phipps (1845–1913), a 'country gentleman' from Westbury, Wiltshire, recording a voyage between October 1867 and February 1868 to Rio de Janeiro and around South America to Panama and onwards to Jamaica. Although Brazil is discussed in a relatively small part of the diary, there are detailed descriptions of the Atlantic voyage and of the city of Rio de Janeiro. In addition, there are several letters written by Phipps during the tour and sent to his father.

*PR/Steeple Ashtun St Mary/730/342 – **Rio Doce Company***
English
This file contains accounts (c. 1838) of the Rio Doce Company and statements by the directors responding to criticisms levelled at the Bahia mining company by its auditors.

*2667 – **Papers of Sir Richard Burton***
English
Following his death, most of the papers of the British explorer,
translator and diplomat Sir Richard Burton (1821–90) were
destroyed by his wife. This collection includes draft letters and a
report (1880–81) on the Littari Mine in Minas Gerais
[*2667/26/2/xiv*], a c. 1865 note book about Burton's term as consul
in Santos [*2667/26/4/1*], and albums featuring photographs of
friends and acquaintances in Brazil [*2667/26/5/1–4* and
2667/26/6/1–4].

COVENTRY

UNIVERSITY OF WARWICK LIBRARY

Modern Records Centre
Coventry CV4 7AL

**www.warwick.ac.uk/services/
library/mrc/mrc.html**

Tel: (024) 7652 4219 • **Fax:** (024) 7652 4211
E-mail: archives@warwick.ac.uk

Open: Mon–Thurs 9am–1pm and 1.30–5pm,
             Fri 9am–1pm and 1.30–4pm.
Closed: Public holidays and one week at Easter.
Admission: Book in advance.

Introduction:

The Modern Records Centre collects and makes available for research original sources for British political, social and economic history, with particular reference to labour history, industrial relations and industrial politics. The archives of hundreds of organisations – in particular trade unions, employers' and trade associations, businesses and political pressure groups – have been deposited with the centre.

Collections:

Brazil-related manuscripts that are held by the Modern Records Centre mainly concern the British motor vehicle industry, once concentrated in and around Coventry. Most Modern Records Centre collections may be searched using the online catalogue *A2A: Access to Archives* (see p. 250).

> *Mss. 313/AS – Association of Brazil Nut Importers*
> *English*
> The collection is limited to transcripts of accounts and abbreviated minutes of annual general meetings during the existence of the Association, 1952–71. It is possible to glean from these documents quantities of Brazil nuts imported to Britain, though not the sources. These documents are part of a wider collection of nut and dried-fruit associations that are held by the Modern Records Centre; the 1941–71 papers of the Edible Nuts in Shell Association [*Mss. 313.EN*] may feature further details of nut (in particular Brazil nut and cashew) imports from Brazil.

BP Archive
English

Although separately administered (tel: 024-7652 4521), the BP Archive shares the searchroom with the Modern Records Centre. The collection documents the history and activities worldwide of BP (British Petroleum) with material covering all aspects of the oil industry. Records created up to 1954 are open for consultation. A separate BP electronic catalogue is maintained. Approximately seventeen records are held relating to Brazil, ten of which are trademark registration certificates while the balance is of more substantive interest, concerning BP's interest in the Brazilian market and prospecting possibilities. Further information is available at the BP website [www.bp.com/company/history/bp/archive_asp].

Mss.226 – British Motor Industry Heritage Trust
English

Almost all the archival material of the British Motor Industry Heritage Trust [www.heritage.org.uk/archive/archive.htm] of Brazilian interest is deposited at the Modern Records Centre. All the files are from the 1950s and concern the export of British-made vehicles and parts to Brazil, discussions regarding the possible manufacture or assembly of British vehicles (Standard-Triumph and Land Rover) and the registration in Brazil of British trademarks. Brazil-related files include:

- *Mss.226/ST/3/0/BR/3 – Standard Motor Co.* – Concerning the visit to Brazil in 1951 by the director of the company with a view to establishing assembly facilities there, building on the successful exports of vehicles from England. Exchange regulations and the availability of machine tools are discussed. In 1953 the project was postponed.

- *Mss.226/ST/3/0/BR/18/5 – Standard Motor Co.* – Survey of future market for motor vehicles in Brazil, 1956.

- *Mss.226/RO/1/1/8 – Rover Co. Ltd* – Detailed board minutes (1952–59) in which overseas (including Brazilian) Land Rover production and assembly possibilities are discussed.

┃ DORCHESTER

DORSET RECORD OFFICE

Bridport Road
Dorchester DT1 1RP

www.dorset-cc.gov.uk/archives

Tel: (01305) 250 550 • **Fax:** (01305) 257 184
E-mail: archives@dorset-cc.gov.uk

Open: Mon–Fri 9am–5pm (Wed 10am–5pm),
               Sat 9.30am–12.30pm.
Closed: Public holidays.
Admission: Proof of identity required.

Introduction:

The Dorset Record Office documents the history of the county and people of Dorset. Material relating to foreign countries is usually held only if the creator of a manuscript has a link with Dorset.

Collections:

Only one, limited, Brazil-related collection has been identified in the Dorset Record Office.

D/COL: C5 – Colfox Manuscripts
English
Amongst the correspondence of Thomas Collins Colfox
(1755–1835) of Bridport, Dorset are four letters (varying from three to fifteen pages in length) from Thomas and Charles Carter in South America. Written in 1809 and 1810, the letters from the brothers discuss political changes and trade (referring to the 'immense and daily influx of British merchandise') and offer detailed impressions of Buenos Aires and Rio de Janeiro by the two British residents of these cities.

DUBLIN

NATIONAL ARCHIVES OF IRELAND / AN CHARTLANN NÁISIÚNTA

www.nationalarchives.ie

Bishop Street
Dublin 8

Tel: (+353 1) 407 2300 • **Fax:** (+353 1) 407 2333
E-mail: mail@nationalarchives.ie

Open: Mon–Fri 10am–5pm.
Closed: Public holidays.
Admission: Proof of identity required.

Introduction:

The National Archives of Ireland (NAI) hold the files of Irish government departments, with material from 1922 to date (although a thirty-year closure rule is in force). Prior to this period, material was held by the Public Record Office of Ireland, but the building housing the collection was destroyed during the civil war that followed the establishment of the Irish Free State in 1921, with the loss of all the records.

Material can be searched using the NAI's web-accessible electronic catalogue and the departmental file catalogues. Only an extremely small proportion of holdings is listed on the electronic catalogue, while many of the entries given in the file catalogues are of limited value in identifying Brazil-related material.

Collections:

There appears to be very little in the way of Brazil-related holdings amongst the NAI's collections. Some relevant pre- and post-1922 material (such as that concerning Irish emigration and trade links with Brazil) is held at the National Archives in London (see p. 131), especially amongst the Foreign Office and Dominions Office archival holdings. The Public Record Office of Northern Ireland (see p. 6) also holds some Brazilian trade-related material within its business history collections.

Department of the Taoiseach
English

The Department of the Taoiseach provides the secretariat to the Taoiseach (the Irish prime minister) and is the channel of communication between government departments and the president. The departmental files are varied and include documents relating to Ireland's international relations.

Only some ten files have a clear focus on Brazil, though some of these basically consist of copies of documents of the Dominions Office (which officially held responsibility for Ireland's external relations during the 1920s and early 1930s) with little, if any, direct bearing on Ireland itself. Examples of files relating to Brazil with a strong Irish subject component (either in terms of subject matter or the creator) include:

- *S 6257* – Commercial Relations between Ireland and Brazil, 16 Oct 1931–7 Jan 1957.

- *S 4844 A* – Consuls in Irish Free State: Brazilian, 1930s.

- *S 15768* – President of Brazil – Election and Death, 24 Aug–11 Nov 1954.

Department of Foreign Affairs
English

Until the 1990s, diplomatic contacts between Ireland and Brazil were generally indirect and limited, overseen initially following Irish independence by the Dominions Office in London and later by the two countries' missions in, respectively, Lisbon and London. Apart from a single file on the visa position of nationals of Brazil and Ireland between 1946 and 1968 [*DFA 99/3/5*], it has not been possible to identify any Brazil-related holdings. Although there are many 1950s and 1960s reports from the Irish Embassy in Buenos Aires, there are no records of any staff tours to Brazil. There are many files relating to individual distressed Irishmen and women abroad (mainly in the United States and England and including no named Brazilian locations), but in most cases it is impossible to identify to what country a catalogue entry refers.

NATIONAL LIBRARY OF IRELAND / LEABHARLANN NÁISIÚNTA NA HÉIREANN

www.nli.ie

2–3 Kildare Street
Dublin 2

Tel: (+353 1) 603 0200 • **Fax:** (+353 1) 676 6690
E-mail: info@nli.ie

Open: Mon–Wed 10am–8.30pm, Thurs–Fri 10am–4pm,
              Sat 10am–12.30pm.
Closed: Public holidays.
Admission: Proof of identity and two passport-sized photographs
              required.

Introduction:

The National Library of Ireland (NLI) was founded in 1877 from the amalgamation of the collections of the Royal Dublin Society and the Joly Library. The NLI collects Irish-interest books and manuscripts, and under copyright legislation it is entitled to receive a copy of every printed item published in the Republic of Ireland. It is not, however, one of the British and Irish copyright libraries (with rights over publications from throughout the British Isles) – that status is held by Dublin's Trinity College Library (see p. 40).

Collections:

Brazil-related manuscript holdings are extremely limited and are held only where the author of a document is of Irish origin or there is an otherwise close connection with Ireland. Post-1990 manuscript acquisitions are listed on the online public-access catalogue (OPAC), with earlier material (to 1975) listed in the fourteen volumes of *Manuscript Sources for the History of Irish Civilisation* (Boston, 1965–79) and (for 1976–90) in the card catalogue in the NLI's Manuscript Reading Room.

Ms. 18,762 – *John J. Byrne-Newell Papers*
English
The collection consists of four files of articles – cuttings from Buenos Aires, Dublin and Irish provincial newspapers as well as unpublished manuscripts – that journalist John J. Byrne-Newell wrote in the 1930s and 1940s on topics relating to the Irish in South America. Most of the articles relate to the history and

contemporary condition of the Irish in Argentina but there are also ones on Bolivia, Brazil and elsewhere.

The drafts of articles relating to Brazil principally examine Irish settlement on the Amazon (1612–23) and Irish mercenaries or farmers in Rio de Janeiro 1827–28. The latter topic is treated in a 27-page manuscript (dated 9 Dec 1943) in which recruitment in Cork, the rebellion in Rio de Janeiro and the subsequent repatriation to Ireland and dispersal to Bahia are described in considerable detail. Unfortunately, it is not entirely clear on what sources the article is based.

Mss. 13,073 to 13,092 – **Casement Papers**
English
Roger Casement (1864–1916) was a British consular official and Irish rebel. In 1906 he was appointed consul in Santos and in 1908 he became the consul in Pará (Belém). He was promoted to consul-general in Rio de Janeiro in 1909, a position he retained until 1913. In 1910 Casement was directed by the Foreign Office to occupy a commission of enquiry sent to the rubber-bearing Putumayo region of the western Amazon (an area straddling the Peruvian–Colombian frontier) to investigate treatment of the local Indian population by the Peruvian Amazon Company. In 1911 Casement was knighted for this and for similar work in Africa. During World War I Casement sided with Germany as a tactic to achieve Irish independence, and in 1916 he was hanged by the British for treason. To damage his reputation, the British publicised the existence of Casement's diaries, which included numerous graphic and coded accounts of his homosexual activities in Brazil and elsewhere (see under National Archives, Kew, p. 165).

There are some 4,000 documents within the collection, mainly covering the years 1889–1916, and the papers are listed in a separate catalogue listing (no. A15). Most of the South America-related material concerns Casement's Putumayo investigations but these documents include drafts of letters and reports on the voyage to the border region. There are also copies of deeds of Casement's appointments to consulships in Brazil as well as some drafts of letters and reports made during his various postings. The 1908–9 files for Pará, for example, include descriptions of life in the city of Pará (Belém) and details of the cost of acquiring wooden sleepers and other materials for the Madeira-Mamoré Railway, amongst other issues.

Ms. 17,805 – **Cornelius J. Cramm**
English
This file contains letters sent to Cornelius J. Cramm of London,
including one dated 20 April 1908 describing Rio de Janeiro in
glowing terms. The author, apparently a contract worker with a
telegraphic cable company, alludes to an Irish community in the
city and states that 'away from the enemies [the British] we
continue our Gaelic studies'.

◆

TRINITY COLLEGE LIBRARY

College Street
Dublin 2

www.tcd.ie/Library/

Tel: (+353 1) 677 2941 • **Fax:** (+353 1) 671 9003
E-mail: mscripts@tcd.ie

Open: Mon–Fri 10am–5pm, Sat 10am–1pm.
Closed: Public holidays.
Admission: Permission to consult manuscripts should be sought in
             writing in advance to the Keeper of Manuscripts.
             Readers should obtain a reader's ticket from the Berkeley
             Library before proceeding to the Manuscripts Room in
             the Old Library.

Introduction:

Trinity College Library (TCL) – the largest research library in Ireland
and one of the most varied in the British Isles – dates back to the
founding of the college in 1591. Since 1801 TCL has been a legal
deposit library of British and Irish publications, although in practice it
has not acquired all items to which it has been entitled.

Collections:

Only two Trinity College Library manuscript collections appear to
contain Brazil-related items, and in these there is disappointingly little
relevant content.

*MS 10355–56, 10404 – **O'Sullivan-Beare Papers***
English
Daniel Robert O'Sullivan (1865–1921) was a medical doctor, army officer and diplomat whose career was largely spent in East Africa and Brazil. He served as British consul or consul-general in Bahia (1907), São Paulo (1910) and Rio de Janeiro (1907–8, 1913–15 and 1919–21). The collection includes few (and largely unremarkable) Brazil-related items. Those that have survived are postcards from Brazil and photographs. The photographs are mainly family studio and group portraits. Other photographs include several images of a general store in Rio de Janeiro (1917–21), diamond mines, Indians and street scenes (1912) and landscapes (various dates).

*MS 959 – **Papers relating to proceedings in South America***
Portuguese and Spanish
These papers concern ecclesiastical, civil and military matters in Spanish and Portuguese America during the first half of the 17th century. The only document concerning Brazil is an unattributed 1625 account, in Portuguese, describing the city of Bahia (Salvador) and its new fortifications.

DUDLEY

BLACK COUNTRY LIVING MUSEUM

Tipton Road
Dudley DY1 4SQ

www.bclm.co.uk

Tel: (0121) 557 9643 • **Fax:** (0121) 557 4242
E-mail: info@bclm.co.uk

Open: Mon–Fri 9am–5pm.
Closed: Public holidays.
Admission: Appointment advised.

Introduction:

Located in the Black Country town of Dudley – now effectively an outer suburb of Birmingham – the Black Country Living Museum attempts to recreate the living and working environment of what was once England's most important iron- and coal-producing regions. The museum has collected material relating to the Black Country since 1975, its collections ranging from complete buildings and large machines to small tools, domestic utensils, photographs and documents.

Collections:

During the 19th and early 20th centuries, Black Country manufacturers exported iron work – such as track for railways, building materials and hardware – throughout the world. Although there are very few items in the collection that relate to Brazil, those that do shed some useful light on sales practices of English exporters.

Archibald Kenrick & Sons Ltd
English
The West Brompton iron founders and hardware manufacturers Archibald Kenrick & Sons traces its origins to the last years of the 18th century. Manuscript holdings relating to the firm cover all aspects of the business, including exports. There are several items [all located in *1990/134/Box 2/Folder 7*] relating to trade with Brazil, including the following:

- Analysis sheet 'Shipment of Hollow-ware to South America', 1878–79.

- Report headed 'Hardware in Brazil' describing types of hardware demanded, the retail trade and competition, and discussing the characteristics required to be a sales representative in Brazil, 1921–22.

- Letter from G.H. Kenrick (São Paulo) to W.B. Kenrick regarding trading prospects in Brazil, 1922.

DUNDEE

DUNDEE CITY ARCHIVE AND RECORD CENTRE

www.dundeecity.gov.uk/archives

21 City Square
Dundee DD1 3BY

Tel: (01382) 434494 • **Fax:** (01382) 434666
E-mail: archives@dundeecity.gov.uk

Open: Mon–Fri 9am–1pm and 2–4.45pm.
Closed: Public holidays.
Admission: Appointment required.

Introduction:

Dundee City Archive and Record Centre holds the official records of the City of Dundee District Council, the former Corporation of Dundee and the core records of the former Tayside Regional Council. In addition, there are records of Dundee businesses and union branches. Material related to other countries is held where there is a connection with Dundee.

Collections:

The city of Dundee (and its jute industry) is better known for its relations with India rather than with South America. Only one Brazil-related collection has been identified.

> *GD/GS/24–27 – **Cia. Anglo-Brasileira de Juta***
> *English*
> This is a small collection of company minutes (1949–66) and miscellaneous related files, including insurance particulars, balance sheets, correspondence and similar records, c. 1919–79. Also held are plans and engineering drawings (1916–50) relating to the company's operations in Taubaté, São Paulo.

UNIVERSITY OF DUNDEE ARCHIVES

Tower Building
Dundee DD1 4HN

www.dundee.ac.uk/Archives

Tel: (01382) 344 095 • **Fax:** (01382) 345 523
E-mail: archives@dundee.ac.uk

Open: Mon–Wed 9am–1pm and 2–6pm (to 5pm outside term),
             Fri 9am–1pm and 2–5pm.
Closed: Thursdays, public holidays and over Christmas
             and New Year.
Admission: Advance notice preferred.

Introduction:

The University of Dundee Archives holds the university's own archives and records of local institutions and businesses, in particular reflecting textile (especially jute and linen), shipbuilding and other industries that contributed much to the growth of the city in the 19th century.

Collections:

Only one University of Dundee Archives' collection features fairly extensive holdings of Brazil-related interest, the city of Dundee (and its former jute industry) being far better known for its links with India than with South America. Some of the other business history collections (a list of which is posted on the archives' website) contain scattered references to exports to Brazil, including late 19th-century records of the Dundee firm James Allison & Sons (Sailmakers) Ltd. [*MS 44*] and amongst the extensive holdings (1855–1966) of the British Jute Trade Association [*MS 144*].

MS 42 – *Giddings & Lewis-Fraser Ltd: Douglas Fraser & Sons*
English

Giddings & Lewis-Fraser Ltd came into being during the course of the 19th century as a result of the gradual amalgamation of a number of businesses in the Dundee area that had specialised in the manufacture of coarse textiles (especially from flax and jute). One of these companies – Douglas Fraser & Sons of Arbroath, which had specialised in the production of canvas, an industry in decline with the advent of steam ships – designed and patented a jute-braiding machine in 1881, manufacturing jute-soled shoes (*alpargatas* or *espadrillas*). Soon the company established factories elsewhere, including in Argentina, Uruguay and Brazil, using machinery supplied from Arbroath.

Brazil-related material includes tenders, legal, financial, business and miscellaneous papers and correspondence. Especially important are letters from Robert Fraser in South America (1889–93), who had been sent out to set up production in the region.

DURHAM

DURHAM UNIVERSITY LIBRARY

Archive and Special Collections
Palace Green Section
Durham DH1 3RN

www.dur.ac.uk/Library/asc

Tel: (0191) 374 3001 • **Fax:** (0191) 374 3002
E-mail: Library@durham.ac.uk

Open: Mon–Fri 9am–5pm, Sat (term time only) 10am–1pm.
Closed: Public holidays.
Admission: Appointment required.

Introduction:

Durham University Library has an important Archive and Special Collection including material of local, regional, national and international importance.

Collections:

Although only one collection featuring Brazil-related content has been identified as being held by Durham University Library, the items are of some considerable historical significance.

Papers of John Ponsonby
English

In 1825, John, Viscount Ponsonby (c. 1770–1855) wrote to George Canning, the British foreign secretary, requesting employment. Ponsonby's first major diplomatic assignment was to travel to Brazil on a special mission, arriving in Rio de Janeiro on 26 May 1826 and departing on 28 August of the same year. Ponsonby later returned to South America, where he served as British minister to Argentina between 16 September 1826 and 31 July 1828 and then minister to Brazil from 20 August 1828 until 28 June 1829. There is a detailed handlist to the papers (c. 1808–50), indexed by name of correspondent, place and subject. While Turkish affairs feature most prominently amongst the Ponsonby papers, the Viscount's South American experiences are well documented.

The Ponsonby Papers form a relatively small – but historically significant – part of the family papers of the Earls Grey of Howick, considered one of England's great political archives covering the 16th to 20th centuries. Included amongst the papers are seven volumes of correspondence [*GRE/E607*] relating to Ponsonby's special mission to Rio de Janeiro and to his period serving as British minister in Buenos Aires. Most of this material (for which a separate descriptive list is available) consists of copies of dispatches sent to George Canning in London and instructions sent by the Foreign Office to Ponsonby. Amongst the papers covering Ponsonby's period as minister in Rio de Janeiro, there are a number of memos, dispatches, original correspondence and contemporaneous copies of letters that were sent to Ponsonby by Brazilian government officials which were translated into English for forwarding to Lord Aberdeen. In addition, there are several series of letters from other correspondents:

- *GRE/E259* – Correspondence (1826–28) between Ponsonby in Buenos Aires and Sir Robert Gordon (the then minister to Brazil) in Rio de Janeiro discussing the conflict between Brazil and Argentina, peace negotiations and general political affairs centring on the two countries.

- *GRE/E375* – Five letters (1828) from Major Alexander McDonald in Buenos Aires regarding a conspiracy to overthrow Dom Pedro I, emperor of Brazil.

- *GRE/E496* – Some twenty letters (20 June 1827 to 23 April 1836) from David Price, an English merchant and banker in Brazil, concerning banking, trade and general affairs of Brazil.

GRE/E87 – Miscellaneous Papers relating to Brazil, 1825–31

In addition to Ponsonby's personal correspondence, there are some fifteen separate reports and other documents on various Brazil-related subjects. Trade issues are especially important amongst these manuscripts, with examples of individual documents being:

- Statement, with abstract, concerning the number of slaves imported from eight regions of Africa into Rio de Janeiro, 1 July 1825 to 1 July 1826.

- Economic statistics and Brazilian naval strengths, 1826–27.

- Statement of the imports and exports trade of Rio de Janeiro, March 1828.

- Address by the British residents of Rio de Janeiro to Ponsonby, 27 June 1829.

EDINBURGH

CENTRE FOR THE STUDY OF CHRISTIANITY IN THE NON-WESTERN WORLD LIBRARY

www.div.ed.ac.uk/ documentscol_4.html

Thomas Chalmers House
16 Bank Street
Edinburgh EH1 2NJ

Address for correspondence:
Centre for the Study of Christianity in the Non-Western World
University of Edinburgh, Faculty of Divinity (New College),
Mound Place, Edinburgh EH1 2LX

Tel: (0131) 650 8902 • **Fax:** (0131) 650 7972
E-mail: actonm@div.ed.ac.uk

Open: Mon–Fri 9am–5pm.
Closed: Public holidays; contact in advance if a visit is planned
             during the Christmas, Easter or summer vacations.
Admission: Appointment advised.

Introduction:

The Centre for the Study of Christianity in the Non-Western World (CSCNWW) exists to advance scholarship in the study of Christianity in Africa, Asia and Latin America. The library supports the CSCNWW's research and teaching activities and is entirely separate from New College Library.

Collections:

The library includes 2,000 missionary magazine titles relating to the churches in Africa, Asia, the Pacific and the Americas, some of which are not held elsewhere. Few of the publications feature much on Brazil, but some of the 19th-century English and Scottish magazines contain reports from missionaries working in Brazil, in particular serving in Pernambuco and the Amazon, some of which are illustrated. The publications are on open shelves. Of the archival collections held by the CSCNWW, only one collection features Brazil-related material.

Evangelical Union of South America
English
Presbyterians were active in Brazil from at least 1855, with the arrival in Rio de Janeiro of Dr Robert Reid Kalley (1809–88) and followers fleeing attacks on their church in the Portuguese island of Madeira. Dr Kalley formed the Fluminense Church (shortly afterward officially renamed the Igreja Evangélica Fluminense) in Rio de Janeiro and conducted outreach work in Petrópolis, Salvador and Recife.

In 1911 the Evangelical Union of South America (EUSA) was formed to unite Presbyterian missionary societies working in the region, including the Help for Brazil Mission that was working in central and northeastern Brazil and closely co-operating with the Fluminense Church. The archives of the EUSA were deposited in August 2002 in the CSCNWW Library by the successor body, the London-based Latin Link. It has not yet established the exact contents of the archive but the collection is very substantial and dates from the mid-19th century. There is much material relating to Brazilian activities, including minute and letter books as well as printed materials such as missionary magazines and several thousand slides and other photographs.

NATIONAL ARCHIVES OF SCOTLAND

HM General Register House
Princes Street
Edinburgh EH1 3YY

www.nas.gov.uk

Tel: (0131) 535 1314 • **Fax:** (0131) 535 1360
E-mail: research@nas.gov.uk

Open: Mon–Fri 9am–4.45pm.
Closed: Public holidays and normally the first two weeks of November (telephone for details of dates).
Admission: Proof of identity required.

Introduction:

The National Archives of Scotland (NAS) – formerly the Scottish Record Office – is primarily a depository of records of the Scottish Office and the devolved Scottish government. The NAS is also the main archive for sources on the general history of Scotland, the country's role in the British Isles and the links between Scotland and other countries over the course of centuries. As such, many private archival collections relating to Scotland have been deposited in the NAS as donations or on long-term loan.

Collections:

In general, the limitations of NAS cataloguing (usually by name of collection or individual) make searching for Brazil-related manuscripts extremely difficult. However, the NAS printed and card catalogues are being entered onto an electronic database, and it is anticipated that online searches will be possible from early 2003. Although there appear to be few Brazil-related collections, at least some valuable material has been identified.

GD233 – *Thomas Cochrane Papers*
English, Portuguese, Spanish
Thomas Cochrane (1775–1860), the 10th Earl of Dundonald, was a distinguished British naval officer who went on to organise the Chilean Navy and from there was recruited in 1823 by the Brazilian government to take charge of its Navy with a view to prosecuting the struggle for independence from Portugal. The Dundonald family have deposited on loan at the NAS several hundred documents relating to the career of Cochrane and covering the period 1810–60.

Within this collection are bundles of letters, financial balance sheets, logs (offering basic navigational information), maps, charts and newspaper reports. The documents cover Cochrane's recruitment into Brazilian service, his efforts to organise the Brazilian naval forces and deal with what are sometimes conflicting instructions from a government that was seeking an accommodation with the Portuguese military, and his resignation from Brazilian service two years later, in 1825. Most of the letters are those sent to Cochrane from Brazilian officials, but there are also some copies of Cochrane's out-going correspondence.

Examples of documents relating to Cochrane's Brazilian service that are found in the collection are:

- *GD233/34/245 (no. 2)* – Letter (31 March 1823) from Luís da Cunha Moreira, minister of the Brazilian Navy, to Cochrane, informing him that he has been admitted to the service of Brazil with a commission of first admiral.

- *GD233/25/466* – Letter (5 May 1823) from Cochrane to the minister of the Brazilian Navy reporting the poor condition of the ships under his command and the equally poor quality of their crew.

- *GD233/20/456 (no. 33)* – Letter (August 1823) from Cochrane to Portuguese residents of Brazil offering them protection if they affirm their loyalty to the Empire and its constitution.

- *GD233/21/454 (no. 4)* – Suggestions (n.d.) by Cochrane for the improvement of the Brazilian Navy – increased pay, the involvement in commerce (for example, the development of a Navy-led whaling industry in southern waters) and the establishment of a naval college on the island of Santa Catarina.

- *GD233/20* – Letters (1824) from the authorities in Bahia, Pernambuco and Paraíba on civil and naval matters.

Although most of the Brazil-related items in the collection were produced between 1823 and 1825, there are some later letters and other documents (1855–65), mainly concerning the Dundonald family's attempts to obtain land and money that they believed was legally owed them by the Brazilian government.

The Cochrane papers are well organised and catalogued. In addition to the general NAS printed handlist that summarises each box or bundle of documents, there is a very detailed catalogue featuring translations into English of the individual Portuguese-language documents. In addition, a catalogue has been published that includes several hundred summaries (*resumos*) in Portuguese of all letters and other documents that form the collection. See *Catálogo do Arquivo Cochrane: Edição Comemorativa do Bicentenário do Nascimento do Primeiro-Admirante Lord Thomas Cochrane (Marqués do Maranhão) 1755–1860* (Rio de Janeiro, 1975).

*AF51/160 – **Emigration: South America: Secretary for Scotland's Correspondence***
English (some in Gaelic)
This file features correspondence and other documents warning of the perils of emigrating from Scotland to Brazil (as well as to Argentina and Chile) between 1889 and 1893. The Brazil-related material concerns the possible recruitment of 2,000 Scottish emigrants for factory and plantation work in São Paolo and includes a warning poster in English and Gaelic.

*GD248/687/21 – **John Grant Letter***
English
Depending on the trade winds, convict ships sailing from Britain to the Australian colonies regularly stopped off in Brazil for repairs and to take on water and food. Dated 9 July 1794, this letter was written by John Grant, a convict bound for New South Wales. Unlike most other convicts on board the ship, Grant is able to go ashore in Rio de Janeiro as he uncovered a mutiny plot on board, a discovery for which he expects to be granted his freedom on arrival in Australia. His letter offers a detailed description of the city and shows that Grant is much impressed by its inhabitants, scenery and buildings.

*CS96/3790 – **Henderson and Campbell, merchants, Pará***
English
Miscellaneous documents from 1829 in relation to Henderson and Campbell, merchants in Pará (Belém) representing George Henderson and Co., a Glasgow merchant house. Documents include a report on the brig *Margaret Richardson* sent from Liverpool to Pará (Belém) to take on cargo, issues concerning debtors in Pará and an account of an expedition from Pará (Belém) to Santarém.

*GD76/454 – **James Henderson Letters***
English
A volume containing twelve letters (1828–44) from James Henderson, Junior, of Messrs. Harrop and Henderson (Belém, Pará), to Henry Flockhart, Annafrech, Kinross, Scotland. The correspondence that relates to Brazil includes a letter from Liverpool (dated 21 June 1834) in which Henderson reports that his ship was unable to sail due to change of wind and he expresses his thoughts on leaving Britain. The five letters from Pará

(1833–35 and 1844) report on health, climate, fauna, British residents, the slave trade, financial matters and local insurrections.

GD1/633/1 and 2 – Francis Erskine Loch Memoir
English
Francis Erskine Loch was a widely travelled commander in the British Navy. Completed in 1835 and based on contemporaneous notes and memories, Loch's memoirs cover the period 19 March 1818 to 29 March 1821. Loch visited the city of Rio de Janeiro and inland areas of the province, and the memoirs include eight pages of descriptions of local customs (including a mention of the ease of hiring an assassin), food, and the conditions endured by plantation slaves.

GD306/22–29 and 32974–32986 – Pará New Gas Company (1890–1907)
English
Documents in this collection include architectural plans for company buildings and for coal and gas wharves in Pará (Belém), catalogues of German- and British-supplied gaslight fittings, tubes, meters and cookers, staff contracts and draft tenders, memoranda and correspondence for new concessions.

Note: Two working days' notice is required to view these documents.

NATIONAL LIBRARY OF SCOTLAND
Manuscripts Division
George IV Bridge
Edinburgh EH1 1EW

www.nls.uk

Tel: (0131) 466 2812 • **Fax:** (0131) 466 2811
E-mail: manuscripts@nls.uk

Open: Mon, Tues, Thurs and Fri 9.30am–8.30pm, Wed 10am–8.30pm, Sat 9.30am–1pm; manuscripts for evening use must be ordered before 4pm.
Closed: Public holidays and normally for one week in early October – telephone for details of dates.
Admission: Proof of identity required; for extended use, two recent passport-size colour photographs are required.

Introduction:

Founded only in 1925 but incorporating the collection of the Advocate's Library that had been in existence since the 1680s, the National Library of Scotland (NLS) is Scotland's largest library and includes some seven million books and 120,000 volumes of manuscripts. As a British legal deposit library (a status inherited from the Advocate's Library that had been one since 1710), the NLS can claim to have one of the most comprehensive collections of material published in the British Isles. The Manuscripts Division of the NLS cares for archival material covering many aspects of the lives, activities and interests of Scots at home and abroad.

Collections:

The cataloguing is remarkably rudimentary, so the identification of relevant individual collections is extremely difficult. There may well be manuscript material relating to Brazil waiting to be uncovered within the NLS's collections, especially relating to the design and manufacture of equipment that was central to Brazil's 19th- and early 20th-century infrastructure modernisation. The worldwide influence of Scottish engineers is certainly well represented and Brazil-related papers may be found, for example, amongst the extensive papers (1786–1955) of the lighthouse-building firm Robert Stevenson and Sons. It is expected that as the NLS catalogues become available online, access to Brazil-related material will be improved. In the meantime, only a few NLS collections of Brazilian interest have been identified.

*Acc. 6905 – **David Angus Papers***
English
The papers of Scottish civil engineer David Angus (1855–1926) cover his career spent mostly in South America (Brazil, Argentina, Paraguay, Chile and Peru) and in Namibia. The collection includes several hundred personal and business letters, private diaries and journals, as well as reports relating to his railways and dockyards engineering work. As a whole, the papers may be the most comprehensive collection of records of an individual British engineer working in South America in the 19th and early 20th centuries.

Some of the most detailed records relate to Angus' Brazilian activities. Angus first sailed to Brazil in 1882, remaining there for four years while working on the construction of the Victoria e Natividade Railway linking Vitória (Espírito Santo) with Minas

Gerais. During these years, Angus was a particularly prolific writer, corresponding with Mary Wilson (his fiancée at home in Scotland) and also recording his experiences of Brazil in his private diaries; Wilson's letters to Angus are also in the collection. Often going into great detail, Angus describes the voyage to Brazil, his impressions of Salvador, Maceió and Rio de Janeiro, pay, and working and living conditions in both Vitória and in often remote railway construction camps. Angus also records engineering problems that he encountered, as well as many observations relating to geological and general natural history conditions of the regions where he worked.

Much later, Angus was employed again in relation to Brazil. In 1924–25 he served as an engineering consultant on the construction of both the Northern Mato Grosso Railway and the Triangulo Mineiro Railway. Included within the collection are several typescript reports describing these projects.

Mss. 5641–5; 5647–8; 5650–1 – Liston Papers: Isabel Bezarra de Seixas Letters
English
Sir Robert Liston (1756–1832) was a British diplomat whose career in the foreign service took him to several European countries. Included in this very extensive collection of private and semi-private papers are fourteen letters written between 1814 and 1817 from Isabel Bezarra de Seixas to her friend Lady Liston (Henrietta Marchant) in Constantinople. The wife of a statesman at the Portuguese court in Rio de Janeiro, Isabel Bezarra de Seixas sent lengthy and very personal letters from Brazil, discussing women in the royal court in Rio de Janeiro, court gossip, official ceremonies, dinners and balls, her own health and the gradually deteriorating health of her husband.

Ms. 3322 – H.M. Tomlinson Papers
English
This collection consists of three letters from Henry Major Tomlinson (1873–1958), a journalist, travel writer and novelist whose work included *The Sea and the Jungle* (London, 1912). The book is widely considered a classic of Amazon travel writing and charts a voyage from England to Porto Velho. The letters, which were sent to his mother in 1910 while Tomlinson was travelling along the Madeira River in the western Amazon, provide

few insights beyond occasional vivid descriptions such as seeing 'black and green butterflies as big as cheese plates – and heat and smell like the palm house at Kew'. Also included in the file are three photographs enclosed with the letters, including one of Tomlinson riding a horse.

Ms. 21206–21237 – **Minto Papers**
English
This collection, in which only a few items relate to Brazil, features the correspondence and papers of the Elliot Murray Kynynmounds, Earls of Minto, and of related families from 1759–1914. *Ms. 21229* features letters to and from the Hon. Sir Charles G.J.B. Elliot, 1864–66, relating to his naval command on the South American Station and the Paraguayan War.

EXETER

DEVON RECORD OFFICE

Great Moor House
Biltern Road
Exeter EX2 7NL

www.devon.gov.uk/dro/homepage.html

Tel: (01392) 384 253 • **Fax:** (01392) 384 256
E-mail: devrec@devon.gov.uk

Open: Mon–Thurs 10am–6pm.
Closed: Public holidays and second week of February.
Admission: Proof of identity required.

Introduction:

The Devon Record Office documents the history of the county and people of the county of Devon. Material relating to foreign countries is usually held only if the creator of a manuscript has a link with Devon.

Collections:

It appears that only one series with Brazil-related material is held by the Devon Record Office.

Addington Family, Viscounts Sidmouth Papers: Political and Personal Papers of Henry Addington, 1st Viscount Sidmouth
English
Henry Addington (1757–1844) served in various senior political positions, including prime minister in 1801–04. Only a very few items within the collection contain references to Brazil. These appear to be limited to the following:

- *152M/C1803/OZ15a–b* – Letter (1803) from Admiral D. Campbell in Lisbon to Addington, describing Brazil as being 'in a state of infancy', stating that the country represents a poor potential market for English exports because of a lack of taste for luxuries.

- *152M/C1808/OF1* – Letter (25 Oct 1808) from Peter Evan Turnball to H. Addington discussing the introduction of a trade agreement between Britain and Brazil.

GLASGOW

GLASGOW UNIVERSITY ARCHIVE
13 Thurso Street   **www.archives.gla.ac.uk**
Glasgow G11 6PE

Tel: (0141) 330 5515 • **Fax:** (0141) 330 4158
E-mail: dutyarch@archives.gla.ac.uk

Open: Mon 1.30–5pm, Tues, Wed and Fri 9.30am–5pm,
             Thurs 9.30am–8pm.
Closed: Public holidays and over Christmas and New Year.
Admission: Appointment strongly recommended and essential for
             Thursday evenings; proof of identity required.

Introduction:

Glasgow University Archive holds the university's own archives and is the most important repository for records documenting Scottish business history, in particular the industries of the west of Scotland – especially shipbuilding and shipping, heavy engineering, railways, architectual ironwork, brewing and distilling, banking, insurance and retailing – in the 19th and 20th centuries.

Collections:

Although it can be safely assumed that many of the business history collections that are held by Glasgow University Archive will feature Brazil-related records, such material has been confirmed only in a few of the collections. A list of the names of the individual businesses for which records are held is posted on the archive's website, from which it may be possible to identify collections worth investigating for additional Brazil-related content.

> *UGD 5, DC 376/4/1 and 2, DC 376/1/1/1 – **Glenfield & Kennedy Ltd***
> *English*
> The Kilmarnock (Ayrshire) firm of hydraulic engineers Glenfield & Kennedy Ltd was created in 1899 from the merger of local engineering works that emerged during the 19th century. The company and its predecessors were important suppliers of

waterworks equipment to Brazil and other Latin American countries prior to 1914; records (1865–1970) include correspondence, sales books and working drawings, some of which relate to Brazilian orders.

UGD 153 – P. & W. MacLellan Ltd
English

P. & W. MacLellan Ltd was one of the numerous engineering firms and foundries functioning in Glasgow during the 19th and 20th centuries. In the late 19th century, the company increasingly concentrated on export markets, successfully securing orders in India. In the early 1890s one of the firm's partners (William MacLellan) travelled to Brazil, where he secured some contracts to supply iron bridges and also major orders for Pernambuco Harbour at Recife. MacLellan's work relating to Brazil can be traced using letter books (1861–1911), contract books and files (1866–1910), bridge contract books (1851–1979) and other record holdings.

UGD 118 and UGD 202 – W. & W. McOnie
English

P. & W. McOnie, engineers, was formed in 1840 in Glasgow and subsequently adopted various variations to the name of the firm according to family involvement, most notably that of W. & A. McOnie. In 1886 the firm became known as W. & W. McOnie. From 1851 until the end of the 19th century and beyond, the firm concentrated on producing machinery for the sugar industry, especially steam engines, sugar mills, steam boilers, waterwheels and evaporating pans for export to Java, Mauritius and Brazil.

The holdings of company records are extensive and it is possible to trace some of McOnie's Brazilian business links, especially through the estate's order books (1851–1938). Other more general holdings include dimension and repair books (1851–1987), letter books (1889–1911) and sugar machinery drawings.

UGD 028 – John Wylie Papers
English

John Wylie was a Glasgow merchant who traded mainly with firms in San Luis Potosí (Mexico), Buenos Aires, Rio de Janeiro and Bahia. Wylie travelled extensively in Mexico, Argentina and Brazil, with correspondence from these places found in letter books for the years 1809–40. Much of the correspondence concerns

Mexico but there are also letters (especially 1809–20) from Brazilian agents and business houses commenting on economic and political issues there, and also letters to English and Scottish suppliers and manufacturers.

GLOUCESTER

GLOUCESTERSHIRE ARCHIVES

Clarence Row
Alvin Street
Gloucester GL1 3DR

www.gloucestershire.gov.uk/archives

Tel: (01452) 425 295 • **Fax:** (01452) 426 378
Email: archives@gloucestershire.gov.uk

Open: Mon 10am–5pm, Tues, Wed, Fri 9am–5pm,
            Thurs 9am–8pm.
Closed: Public holidays.
Admission: Proof of identity required.

Introduction:

The Gloucestershire Archives holds records concerning the people and the county of Gloucestershire. Material relating to other parts of England and the world is normally held only when the originator of the documents has a connection to Gloucestershire.

Collections:

Only one collection, held by the Archives, has been identified as featuring some material relating to Brazil.

> *D1571/F508–552 – **Walter Grimston Bucknall Estcourt***
> *English*
> Walter G.B. Estcourt (1807–45) was born in the Gloucestershire village of Shipton Moyne. He joined the British Navy and by the time of his death he had achieved the rank of Commander. His papers provide an excellent account of his naval career, including a tour of duty that took him to Brazil.

- *D1571/F513* – Description of a voyage from Rio de Janeiro to Chile, via Cape Horn, 1825.

- *D1571/F514* – Details of sea, weather conditions, bearings and progress from Esquimbo (Guyana) to Rio de Janeiro in the HMS *Briton*, 1826.

- *D1571/F528* – Admiralty instructions (1844–46) for the HMS *Eclair*, including many concerning the 1817 treaty with Brazil for the suppression of the slave trade.

GUERNSEY

THE ISLAND ARCHIVES

St Barnabas
Cornet Street
St Peter Port
Guernsey GY1 1LF

Tel: (01481) 724 512 • **Fax:** (01481) 715 814
E-mail: archives@gov.gg

Open: Mon–Fri 8.30am–4.30pm.
Closed: Public holidays.
Admission: It is advisable to make an appointment.

Introduction:

The Island Archives hold, or has responsibility for, records of the States of Guernsey and the Royal Court, as well as other historical collections that have been acquired from institutions, businesses and individuals relating to the self-governing territory.

The Greffe

Researchers investigating Guernsey merchants' links with Brazil should be aware of the *Amirauté* series of court records, held at The Greffe, Royal Court House, St Peter Port (Mon–Fri 9am–1pm and 2–4pm). Spanning the years 1653 to 1968, these are texts of legal procedures involving merchants and shipping companies. The series remains unindexed and a search for relevant documents will involve examining individual *Amirauté* volumes. Until 1948, virtually all these records, like most other official papers in Guernsey, were recorded in French.

Note: The Island Archivist also holds the title of Archiviste de la Cour Royale. Enquiries concerning research at the Greffe should be addressed to the Island Archives.

Collections:

In the 19th century, Guernsey merchants maintained close ties with Latin America, in partnership with agents in the region, including some from the Island. A triangular trade developed, enduring until the 1870s, with Guernsey-based ships carrying mixed cargoes from Britain and France to Newfoundland. From there salt-cod was carried south to Brazil where coffee was loaded for delivery to Europe.

The Brazil-related documents in the Island Archives are largely related to trade relations with material largely consisting of individual documents. The most significant are described below but other items also exist that shed light on the trading network of which, especially in the early 19th century, Guernsey and Brazil were part (see, for example, *AQ 025/04-04* dated 1827; *AQ 025/02-02* dated 1837; *AQ 846/16-02* dated 1837; and *AQ 031/25* dated 1839).

Note: Apart from naturalisation and aliens' registration documents, no Brazil-related material has been identified in the Jersey Archive [http://jerseyheritagetrust.jeron.je], in the neighbouring Channel Island of Jersey which, in the 19th century, maintained Atlantic trading links with Québec rather than with Latin America.

DC / HX – *Hôpital de St Pierre Port*
French

References to Brazil can be found in the deliberations (1741–1948) of the Hôpital de St Pierre Port, the town workhouse. About three-quarters of the archive has survived, with the extremely detailed recordings of deliberations now also available in English précis. The volumes covering the years 1801–29 include arrangements to assist inmates of the Hôpital to leave the island. Guernsey merchants in Brazil occasionally offered apprenticeships to young boys and their circumstances are discussed: for example, Thomas Le Gallez, aged 15, was sent to Bahia in April 1822 to join Mr Thomas Lihou [*Deliberations B, DC /HX 79–02, p. 352*]; Pierre Langdon, aged 15, and Pierre Sauvarin, aged 13, were sent in June 1822 to be apprenticed to a Mr Gemmill [*Deliberations C, DC / HX 135–02. p. 8 and p. 11*].

DC2 / 045-01 – **Letter from Peter Dobrée (Guernsey) to Samuel Dobrée, 25 December 1807**
English

A letter congratulating the author's son for being on board the ship conveying the King of Portugal into exile in Brazil. Dobrée writes that "[t]his is an event of vast importance to England, as it will throw the vast rich trade of the brazils [*sic*] in our hands."

AQ 276/19 – Accounts ledger, Elias Guerin(?), 1814–27
English
This ledger lists cargoes such as sugar, coffee, wine and brandy shipped to and from Guernsey and various locations, with names of ships and captains. The ledger provides an indication of an individual Guernsey merchant's extensive trading connections, including with Brazil and other parts of the world.

AQ 79/38 – Letter from John Mansell (Guernsey) to Alfred Grut (Rio de Janeiro), 19 November 1822
English
A letter enquiring as to the safe arrival of Alfred Grut in Rio and asking for information as to what European goods were demanded by the Brazilian market. Mansell notes that Guernsey merchants Priaulx, Tupper & Co. had for some time traded in Brazil and that Rio was a regular port of call for Guernsey ships carrying wine, spirits and salt and returning with coffee.

AQ 509/03 – Letters to Brazil from W.S. and J.E.B. Guild, 1877–81
English and Portuguese
The ninety letters in this collection were written by brothers attending Elizabeth College to their parents in Petrópolis and Rio de Janeiro. The letters to the boys' father are in English while those to their mother are in Portuguese, suggesting that her side of the family was Brazilian. It is unclear whether the family had pre-existing connections to Guernsey. They were likely attracted to the Island by the College's reputation, the lower fees than of similar schools in England, as well as by Guernsey's mild climate and the possibility of learning French, of which a dialect – *Gèrnésiais* – was widely spoken. The rather charming letters discuss College life, special events such as day trips, Guy Fawkes Night and the boys' attempts at celebrating Brazilian independence as well longing for family and servants in Brazil.

AQ 87/24 – Log book of the brig Star of the West, 1879
English
Built in Guernsey in 1869, the *Star of the West* undertook 21

overseas voyages until 1882, including many trans-Atlantic crossings. This log documents a typical voyage: the ship set sail from Guernsey in April 1879 carrying a cargo of railway sleepers from London for delivery to Cadiz, Spain; there tubs of salt were loaded and transported to Rio Grande, arriving in August; the ship then sailed, via Pernambuco, to Puerto Rico where it collected sugar for delivery in Scotland.

◆

PRIAULX LIBRARY
Candie
St Peter Port
Guernsey GY1 1UG

www.priaulx.gov.gg

Tel: (01481) 721 998 • **Fax:** (01481) 713 804
E-mail: priaulx.library@gov.gg

Open: Mon–Sat 9.30am–5pm.
Closed: Public holidays.
Admission: No advanced notice or identification is required.

Introduction:

Established in 1887, the Priaulx was the first free lending library in Guernsey. Today the Library houses the Island's local studies collections with a large number of books and journals concerning all aspects of Guernsey's life and history. The Priaulx is also the principal repository for the Island's collection of newspapers, dating back to their first production with, in 1791, *La Gazette de Guernesey* [*sic*], to the present day.

Collection:

Only one manuscript collection has been identified in the Priaulx Library as featuring Brazil-related references.

The Carteret Priaulx Commerce Papers (1686–1927)
French and English
This collection of letters and circulars sent to and from the Guernsey merchant house of Priaulx, which later became Carteret Priaulx & Co. and then Priaulx Lauga & Co. The papers have been

indexed from 1720 to 1837 according to the name of the foreign merchant house or subsidary and the town where it was located. All the papers have been transcribed and, if in French, translated in full or part. The following are examples of the approximatly ten Brazil-related documents that have so far been identified:

- *18 November 1808, Rio de Janeiro, William Morganson & Co.:* A letter warning that, since the arrival of the Prince Regent and the Court, there has been too much cargo arriving from Europe and the market was for the time being saturated.

- *8 April 1809, Rio de Janeiro:* An account describing the quality of goods produced in Brazil for both the export and the home markets as well as an assessment of commodities that were in demand.

- *3 February 1832, Rio de Janeiro:* Prices and demand for olive oil, codfish, salt, cheese, gin and other imports from Europe as well as the availability for export of Brazilian sugar, hides and coffee (the latter commodity in much demand in the North America).

- *15 and 25 June 1835, Bahia, Priaulx & Le Quesne:* A note referring to sugar prices, explaining that oil, brandy and port wine were all demanded but that there was sufficient local stock of flour.

HATFIELD

HATFIELD HOUSE

Hatfield
Hertfordshire AL9 5NF

www.hatfield-house.co.uk

Tel: (01707) 287 005
E-mail: library@hatfield-house.co.uk

Open: Mon–Fri 10am–5pm, strictly by appointment.
Closed: Public holidays.
Admission: A letter of enquiry addressed to the Librarian and Archivist to the Marquess of Salisbury is required; the letter should outline the subject of research, the material to be consulted and any plans for publication.

Introduction:

Hatfield House was built in 1611 by Robert Cecil, 1st Earl of Salisbury, the chief minister to King James I. Since that time the house has remained in family ownership. It is currently home to the 6th marquess and is run, in part, as a tourist attraction.

Collections:

The archive features family and estate papers from the 13th century, with most dating from the 17th century onwards. Brazil-related papers are few in number and relate only to the 1st and 3rd marquesses.

Salisbury Papers: 1st Marquess
English
Robert Cecil, 1st Earl of Salisbury (1563–1612), was an English parliamentarian and a key adviser to Queen Elizabeth I. By about 1589 he had begun performing the duties of secretary of state, a position to which he was officially appointed in 1596. On the death of Elizabeth in 1603, James I ascended to the English throne, with Cecil maintaining his position of influence, especially in foreign affairs.

While papers relating to the West Indies appear prominently within the collection, there are only a few items of Brazilian interest, mainly concerning trade and piracy. These appear to be limited to the following:

- *Salisbury (Cecil) III: p. 423* – Petition for the release of two Hamburg ships trading with Brazil, 18 Feb 1588 or 1599.

- *Salisbury (Cecil) IV: p. 200* – Burghley and the Lord Admiral to Sir Walter Raleigh regarding attempts to capture treasure ships from Havana and Brazil, 23 May 1592.

- *Salisbury (Cecil) XVIII: pp. 371–72* – Draft letter (1606) from James I to the States-General requesting a passport and safe conduct for William Barnes to enable him to export sugar, brazilwood and cotton from Brazil in Portuguese ships to Lisbon for transhipment in English ships to England.

- *Salisbury (Cecil) XVIII: p. 432* – Copy of a memoir (1606) from the Spanish ambassador regarding piracy by British ships on Spanish and Portuguese vessels coming from Brazil.

- *Salisbury (Cecil) XIX: pp. 473–74* – Report (mid-1607) on a project to allow Portuguese Jews into England, which might divert trade with Brazil to England, to Spain's detriment.

Salisbury Papers: 3rd Marquess
English

Robert Arthur Talbot Gascoyne-Cecil, 3rd Marquess of Salisbury (1830–1903), was one of Britain's most influential 19th-century political figures, having served three times as prime minister (1885–86, 1886–92 and 1895–1902) and four times as foreign secretary (1878, 1885–86, 1886–92 and 1895–1900). Until 1975 the private papers of the 3rd marquess were held on loan in the Library, Christ Church, Oxford, but they have since been returned to the family home. The papers are listed in J.F.A. Mason (1963), *Calendar of the Private Foreign Office Correspondence of Robert, Third Marquess of Salisbury*, two volumes (London).

The extremely limited material of Brazilian interest covers the years 1895–98, largely concentrated within one volume of papers [*3M/A130*]. The only material of some historical significance are the letters confirming Britain's formal renunciation of claims to the sovereignty of the Atlantic island of Trinidade. Otherwise, Brazil-related material is limited to correspondence regarding political relations between Brazil and Italy. Elsewhere in the collection [*3M/A126*] there are brief, though largely inconsequential, references to Japanese emigration to Brazil.

HULL

RECKITT'S HERITAGE

Reckitt Benckiser
Dansom Lane
Hull HU8 7DS

Tel: (01482) 582 910 • **Fax:** (01482) 582 532
E-mail: Gordon.Stephenson@ReckittBenckiser.com

Open: Wed and Thurs 9.30am–4.30pm.
Closed: Public holidays.
Admission: By appointment only.

Introduction:

A joint venture between Reckitt & Sons Ltd and J. & J. Colman saw the establishment in 1923 of a company called Atlantis (Brazil) Ltd, situated in Santo André, outside of the city of São Paulo. Factories were subsequently acquired or built in Mauá and elsewhere in Brazil. The first product made locally was Reckitt and Colman's 'Laundry Blues' washing detergent. Other products (including 'Brasso' and 'Coleman's Mustard') that were produced by the company at that time were imported from England. The company still manufactures and trades in Brazil under the name of Reckitt Benckiser (Brasil) Ltda.

Collections:

Records relating to Brazil held by the Reckitt's Heritage archive are particularly useful for the 1920s and 1930s when Brazilian operations were closely directed or overseen from England. Material (in English) includes accounting records (1924–69), board minutes, correspondence with suppliers, new product launch details, photographs of staff, buildings and products, and technical drawings of machinery, layouts and site plans.

UNIVERSITY OF HULL

Brynmar Jones Library
Cottingham Road
Hull HU6 7RX

www.hull.ac.uk/archives

Tel: (01482) 465 265 • **Fax:** (01482) 466 205
E-mail: archives@acs.hull.ac.uk

Open: Mon–Fri 9am–1pm and 2–5pm.
Closed: Public holidays and Christmas to New Year.
Admission: Appointment and proof of identity required.

Introduction:

The University of Hull's Brynmar Jones Library has been collecting manuscripts since 1927. Its holdings relate to the city of Hull, the northeast of England and overseas countries, in particular Australia and Southeast Asia.

Collections:

Only two manuscript collections that are held by the library have been identified as containing some Brazil-related content.

Hotham Family Papers
English
Included amongst the Hotham family papers are letter books and other manuscripts created by Sir Charles Hotham (1806–55), whose career was divided between the Royal Navy and colonial administration in Australia. Brazil-related material is limited to correspondence created while Hotham was in command of naval vessels serving in South American and West African stations.

The South American letter book [*DDHO/10/6*] covers the period from December 1842 to July 1846, while Hotham commanded the HMS *Gorgon*. They mainly concern Argentina and Paraguay but Brazilian naval affairs (including references to the slave trade) are also the subject of correspondence.

The West African letter book [*DDHO/10/7*] covers the period August 1846 to September 1848, while Hotham commanded the HMS *Devastation*. Although they primarily concern West Africa and the mid-Atlantic island of St Helena, an important part of the correspondence concerns the suppression of the Atlantic slave trade, with some letters written in Bahia.

Palmes Family Papers
English

These papers include a journal, believed to be written by
William Lindsay Palmes (1813–51) of Naburn, in East Yorkshire,
describing an 1842 voyage from Santa Cruz, Canary Islands
to Rio de Janeiro, and Palmes' stay there.

LEEDS

LEEDS DISTRICT ARCHIVE

(West Yorkshire Archives Service)
Chapeltown Road
Sheepscar
Leeds LS7 3AP

www.archives.wyjs.org.uk

Tel: (0113) 214 5814 • **Fax:** (0113) 214 5815
E-mail: leeds@wyjs.org.uk

Open: Mon, Tues, Thurs and Fri 9.30am–5pm.
Closed: Public holidays and 4–8 Feb.
Admission: Appointment required.

Introduction:

The Leeds District Archive is one of six constituents of the West York-shire Archive Service (see also under Bradford, p. 14). The archive's core holdings are the records of the city of Leeds, but the records of churches, local families and estates, and businesses and voluntary organisations have also been deposited here.

Collections:

From the 18th century until well into the 20th century, Leeds was one of England's most important industrial centres, noted especially for strong textile, clothing, engineering and mining businesses, all sectors for which exports to Brazil would have been significant at various times. Leeds District Archive holds the records of many local and regional businesses, of which others could be assumed to include Brazilian content of the kind described on p. 79. Of more obvious relevance to Brazil are the papers of George Canning, one of the most important political figures in relation to early 19th-century Latin American history. The archive also holds the papers of Augustus Stapleton (1800–80), George Canning's private secretary during the 1820s, but no material relating to Brazil has been identified within that collection.

George Canning Papers
English

The archive holds the bulk of the diaries and private papers of George Canning (1770–1827), whose political career included the post of foreign secretary between 1807 and 1809 and again between 1822 and 1827, key periods during which Brazil was gradually severing its ties with Portugal and developing into one of Britain's most important trading partners. Most of the material was transferred to the archives from Harewood House, near Leeds, which now retains only a bound set of dispatch books for their decorative value. These papers are, however, largely duplicates of documents found amongst the Foreign Office holdings at the National Archives (see p. 135).

Material relating to Brazil (1807–26) is a major part of the collection but many documents concern the independence (as well as other issues) of Spanish America or consist of personal correspondence with family members and British political figures (some of which, such as with Prime Minister Palmerston from 1824 to 1827, relate to Brazil). Although some of the Brazil-related documents are contemporary copies of Foreign Office items (see under National Archives, p. 131), most are not to be found elsewhere. The papers can be identified using a card index of names of correspondents and a handlist giving descriptions of bundles of documents (which range from a single letter to a hundred or more). The following list represents the main Brazil-related Canning Papers:

- George Canning's private diaries, 1792–1815, 1818–21, 1823.

- Correspondence with Viscount Strangford (British minister in Lisbon and then, following the transfer of the Portuguese court to Brazil, in Rio de Janeiro) concerning Portugal and Brazil, 1807–10.

- Correspondence with John Charles Villiers, Chevalier d'Almeida and others concerning Portugal and Brazil, 1807–10.

- Correspondence with Sir William A'Court, British ambassador in Lisbon, 1824–27.

- Correspondence with Sir Edward Thornton, British ambassador to the Portuguese court in Rio de Janeiro and in Lisbon, 1823–25.

- Correspondence with Sir Robert Gordon, minister to Brazil, 1826–28.

Hathorn, Davey & Co. Ltd
English

Manufacturers of steam-powered pumping machinery since the mid-19th century, Hathorn, Davey & Company started to export to the Brazilian market at the end of the same century. In addition to catalogues (from 1900), drawings of equipment and scrapbooks of newspaper and trade journal cuttings relating to the company, a complete set of order books (from 1852) survives which contain references to equipment sold to and orders received from Brazil and elsewhere.

Hunslet Engine Co. Ltd
English

During the 19th century the Hunslet Engine Company was a major supplier of steam locomotives to railway companies, estates and plantations in Latin America, not least Brazil. Included in this comprehensive collection are the records of other engine manufacturers that were later absorbed into Hunslet (Avonside Engine Co., 1864–1934; Kerr Stuart & Co., 1886–1930; Kitson & Co., 1839–1938; Manning Wardle & Co., 1858–1926). Of particular relevance are the order books which contain references to equipment sold to and orders received from Brazil and elsewhere and details of shipments. In addition there is a very complete set of technical data relating to the orders.

LEIGH

WIGAN ARCHIVES SERVICE

Town Hall
Leigh
Lancashire WN7 2DY

www.wiganmbc.gov.uk

Tel: (01942) 404 430 • **Fax:** (01942) 404 425
E-mail: heritage@wiganmbc.gov.uk

Open: Mon, Tues, Thurs and Fri 10am–1pm and 2–4.30pm.
Closed: Public holidays.
Admission: By appointment only; documents can be produced only
             by prior arrangement with the archivist.

Introduction:

The Wigan Archives Service's primary purpose is to collect, preserve, catalogue and make available to the public local records of the district it serves. These records include archives of the local authority itself, schools, churches, businesses, solicitors, families, estates and individuals as well as maps, photographs and ephemera.

Collections:

The archive holds a large collection of diaries, journals and letter books donated by Edwin Hall, a local book collector. Only a few items concern the Wigan area; most relate to other parts of Britain or to foreign countries. One significant item has been identified relating to Brazil.

*DDZ/EHC/27/M795 – **Mrs S.M. Miers Diary***
English
A 478-page diary (July 1850–June 1860) of Mrs S.M. Miers, the wife of Francis Charles Miers, a shipbuilder. The diary records, often in great detail, the Miers' marriage preparations, voyages in 1850 and 1853 between England and Brazil, and ten years of domestic life in Rio de Janeiro of a devoted wife and mother. The diary is an important document describing the closeted life of an upper-middle-class woman in Rio de Janeiro's British community in the mid-19th century.

LERWICK

SHETLAND ARCHIVES

Hay's Dock
Lerwick
Shetland Islands ZE1 0WP

www.shetland.gov.uk/archives

Tel: (01595) 695 057
E-mail: info@shetlandmuseumandarchives.org.uk

Open: Mon–Thurs 9am–1pm and 2–5pm, Fri 9am–1pm and
2–4pm.
Closed: Public holidays.
Admission: Readers are advised to contact the archives prior to
visiting.

Introduction:

The Shetland Archives documents the history of the Shetland Islands.
Material relating to other parts of Scotland and to foreign countries is
usually held only if the creator of a manuscript has a close connection
with the Shetland Islands.

Collections:

It appears that only one series with Brazil-related material is held by the
archives.

*D.6/142 – **Recruiting for the Brazilian Navy in Orkney and Shetland, 1836–40***
English
This comprises notorial copies of correspondence concerning
attempts to find employment for Shetland and Orkney islanders in
Brazil. Although recruits were officially travelling to Brazil to
establish a sperm whale industry on the island of Santa Catarina,
the real purpose of the recruitment efforts was to provide men for
service in the Brazilian Navy. The items held in Lerwick offer very
little in the way of insights into the emigration scheme; more
detailed records are found at the National Maritime Museum,
London, p. 174. No records relating to this scheme are held by the
Orkney Archives in Kirkwall [www.orkneylibrary.org.uk].

LIVERPOOL

LIVERPOOL RECORD OFFICE

Central Library
William Brown Street
Liverpool L3 8EW

archive.liverpool.gov.uk

Tel: (0151) 233 5817 • **Fax:** (0151) 207 1342
E-mail: RecOffice.central.library@liverpool.gov.uk

Open: Mon–Thurs 9am–7.30pm, Fri 9am–5pm, Sat 10am–4pm.
Closed: Public holidays and third and fourth weeks of June.
Admission: Proof of identity required.

Introduction:

The Liverpool Record Office holds material relating to Liverpool and its links with other parts of England and the world. The collection includes books, maps, newspapers from 1756, port and city directories, census returns and family and business history manuscripts.

Collections:

Only one Liverpool Record Office collection includes substantial Brazil-related material, although Brazil features marginally within the manuscripts of several others.

*387 BOO – **Booth Steamship Co. Ltd***
English
The origins of the Booth Steamship Co. extend back to 1863 when the brothers Alfred and Charles Booth established a partnership with the main purpose of importing leather to England from the USA. In 1865 the first two ships were acquired and by 1871 the brothers had expanded their business interests to include a regular Liverpool-to-northern-Brazil shipping service. The Booth Steamship Co. Ltd was incorporated in 1881 with Alfred Booth & Co. having a majority shareholding. By the time of the Amazon rubber boom (1890s and early 20th century) the Booth Steamship Co. was positioned as the most important such operation in the region, dominating trade between the Amazon and England and

owning fourteen ships. In 1901 the Booth Iquitos Line was established as a separate river operator to link the Peruvian Amazon region with the Atlantic, but was absorbed into the Booth Steamship Co. in 1913. The company was heavily involved in the modernisation of Amazon river ports, not least through the establishment in 1902 of the Manaus Harbour Company, a venture in which it held for some time a controlling interest.

The two world wars contributed to a decline in the importance of the Booth Steamship Co., with many of the ships requisitioned for the war efforts. Some of the ships were lost and the shipping company was unable to fully recover.

The records in this collection are from 1866 to 1971 and constitute one of the most complete sets of transport history records in Britain relating to Brazil. (See also under Merseyside Maritime Museum. p. 85.) Of particular significance are the following:

- *387 BOO / 1 and 2 – Minutes of General Meetings* (1901–71; 1 vol.) and *Directors Minute Books* (1901–40; 4 vols) – Containing minutes of annual general, extraordinary, and board meetings.

- *387 BOO / 3 – Steamers' Voyages* (1866–1943; 21 vols) – Each volume arranged alphabetically by the name of the vessel. Details are given for each voyage of time and date of arrivals and departures at/from ports, speed, amount and cost of coal consumed and sometimes names of officers and engineers. Six early volumes (for 1866–1901) provide details of cargo carried and costs incurred.

- *387 BOO / 4 – Ships Particulars* (1902–22; 2 vols, 6 folders) – Details of individual vessels including name and date of builder, dimensions, technical specifications and some scale drawings.

- *387 BOO / 5 – Correspondence relating to Manaus* (1902; 17 documents) – Letters in English from Brazil and Germany concerning shipping and dock developments in Manaus. Many of the letters express the frustration of

> Booth managers for being sent unsuitable equipment, while some correspondence provides insights into Anglo-German rivalry in the Amazon.
>
> - *387 BOO / 6 – Newspapers, scrapbooks, etc.* (1903–54; 7 vols) – Extensive newspaper and periodical cuttings relating to the Booth family, their business interests and company employees.
>
> - *387 BOO / 7 – Photographs* (1910–22, 1926; 3 vols) – Although many of the photographs relate to Booth's interests in the Peruvian Amazon, images of Brazil are well represented. Included are pictures of ports and Booth-linked facilities in Ceará, Maranhão, Porto Velho, Pará and elsewhere.

387 MD 37 – Journal of the ship Crown
English

This is a journal that was kept by Joseph Pinder, Master of the Crown, during a voyage from Liverpool to Demerara (British Guiana) and back to Liverpool between 12 May 1826 and 19 October 1826. Included is a vivid, twenty-page description of life in Maranhão, including discussions on general commerce of the province (and trade with Britain in particular), the conditions endured by slaves and criminals, and the lifestyle of upper-class Brazilian women.

George Benvenuto Buckley Mathew
English

George Benvenuto Buckley Mathew (1807–79) was a British diplomat who served in many parts of Latin America, including minister in Rio de Janeiro 1867–79. The collection covers Mathew's entire diplomatic career and includes a few official and private letters received while in Rio de Janeiro. (See also under Glamorgan Record Office, p. 26.)

*920 DER (15) – **Edward Henry Stanley, 15th Earl of Derby***
English
Edward Henry Stanley (1826–93) served as foreign secretary from 1866 to 1868, and again from 1874 to 1878, the first period in office covering the Paraguayan War. This substantial collection of official and semi-private letters includes some Brazilian material within six volumes of South American or other general foreign correspondence. Amongst the papers are general in-coming South American letters [*920 DER (15) 12/1/1*], letters from the British minister (Buckley Mathew) and consuls in Brazil [*920 DER (15) 5&6* and *920 DER (15) 16/1/1*] and copies of out-going letters from Stanley [*920 DER (15) 13/5* and *920 DER (15) 16/17/3*].

MERSEYSIDE MARITIME MUSEUM

Maritime Archives and Library
Albert Dock
Liverpool L3 4AQ

**www.liverpoolmuseums.org.uk/
maritime/archive**

Tel: (0151) 207 0001 ext. 4418 • **Fax:** (0151) 478 4590
E-mail: maritime@nmgmnh1.demon.co.uk

Open: Mon–Thurs 10.30am–4.30pm.
Closed: Public holidays.
Admission: Proof of identity required.

Introduction:

The Merseyside Maritime Museum's Maritime Archives and Library contains printed books, pamphlets and business and personal records concerning the port of Liverpool and its relationship to the rest of Britain and overseas. The archives do not hold lists of passengers, emigrants and mariners, nor are there many pictures of the port of Liverpool.

Collections:

Many records of shipping companies connected with Liverpool have been deposited with the archive, but Brazil-related material is limited.

Lamport and Holt Line
English

The Lamport and Holt Line was founded in 1845 and was a pioneer in trade between England and Brazil. In addition to Liverpool-to-Brazil services, the company (or its subsidiaries) from the 1860s linked Brazilian ports with London, Glasgow, Antwerp and New York. Particularly notable are the company's pioneering position in the development of the United States as a market for Brazilian coffee and its role in opening the Amazon to direct overseas trade. The archives hold material relating to both the Lamport and Holt Line and its associated companies for the period between 1865 and 1977 and are largely in the form of routine ledgers and basic minutes of board meetings.

Manaus Harbour Co. Ltd
English

The Manaus Harbour Co. Ltd collection is limited to printed accounts and reports for the years 1904–05.

Anglo-South American Airlines Ltd
English

Archival holdings relating to Anglo-South American Airlines Ltd are limited to very basic staff attendance records (1943–57), minutes of directors' meetings (1945–56) merely accepting annual or quarterly reports (the reports themselves have not been preserved), and routine correspondence (1943–57).

Booth Steamship Co. Ltd
English

The Booth Steamship Co. Ltd collection is limited to printed annual reports and accounts for the years 1901–42. (See also under Liverpool Record Office, pp. 82–84.)

Liverpool, Brazil & River Plate Steam Navigation Co.
English

Archival holdings relating to the Liverpool, Brazil & River Plate Steam Navigation Co. are limited to the memorandum and articles of association (1865 and 1911–13), basic minutes for board of directors (1908–77), accounting records, directors' attendance registers, balance sheets and profit and loss accounts (1910–36). The records shed very little light on the shipping company's operational details.

Pacific Steam Navigation Co.
English
Established in 1840, the Pacific Steam Navigation Co. (PSNC) mainly served the west coast of South America. Rio de Janeiro and Santos, however, were also regularly scheduled ports of call for PSNC ships, although these Brazilian connections are not reflected in the surviving documents.

◆

UNIVERSITY OF LIVERPOOL LIBRARY

Special Collections and Archive **sca.lib.liv.ac.uk/collections/**
PO Box 123
Liverpool L69 3DA

Tel: (0151) 794 2696 • **Fax:** (0151) 794 2681
E-mail: archives@liv.ac.uk

Open: Mon–Fri 9.30am–5pm.
Closed: Public holidays.
Admission: By appointment only; proof of identity required.

Introduction:

The library's archive contains material on a wide variety of themes, many of national or international significance, although the emphasis is on holdings with a Liverpool connection.

Collections:

The Brazil-related manuscript collections that are held by the University of Liverpool Library are few in number but all are of some considerable significance.

MS.5.21 (12 and 13) – **English in the Amazon**
English
Two manuscript drafts of a document (c. 1630) addressed to Charles I regarding the establishment of an English colony in northern Brazil. The documents amount to a total of fourteen fragile pages, the text of which is extremely difficult to decipher.

John Pascoe Grenfell Papers
English (some Portuguese)

Born in London in 1800, John Pascoe Grenfell joined the East India Company at the age of 11, travelling to India several times, first as a midshipman and then as a mate. In 1819 he entered the service of the Republic of Chile under the command of Lord Cochrane, admiral of the Chilean naval forces, and took part in the war of independence against Spain. On the conclusion of the war in 1823, Grenfell returned to Liverpool, but by the end of the year he had volunteered for service in the new Brazilian Navy and was engaged, again under Admiral Lord Cochrane, to take part in Brazil's struggle against Portugal.

Grenfell rose to the rank of commander after having compelled the surrender of the Portuguese forces at Pará and the adhesion of the province of that name to the new government. In 1844 he was made rear-admiral and two years later he was appointed Brazil's consul-general at Liverpool. Shortly after, however, Grenfell was recalled to South America, where he participated in Brazil's conflict with Argentine forces and reached the rank of vice-admiral. He returned to Liverpool to resume his appointment as vice-admiral, retaining his position until his death in 1869.

The papers are held unsorted in four boxes and total some 586 documents spanning the years 1820 to 1852. Most material (logs, official and private correspondence, newspaper clippings) relates to Grenfell's career in the Brazilian Navy from his initial recruitment. There is a complete absence of material relating to Grenfell's activities as Brazilian consul-general in Liverpool (the limited consular material that has survived is held by a private collector in São Paulo). Examples of especially significant documents include:

- Grenfell's personal defence put at his 1824 court martial in Rio de Janeiro.

- Logs of the four ships commanded by Grenfell between 1823 and 1826, including the period of the struggle for independence.

- A set of 150 letters from Lord Cochrane, mainly covering the years 1847 to 1868 – a mix of reminiscences and pleasantries and discussions of awards being granted to the two former naval officers.

- Letters between Grenfell and other officers in the Brazilian Navy.

- Documents relating to the struggles for the restoration of Pará in 1823.

- Documents relating to the attack on the forces of Admiral Brown (of Argentina) in 1826.

- Documents relating to the pacification of Rio Grande in 1846.

- Letters to Grenfell from Dom Saturnino Souza e Oliveira (president of the province of Rio Grande do Sul) and from the Barão de Caxias regarding the military situation in the south of Brazil.

*TM/12 and TM/14 – **Liverpool School of Tropical Medicine: Research Laboratory, Manaus, Brazil***
English
In 1905, the Liverpool School of Tropical Medicine sent an expedition to Brazil to study yellow fever in the Amazon. Based in Manaus, the expedition initially used local laboratory facilities for the team's work but by 1910 a separate research facility had been established providing a secure scientific base. Liverpool maintained its Manaus Research Laboratory (MRL) until 1931, by which time the school's main overseas centre was located in Sierra Leone.

Any records that may have existed at the MRL appear to have been lost but a number of useful files containing reports, correspondence and photographs are in the Liverpool School of Tropical Medicine's archive. Included amongst the general holdings are notes on the prevention of malaria and yellow fever, illustrations (c. 1910) of the anopheles mosquito and the tiger mosquito, and a six-page report (1920–21) on Liverpool's Amazon work by Dr Wolferston Thomas (1875–1931), a member of the 1905 expedition and between 1914 and 1931 the director of the MRL.

Amongst the files of private papers of former Liverpool School of Tropical Medicine employees is important material relating to the MRL. There are portraits of Dr Thomas in Brazil, photographs of his smallpox hospital (later a home for destitute people) and of his tombstone in Manaus, and letters written after his death attesting to his work. Dr Rupert 'Tim' Gordon (1893–1961) left 26 letters sent from Brazil to family members recording his voyage from Liverpool to Manaus via Belém, his daily life in Manaus, observations on the British community in the town and comments on the Brazilian way of life. In other notes and a report on Brazil, he describes Amerindian methods of fishing by poisoning the river, and he discusses his work as a research assistant at the MRL. There is an album of photographs of views of Manaus and the wider Amazon region, rubber collection, fishing, and Dr Gordon's colleagues.

LONDON

BANK OF ENGLAND

Archive Section (HO–SV)
Threadneedle Street
London EC2R 8AH

www.bankofengland.co.uk

Tel: (020) 7601 4889/5096 • **Fax:** (020) 7601 4356
E-mail: archive@bankofengland.co.uk

Open: Mon–Fri 10am–4.30pm.
Closed: Public holidays.
Admission: By appointment only.

Introduction:

The Bank of England was founded in 1694 as the first public bank in the British Isles. Since that time the Bank has been at the centre of the British banking system and during the 18th century it developed its main function of acting as banker to the government and to the banking system. Included in its responsibilities were managing the national debt and issuing sterling notes in England and Wales.

Over the course of centuries, the Bank's roles and responsibilities gradually became more complex. From the beginning of the 20th century, an increased interest in economic matters and statistics, both domestic and international, was reflected in the work of the Bank. In the period between the two world wars, the special importance placed by the Bank on relations with other central banks was formalised by the creation in 1927 of a Central Banking Section, while in 1932 the Overseas and Foreign Department was established, later renamed the Overseas Department and in 1980 reorganised into a number of International Divisions.

Collections:

The Bank of England has an extensive archive covering all aspects of its administration from its foundation to the present. Although much of the material held by the archive concerns the internal workings of the Bank, external relationships are well documented. However, there is little archival material covering the Bank's pre-20th-century international interests and links. Brazil-related collections cover the years 1923 to 1980. The archive also holds official and semi-official papers of many former employees. The papers of Sir Otto Niemeyer [*OV9*], discussed below, include Brazil-related material. Researchers have access to most records over thirty years old.

The archive's catalogue – a set of bound lists – may be consulted in the search room; although not indexed, the 'supplementary notes' provide some indication of the contents of the files. The useful *Guide to the Archives* (London, n.d.) may be downloaded from the Bank's website and is available in printed form from the Bank.

- ## OV – Overseas Department

OV103 – Brazil – 1923–80
English
These 71 files, discussed in greater detail below, are divided between those that cover general financial and economic correspondence, etc., and those with more specific areas of concern. Some subjects (for example, negotiations about Brazil's sterling balances) appear in one group of files at one period and in another group at another. There is also considerable overlap between groups, with many copies of the same documents in different files.

OV103 / 1 to 14 – Brazil: Country Files – 29 Aug 1927–13 Aug 1964
The fourteen files, arranged by date, cover a range of financial and economic matters. They usually contain documents relating to more than one topic and are sometimes quite substantial. Documents include correspondence between Brazilian government and Bank of England officials and reports discussing visits to Brazil. Topics covered include:

- Brazilian loans outstanding, 1928.

- A note about the functions of the Banco do Brasil, October 1929.

- Sir Otto Niemeyer's visit to Brazil (including a copy of his report), 1931.

- A paper on coffee, 1934.

- A history of the Brazilian exchange system from 1906, November 1947.

- British investments in Brazil, 1948.

- A visit by Bank of England officials seeking to introduce some order into Brazilian financial chaos, 1951–52.

OV103 / 15 to 30 – Brazil: Financial (Including Trade) Relations with the United Kingdom – 11 Jan 1940–31 Jan 1955
English
Thirteen of the files (1940–48) concern the Brazilian foreign debt and the Anglo-Brazilian Payments Agreements overseen by the Bank of England and the Banco do Brasil. Three of the files (1949–55) document general financial (including trade) relations between Brazil and the United Kingdom.

OV103 / 31 to 39 – Brazil: Central Bank (Banco do Brasil) –
10 Feb 1925–27 April 1965
English
The files document the Bank of England's relationship with the Banco do Brasil. The Banco do Brasil's function as a central bank is discussed, and there is correspondence reporting on senior officers of the Brazilian bank.

OV103 / 40 to 66 – Brazil: Foreign Debt – 7 Aug 1931–13 Dec 1965
English
The files document technical discussions relating to the negotiation and management of Brazil's external debt. Three files [*OV103 / 40–42*] consist of cables to and from Sir Henry Lynch (1878–1958) and mainly relate to Brazil's inability to service its debt. Lynch was senior partner of Davidson, Pullen and Co. (Rio de Janeiro), one-time president of Brazil's Chamber of Commerce, and, either formally or informally, Rothschild's representative in Brazil. Other files deal with bonded debt [*OV103 / 45 to 55*]. Several files concern specific claims by British investors in British- or US-registered companies, sometimes including detailed histories of the claims. Company-specific files include:

- *OV103 / 56–7* – Brazil Railway Company, 31 Dec 1938–16 May 1956.

- *OV103 / 63* – Paraná Plantations, 19 Jan 1943–19 May 1944.

OV103 /67 to 71 – Brazil: Miscellaneous – 1924–64
English
The earliest Brazil country-specific file is represented in this category. Dated 23 Feb–21 March 1924, the file [*OV103 / 67*] relates to the Montagu Report. E.S. Montagu led a financial mission to Brazil which made two reports, one to the Brazilian president and one to the London merchant banks Rothschild, Barings and Schroders, both arguing on behalf of British companies doing business in Brazil. Sir Charles Addis, a director of the Bank of England, was a member of the mission and provided a historical survey of currency, exchange and banking in Brazil (see p. 195).

*OV9 / 293 to 295 – **Sir Otto Niemeyer's Papers: Mission to Brazil, 1931***
English
Sir Otto Niemeyer (1883–1971) joined the Bank of England as an adviser in 1927 and in 1938 he was appointed a director, a position he held until his retirement in 1952. Niemeyer particularly worked on the international side of the Bank's business and was invited by a number of overseas countries to report on their financial and economic problems.

Niemeyer was invited to visit Brazil in 1931 to advise on such financial reforms as he saw necessary to secure the maintenance of budget equilibrium and a number of other matters. Niemeyer's report appeared in July 1931 and it recommended that Brazil should phase out its coffee price support (valorisation) policies, bring the government's finances under control and curtail independent foreign borrowing by states and municipalities. It also included complete draft statutes for the creation of a Brazilian central bank, totally independent from the government but with significant foreign influence, as well as the recommendation that Brazil should return to the gold standard.

In addition to material found in Brazil country files (in particular *OV103 / 1, 39 and 69* – see p. 93), there are three Niemeyer files devoted to the Brazilian mission and its aftermath:

- *OV9 / 293* – Letters and memos (10 Jan–30 May 1931) concerning travel and personnel arrangements for the Brazilian mission.

- *OV9 / 294* – Correspondence (6 March–26 July 1931) with the Brazilian minister of finance concerning budgets, exchange control, the establishment of a central reserve bank and other mission interests. Also in the file are assorted memos and documentation, newspaper clippings discussing the mission and a copy of Niemeyer's completed report.

- *OV9 / 295* – Documents relating to the Banco do Brasil, including assorted statistics on Brazilian banks, details of currency issue and Brazil's foreign exchange position. Also correspondence and reports (1933) concerning the Brazilian government's debt and budget and coffee price statistics.

*OV9 / 92 to 96 – **Sir Otto Niemeyer's Papers: Council of Foreign Bondholders: Brazil – 11 June 1936–31 Dec 1941***
English
Only three files featuring documents relating to Sir Otto Niemeyer's membership of the Council of Foreign Bondholders are devoted to Brazil. Correspondence, reports, etc. in these files examine Brazil's means of paying its external debt and the position and order of priority of Brazil's various loans.

◆

BARING ARCHIVE
ING-Barings
60 London Wall
London EC2M 5TQ

Tel: (020) 7767 1944 • **Fax:** (020) 7767 7131
E-mail: archive@ing-baring.co.uk

Open: Mon–Fri 10am–4pm.
Closed: Public holidays.
Admission: By appointment only; letter of recommendation required.

Introduction:

Barings, one of Britain's most renowned merchant banks, was established by the Baring family in Exeter in 1762. From the early 19th century until its dramatic collapse in 1995, the bank played central roles in the financing of international trade, infrastructure and the negotiation of government loans. During the 19th and the early 20th centuries, Barings specialised geographically in the finance of the USA, Canada, Russia and Argentina and was known especially for its role in railway development. Although Brazil was always marginal in terms of Barings' overall operations (and, similarly, Barings was rarely a significant financial partner for Brazil), the bank maintained some business dealings with the country.

Collections:

Although Brazil-related papers are a minor part of the archive's holdings – a reflection of Barings' marginal role in Brazil – the files are not without importance, especially those created in the early 19th and the early 20th centuries. The collection may be accessed through the electronic catalogue (not online), which provides detailed listings of the contents of the individual volumes of documents.

HC4 – House Correspondence: Brazil
English
This is a bundle of Brazil-related correspondence made up of ten distinct series of letters from Barings' clients in Rio de Janeiro and Bahia. The correspondence, primarily relating to Brazilian exports – or potential exports – is strongest for the 1830s but there are some letters from other early and mid-19th century decades. Some letters stand out as being particularly informative, examples of which are:

- *HC4.2.3 and HC4.2.4* – Letters (1837 and 1838) from John James Sturza in Bahia concerning a proposal to establish steam navigation and to set up diamond- and gold-mining operations in the province.

- *HC4.2.6* – An 1838 series of letters from Henry Bellamy Webb reporting on the coffee trade and merchant houses in Rio de Janeiro and on the state of exchange.

Partners Files Main Series: Brazil

English

Although Barings' relationship with Brazil was limited, there were some substantial 20th-century business dealings, some of which generated files with considerable correspondence, memos, reports, etc. The main relevant ones are outlined below:

- Brazil Government 7.5% Coffee Loan – 12 vols (1922–35)

- São Paulo State 8% Loan 1921 – 3 vols (1921–46)

- São Paulo State 6% Loan 1928 – 2 vols (1928–31)

- São Paulo State Coffee Credit – 2 vols (1929–31)

- São Paulo State Coffee Realisation Loan 1930 – 11 vols (1930–38)

These files contain a wealth of detailed information in the form of correspondence and cables between London and Barings' representatives in Brazil and the Brazilian and São Paulo governments and agencies, in particular relating to the stabilisation of coffee prices and coffee valorisation loans. Bound together with this material are related documents, including draft agreements, contracts and newspaper cuttings, concerning the original bond issues and the subsequent restructuring of the debts. Each volume is indexed by subject and name of correspondent.

Brazil Iron Ore Project (1909–55)

English

This is a vast resource (sixteen volumes) on the finance and development of iron ore extraction and of associated transport facilities in Brazil. Although iron ore sources throughout Brazil are discussed, the bulk of the material in this collection concerns the Itabira Iron Ore Company in Minas Gerais, associated railway developments (including the Brazil Victoria Minas Railway) through Espírito Santo, and port facilities in the state capital, Vitória. Thirteen of the volumes cover the early years (1909–18) of the project and include geological and engineering reports, financial assessments, correspondence and maps, plans and newspaper cuttings. The collection is unparalleled as a resource documenting each stage of the development (and eventual winding down) of a major British business operation in Brazil.

Note: Substantial files concerning the Itabira Iron Ore Co. (1919–63) are found among the Percival Farquhar Papers at Yale University Library [www.library.yale.edu/latinamerica/mss.html].

◆

THE BRITISH LIBRARY

Manuscripts Collections
96 Euston Road
London NW1 2DB

www.bl.uk

Tel: (020) 7412 7513 • **Fax:** (020) 7412 7745
E-mail: mss@bl.uk

Open:	*Manuscripts Reading Room* – Mon 10am–5pm, Tues–Sat 9.30am–5pm.
	General Humanities Reading Rooms – Mon 10am–8pm, Tues–Thurs 9.30am–8pm, Fri–Sat 9.30am–5pm.
Closed:	Public holidays.
Admission:	Interview required to determine that the material to be consulted is not available elsewhere or requires the facilities of a large research library. Academic staff and postgraduate students are usually issued with passes valid for five years. Readers who have a long distance to travel are advised to obtain confirmation in writing in advance that the manuscripts they require are available.

Introduction:

In 1753 the British Museum was founded, with a library (the British Museum Library) that included in its remit the manuscripts collections. The foundation manuscripts collections are those of Sir Hans Sloane, Robert and Edward Harley and Sir Robert Cotton and still bear their names, while another important early collection is that of Francis Egerton. Since the foundation of the museum, the manuscripts collections have been continuously added to by donation, bequest and purchase. Most of the items acquired in this way become part of the Additional (Add.) collection, now by far the largest of the collections. In 1973 the British Library was established, with the manuscript holdings of the British

Museum Library becoming the basis of the collections of the Department of Manuscripts.

Note: Although the India Office Library is now held at the British Library, these collections are historically and entirely separate from each other, with their own cataloguing systems and reading room facilities. For these reasons the India Office Library (Oriental and India Office Collections) is discussed as a separate entry (see p. 121).

Collections:

Manuscripts held by the British Library are related to all disciplines and range in origin from the 4th century to the present day. The Department of Manuscripts holds a considerable number of items of Brazilian interest. The foundation collections (Cotton, Egerton, Harley and Sloane) include individual journals of voyages, letters, copies of rare documents from Spanish and Portuguese archives and official transcripts of government reports relating to Brazil. More such items (and some extensive collections) are to be found throughout the varied series of Additional manuscripts, which also include the private papers of British politicians and diplomats.

Although the British Library's Brazil-related holdings of manuscripts are limited when compared to the collections relating to Spanish America, many important documents are held either as part of named collections of papers or as miscellaneous items. There are few literary or scientific manuscripts, the collections instead being strongly biased towards the political and historical. Even in this regard, collections are uneven. Twentieth-century material is minimal, and while there are some significant 16th- and 17th-century manuscripts, most Brazil-related documents date from the 18th and 19th centuries. While manuscript records of government departments or of public institutions are not to be found at the library, it is still possible to find much correspondence that relates to political affairs. Many of the manuscripts of Brazilian interest fall into this category and include the correspondence of the British diplomats who served in Brazil and of government ministers. The slave trade is a recurring theme in many of these series of manuscripts – usually from the perspective of the abolitionists but occasionally from that of the traders.

FINDING AIDS:

Located in the Manuscripts Reading Room, in the British Library building at St Pancras, are the main index to manuscripts as well as descriptive catalogues and indexes to the individual collections arranged by name of collection. These are now supported by the Manuscripts Online Catalogue (molcat) [http://molcat.bl.uk/], the automated finding tool for most of the collections. With a few exceptions (most notably the Cotton and Harley collections), all the manuscript catalogue descriptions have been entered onto molcat. Molcat is searchable using keywords (consider English and Portuguese alternatives as well as other subject or name permutations – e.g. 'Amazon', 'Amazonia', 'Grão Pará') or one may search for a specific manuscript accession number within a selected collection.

Another valuable manuscript finding aid is Oliveira Lima's *Relação dos manuscriptos portuguezas e estrangeiros de interesse para o Brazil existentes no Museu Britannico de Londres* (Rio de Janeiro, 1903). The publication is a thorough annotated listing of largely 17th- to early 19th-century English, Portuguese, Spanish, French and Brazilian manuscripts that the library holds relating to Brazil. It includes very little material that was created later in the 19th century and, of course, no 20th-century listings.

Peter Walne's *A Guide to Manuscript Sources for the History of Latin America and the Caribbean in the British Isles* (London, 1973) is also an important finding aid. There are 66 pages of manuscript listings devoted to the library, a large proportion of which relate to Brazil, with more 19th-century items having been deposited and catalogued since Lima's guide was published. Note that the *Guide* states that the manuscripts are at the British Museum, whereas they have since been transferred to the British Library at St Pancras. ▩

● **Cotton Manuscripts**

The contribution made by the politician and antiquarian Sir Robert Cotton (1571–1631) to the British Museum is particularly noted for its Anglo-Saxon charters and medieval manuscripts. Also amongst the Cotton collection, however, are scattered 16th- and early

17th-century manuscripts relating to trade and Sir Walter Raleigh's voyages to the West Indies and Guiana. But apart from a few 16th- and 18th-century maps, one of the very few Brazil-related items appears to be a letter in Portuguese from Lisbon dated 6 Dec 1594 discussing trade with Brazil [*Cotton Galba D. X. f. 118b*].

• Egerton Manuscripts

This collection takes the name of Francis Egerton (1756–1829) who bequeathed to the British Museum 67 manuscripts and £12,000 to produce an income to purchase more items. Apart from a series of Spanish State Papers (see below), few of the Egerton Manuscripts relate to Brazil. There are, however, several important 18th-century diaries kept by English mariners circumnavigating the globe (including on Captain Cook's voyages) that include some entries made in Brazilian ports. Examples of isolated manuscripts (both in English) specifically dealing with Brazilian affairs are:

- *Eg. 742* – Reply of Queen Elizabeth I to the Portuguese Ambassador concerning the commerce of English ships along the coasts of Brazil, Africa and India, 1562.

- *Eg. 2395, f. 46* – Privileges granted to Dutch Jews in Brazil, c. 17th century.

*Eg. 1131 to 1136 – **Spanish State Papers: Papeles Varios de Portugal** Spanish*
A major six-volume collection made up of several hundred *Consultas* (reports to the king in Council), letters and other State Papers from 1620–26 when Portugal was under the domination of Spain. The documents (originals or official copies) include reports relating to Brazil and other Portuguese colonies. Subjects are varied, including the state of Brazilian defences, the Dutch presence in Bahia and losses suffered by individual petitioners. A separate index for the *Consultas*, a listing of individual documents, is available for consultation in the Manuscripts Reading Room.

- ### Harley Manuscripts

  The personal libraries of the 1st and 2nd Earls of Oxford, Robert Harley (1661–1724) and Edward Harley (1689–1741) were amongst the British Museum's foundation collections of manuscripts. Manuscripts include 17th-century accounts of the English and Spanish presence in the Americas, including some by Sir Walter Raleigh regarding Guiana. The only specifically Brazil-related document appears to be an early 17th-century document [*Harl. 1583, f. 196*] in English relating to the establishment by Duke Lennox and Richmond, Earl of Arundel, and other members of the nobility, of an English colony on the Amazon River.

- ### Sloane Manuscripts

  Within the personal library of Sir Hans Sloane (1660–1753), medical doctor, scientist, collector and a founder of the British Museum, are papers detailing Sir Walter Raleigh's 17th-century Guiana voyages but little appears to relate to Brazil apart from the following items, all in English:

  - *Sloane 2496 – The voyages, commanders, and successes of the Queen's ships in the time of the war with Spain, 1585–1603. The discoveries of divers countries, and the enterprizes of the Spaniards and Portuguese, in their conquest of the Indians.*

  - *Sloane 159, f. 20* – Letters patent from King Henri IV of France, and ordinances and commissions relating to the colonisation of Guiana, Brazil and Peru, 1602–10.

  - *Sloane 608, ff. 151–91b – History of J. de Léry's voyage to Brazil in 1577*, translated by Dr D. Foote, 1674.

- ### Additional Manuscripts

  The Additional series (Add.) is by far the largest collection and comprises all the manuscripts acquired by gift, purchase or bequest since 1756, other than the Egerton Manuscripts and a few other separate collections. Brazil-related material mainly takes the form of individual or small groups of documents found scattered amongst series of private papers and items acquired on their own. There are, however, a few manuscript series in which Brazil is of central importance. The series or items described here are either the most significant of the Brazil-related Additional collections, or are representative of the variety of material within this immense and diverse collection. More comprehensive searches should be made using the finding aids (see p. 100), from which a more thorough inventory of Brazil-related material emerges.

Add. 43039 to 43358 – **Aberdeen Papers**
English (some French and Portuguese)
The political career of the Edinburgh-born statesman George Hamilton Gordon, 4th Earl of Aberdeen (1784–1860), followed a period in the foreign service in Europe. The election to an English seat in the House of Lords enabled Aberdeen to take government positions, serving twice as foreign secretary (1828–30 under the Duke of Wellington and 1841–46 under Sir Robert Peel) and later as prime minister (1852–55). As foreign secretary, Aberdeen is remembered for the Slave Trade (Brazil) Act of August 1845 – the so-called 'Aberdeen Act' – which authorised the British Navy to treat Brazilian slave ships as pirate vessels and send them for condemnation in British vice-admiralty courts in St Helena and elsewhere. When Aberdeen was prime minister, Brazil was relegated very much into the background, with interest in foreign affairs instead dominated by Britain's relations with Russia and by Aberdeen's eventual resignation due to criticism of his government's handling of the Crimean War.

There are 320 volumes of Aberdeen Papers. Manuscripts of Brazilian interest are mainly found within the 108 volumes of official and semi-official correspondence and other papers generated during Aberdeen's tenures as foreign secretary [*Add. 4380–43122* for 1828–30 and *Add. 43123–43187* for 1841–46]. Scattered Brazilian references are also found within the volumes of general correspondence, diaries and letter books.

Volumes covering Aberdeen's first tenure as foreign secretary include correspondence from two British envoys to Brazil, John Ponsonby (Sept 1828–Aug 1830) and Viscount Strangford (Aug 1828–May 1829) and Brazilian special envoy to London, Manoel Rodrigues Gameiro Pessoa (June–Oct 1828), amongst others [*Add. 43081*]. There are letter books containing copies or abstracts of Aberdeen's official correspondence to and from Brazil, 1828–30 [*Add. 43094–43095*] and the correspondence of Aberdeen's brother, Sir Robert Gordon, while serving as minister to Brazil (see under separate heading, p. 108).

Of particular importance in relation to Aberdeen's second period as foreign secretary are correspondence and other papers relating to the suppression of the Atlantic slave trade, some volumes of which are specifically of Brazilian interest:

- *Add. 43124* – Papers relating chiefly to Brazil, 1841–48. Included is correspondence with (1) Charles James Hamilton, sometime minister to Brazil, 1842–46, *ff. 1–134b*; (2) Henry Ellis, relating to his unsuccessful special mission to Brazil, 1842–43, for the negotiation of a commercial treaty, *ff. 135–210b*; (3) John Hobart Caradoc, sometime minister to Brazil, 1841–48, *ff. 211–316b*; (4) Marques José Lisbôa, Brazilian minister in London, 1846, *ff. 317–353b*.

- *Add. 43125* – Papers relating to the slave trade with Brazil, compiled officially for use in connection with the negotiations consequent upon the termination in 1845 of the Anglo-Brazilian Convention of 1826 for the suppression of the trade. Included amongst the papers are (1) copies and abstracts of the King's (or Queen's) Advocate on contested questions relating to captured Brazilian slave vessels, 1827–44, *ff. 3–89b*; (2) extracts from Parliamentary Papers containing decisions of the British Government upon the contested questions relating to captured Brazilian slave ships, 1825–39, *ff. 90–132b*; (3) papers relating to the Brazilian Slave Trade Act of 1845; (4) papers showing co-operation of the Spanish and Portuguese authorities in the suppression of the slave trade, 1845–46, *ff. 259–318b*; (5) returns showing numbers of British warships employed in the suppression of the slave trade, 1837–44, *ff. 344–45b*.

- *Add. 43158–43159* – Letter books containing copies or abstracts of official correspondence to and from Brazil, Jan 1842–Dec 1845.

- *Add. 43160* – Letter book containing copies or abstracts of official correspondence to and from Brazil in relation to Henry Ellis' unsuccessful special mission for the negotiation of a commercial treaty, Aug 1842–April 1843.

- *Add. 43245* – Papers relating to the Brazilian slave trade, 1845–46.

Add. 37042 to 37044 – British Guiana Papers
Portuguese (some English)

A collection of transcripts of official and other documents relating to the Portuguese occupation of Maranhão, Grão Pará and adjoining parts of northern Brazil, 1624–1822. Most of the several hundred documents (1,191 folios in three volumes) were copied from Portuguese archives, and the transcripts were made for the British government to use in the 1903 arbitration on the boundaries of British Guiana.

Although the ultimate purpose was to examine the historical justification of Brazil's territorial claims, the subject matter of the transcripts is wide-ranging, with the title or topic, author, addressee and date of each document catalogued (molcat accessible). The enslavement of Indians, Spanish and Dutch encroachment into the region, the activities of Jesuit missionaries and Portuguese military preparedness are the main subjects, with examples of individual documents being:

- *Add. 37042, f. 5* – Extract from a royal letter on the reservation of the captaincies of Grão Pará and Maranhão to the Crown, and their boundaries, 1633.

- *Add. 37042, ff. 17, 21, 35* – Petition of Peter Sotman (or Suetman or Setman), an Irishman, to the king, to be allowed to settle the Ilha de Joannes, 1643. Royal licence to allow Sotman to settle at the mouth of the Amazon with 400 companions, 1643. Petition from João Delgado Figueira urging the rescinding of the grant, 1644.

- *Add. 37042, f. 39b* – Report concerning gold mines on the Amazon and the Tocantins, 1645.

- *Add. 37042, f. 62* – Appeal by Father Antonio Vieira to the Senate of the chamber in Pará against breaking promises made to the Indians and the laws for their protection, 1661.

- *Add. 37043, f. 3* – Letter from the king to the governor of Maranhão, asking the name of a missionary who refused to supply Indians to the expedition of Sergeant-Major Belchior Mendes de Moraes against the Mayapepemâ Indians on the Rio Negro, 1730.

- *Add. 37044, f. 28*– List of 'villas' and 'lugares' in the captaincy of the Rio Negro, 1773.

- *Add. 37044, f. 54* – Report by Filippe Sturm to the governor of Grão Pará, on his expedition against the Spanish and the building of a new fort at the mouth of the Tacutú River, 1776.

- *Add. 37044, ff. 152, 170, 177, 391* – On a revolt by Indians on the Rio Branco, their transfer to other districts, and their land being given to another tribe, 1782–90.

Although not part of this collection, other significant documents held by the library that have a bearing on the British Guiana–Brazil boundary issue include the following:

- *Add. 34205* – Journal of Sir Robert H. Schomburgk's expedition to explore the boundaries of British Guiana, 1843 (see also under University of Birmingham Library, p. 11 and Royal Geographic Society, p. 192.)

- *Add. 16936–16939* – Drawings (chiefly coloured) and sketches by E.A. Goodall illustrating the scenery of the interior of British Guiana and manners of the inhabitants, made when he was draughtsman for the expedition of Sir Robert H. Schomburgk.

Add. 69868 to 69883 – **Coke Papers**
English
Formerly held at Melbourne Hall in Derbyshire, this series of
papers includes the incoming correspondence of Sir John Coke
(1563–1644), the secretary of state to King Charles I at a time of
English interest in the Amazon River and the Dutch occupation of
northeastern Brazil. These manuscripts are listed, with a précis of
each item, in *The Manuscripts of Earl Cowper preserved at
Melbourne Hall, Derbyshire*, vol. II (London, 1888). Brazil-related
documents appear to be limited to the following:

- Letter from the English diplomat Francis, Lord Cottingham
  (1578–1652) to Sir John Coke concerning an attempt to
  establish a colony on the Amazon River and referring to
  eight of the best men having been killed by 'savages',
  22 June 1633 [*Cowper*, II, p. 21].

- Letter from Viscount Conway and Kilulta to Sir John Coke
  concerning news of the Dutch capture of Brazil, 17 Aug 1637
  [*Cowper*, II, p. 165].

- Report on the activities in Brazil of the Dutch West India
  Company and Pernambuco governor, Count Johan-Maurice
  of Nassau, and of the blockade of Bahia, 1638 [*Cowper*,
  II, p. 207].

Add. 5885 to 59478, 69038 to 69411 – **Dropmore Papers**
English
This collection consists of some 640 volumes of correspondence
and other papers. Included are the papers of William Wyndham
Grenville, Baron Grenville (1759–1834), whose political career
included the posts of foreign secretary (1791–1801) and prime
minister (1806–07).

Cataloguing limitations make the identification of documents of
Brazilian interest difficult but some relevant material certainly
exists. Apart from a few documents identifiable with molcat, the
most useful index for the Dropmore Papers is the Historical
Manuscripts Commission's ten-volume *The Manuscripts of
J.B. Fortescue, Esquire, preserved at Dropmore (1892–1927).*

Although there are numerous papers included relating to Spanish America and the West Indies, there is little of Brazilian interest. Of some significance, however are several letters (dated 14, 24 and 28 November 1807 and 3 January 1808) to Lord Grenville mentioning the flight of the Portuguese court from Lisbon to Brazil (see vol. IX, pp. 143, 151, 152, 165).

Also of value is a 47-page outline, dated 25 June 1806, of a scheme presented to Lord Grenville to transport the Prince Regent of Portugal, or his son, to Brazil and to send a military force to assist the emancipation of Spanish and Portuguese South America with the intention of opening up the region to direct British trade [*Add. 59285 Vol. 431*]. The scheme proposes that Britain should establish naval and commercial stations in Bahia and, if possible, Rio de Janeiro and the island of Santa Catarina. There is no indication as to the origin, or authorship, of the scheme.

Add. 44086 to 44835 – **Gladstone Papers**
English

These are the papers of William Ewart Gladstone (1809–98), whose political career culminated as prime minister but who held many other government positions, including vice-president and president of the Board of Trade (1841–45). There are only a very few Brazil-related items [especially *Add. 44733*, with isolated papers in *44729, 44730, 44777*] within this very large collection, and they concern almost exclusively British-Brazilian commercial relations – specifically memoranda of discussions regarding the negotiations of a new trade treaty, in particular the terms and levels of customs duties for sugar and other products over the years 1841–44.

Add. 43214 to 43215 – **Sir Robert Gordon**
English

The diplomat Sir Robert Gordon (1791–1847) – the brother of Lord Aberdeen – served as minister to Brazil between 1826 and 1828. Included within the Aberdeen Papers (see pp. 103–5) are two volumes of correspondence between Gordon and Lord Ponsonby, the Foreign Office and naval officers in the South Atlantic:

- *Add. 43214* – Correspondence (1826–28) of Sir Robert Gordon in Rio de Janeiro (1) with George Canning and John William Ward, Viscount Dudley, successive foreign secretaries and also their under-secretaries of state, ff. 1–151; (2) with Rear Admiral Sir Robert Waller Otway, commander-in-chief of the South America Station; and (3) with several subordinate officers, ff. 152–316. Subjects are varied but include an acrimonious exchange of notes in 1828 between Gordon and Otway over the responsibility for the repatriation of Irish immigrants, or mercenaries, to Cork.

- *Add. 43215* – Correspondence (1826–28) between Sir Robert Gordon in Rio de Janeiro and John Ponsonby, the British minister in Buenos Aires, discussing the military conflict between Brazil and the United Provinces of the Rio de la Plata.

Add. 41511 to 41563 – Heytesbury Papers
English (some French)

This series of papers includes correspondence of Sir William A'Court, 1st Baron Heytesbury (1779–1860), while British ambassador to Portugal, with foreign secretaries John William Ward (later Earl Dudley) and George Canning between 1824 and 1828 [*Add. 41547–41555*]. Included in these volumes is considerable correspondence relating to Brazil, in particular attempts being made to reconcile Portugal with the newly independent country.

Add. 52115 – Holland House Papers: Pedro II, Emperor of Brazil
French

This file comprises fourteen letters from the emperor of Brazil to Lady Margaret Holland, socialite wife of Conservative politician Sir Henry Holland, and a copy of a letter to Dom Pedro II, all dated between 1874 and 1887. Dom Pedro II's letters were sent from Rio de Janeiro, Petrópolis, London and Italy and are very domestic in content, mainly featuring formal pleasantries. Apart from some discussion of 'the Irish question', the letters contain minimal political or social commentary.

Add. 13974 to 13986 – **Kingsborough Papers**
Spanish and Portuguese
These papers are a collection of both original and copies of
17th- and 18th-century documents acquired by Edward King,
Lord Kingsborough (1795–1837), from archives in Spain.
Kingsborough, who developed a fascination for Mexican
antiquities and for the history of New Spain, is credited with
having preserved, in his copies, often fragile documents relating to
Spanish and Portuguese America. Documents in the collection
that directly or indirectly relate to Brazil mainly focus on Jesuit
activities and territorial demarcations between the Spanish and
Portuguese and include general descriptive tracts of the country.

Add. 39105 to 39107, 39110 to 39113, 39115 – **Layard Papers**
English
These are semi-official papers of Sir Austen Henry Layard, MP,
who served as under-secretary of state for foreign affairs, 1852 and
1861–66. They include miscellaneous correspondence from Latin
America, especially of British diplomatic representatives in the region.
Of Brazilian interest is the correspondence of William Dougal Christie,
the British minister to Brazil in the early 1860s, who pressured Brazil
to undertake measures to end slavery. In 1863 he ordered the seizure
by British ships of several Brazilian vessels outside the port of Rio
de Janeiro – the so-called 'Christie Affair' – to suggest British
willingness to apply force with regards to slavery. This led to Brazil
suspending diplomatic relations with Britain. The copies of letters
from Christie, many of which refer to the events surrounding this
particularly fractious period in British-Brazilian relations, include as
their addressees Layard, Lord Russell (as foreign secretary, see under
National Archives, p. 153) and the United States minister in Brazil.

Add. 20107 to 20233 – **Lowe Papers**
English
This series includes correspondence (mainly in-letters) and
miscellaneous papers of Sir Hudson Lowe (1769–1844), an officer
of the British Army and colonial administrator. Brazil-related
correspondence makes up only a small proportion of the collection
(27 volumes covering 1794–1822) and consists of letters received
by Lowe while he was governor of the mid-Atlantic island of St
Helena, where the former French emperor Napoleon Bonaparte
was being held captive by the British.

The 1816–18 letters, from Henry Chamberlain, British consul-general in Rio de Janeiro, report on defence, trade (in particular the possibility of introducing Brazilian plants and cattle to St Helena), Portuguese-Brazilian political developments and intelligence concerning the possibility that Bonapartist exiles in Rio de Janeiro, Pernambuco or Bahia were going to mount an attempt to free their former leader. [See *Add. 20115, ff. 298, 378, 381; Add. 20121, f. 44; Add. 20123, f. 293; Add. 20124, f. 156; Add. 20139, ff. 105, 108b; Add. 20147–20150 (passim); Add. 20200, f. 123; Add. 20233, ff. 11, 77, 81, 101.*]

Add. 64076 – **Macdonell Papers**
English
These are the correspondence and papers of Sir Hugh Guion Macdonell, a British diplomat serving in South America and Europe in the late 19th and early 20th centuries. Although Macdonell's period of service as minister in Rio de Janeiro (1885–88) coincided with the final abolition of slavery, papers relating to Brazil in the collection are very few in number and are personal in content.

Add. 40181 to 401617 – **Peel Papers**
English
The extensive collection of papers of Sir Robert Peel (1788–1850), who became prime minister in 1841, include limited correspondence relating to negotiations with Portugal and Brazil over the suppression of the slave trade, 1810–45, and specifically to the Slave Trade (Brazil) Act of August 1845 [scattered in *Add. 40499, 40568, 40570–40572, 40576* and *40612*].

Add. 49987 and 49988 – **Wellesley Papers**
English
The political career of Richard Colley Wellesley, 1st Marquess of Wellesley (1760–1842), was mainly linked with Indian and colonial affairs but also included the post of foreign secretary (Dec 1809–Jan 1812). Wellesley's Brazil-related papers mainly consist of drafts of correspondence concerning the slave trade, general trade matters (including discussions relating to negotiating a commercial treaty), shipping and the opening of British consulates in Brazil. [See *Add. 49987 Wellesley Letter Books, vol. IX, to Brazil, 1810* and *Add. 49988 Wellesley Letter Books, vol. X, to Brazil, 1811–12.*]

*Add. 30095 to 30144 – **Wilson Journals***
English
The journals and other papers of General Sir Robert Thomas Wilson (1777–1859) include many references to diplomatic and commercial negotiations with Portugal but only occasional references to Brazil. One journal entry is a lengthy description of the province of Bahia, where Wilson visited in Nov 1805 while serving at the Cape of Good Hope, southern Africa [*Add. 30097, ff. 8–18*]. Wilson comments on the port of Bahia (Salvador), its defences, the lack of Brazilians in government administration, the 'low moral standards' of the inhabitants and agricultural production, especially sugar and fruit. He was also impressed by the quality of the locally produced red wine.

● *Miscellaneous Papers*

Many manuscripts of Brazilian interest are single items that appear to be completely unrelated to the other collections of papers, having been acquired independently by the library. Some such manuscripts are, however, of considerable importance or interest. The following list represents just a small proportion of such holdings – others can be identified via Department of Manuscripts finding aids (see p. 100).

- *Add. 31237, f. 182* – An unattributed document on '*the necessity of abolition of slave trade to Brazil as a preliminary to commercial treaty with Britain, 1808*'.

- *Add. 33931 and 35300 – Views in and near Rio de Janeiro, 1792, being original drawings made by Sir John Barrow, William Alexander, Samuel Daniell, and Capt. Henry William Parish, travelling to China under Earl Macartney in 1792–93.*

- *Add. 34744, ff. 38–44* – Correspondence of naturalists Sir Joseph Banks and Dr Daniel Charles Solander concerning their reception at Rio de Janeiro on board the *Endeavour*, 1768.

- *Add. 42138, A, B* – Pocket book of naturalist Henry Walter Bates, used during his travels in Brazil, 1848–59. Apart from brief notes of journeys from Ega to Óbidos (3–18 Feb 1859) and from Pará (Belém) homewards later that year, the entries are confined to business records such as accounts, receipts of parcels and consignments of collections (see also under Natural History Museum, p. 178).

THE BRITISH POSTAL MUSEUM & ARCHIVE

Feeling House
Phoenix Place
London WC1X 0DL

www.postalheritage.org.uk

Tel: (020) 7239 2570 • **Fax:** (020) 7239 2576
E-mail: info@postalheritage.org.uk

Open: Mon–Wed and Fri, 10am–5pm, Thurs 10am–7pm.
Closed: Public holidays.
Admission: Appointments not required.

Introduction:

The British Postal Museum and Archive (BPMA) records British postal services from the 17th century to the present day. The BPMA is perhaps the largest source of postal and philatelic history in the world and represents a valuable business, transport and local-history resource.

Collections:

The BPMA's collections are in two complementary parts – the Museum collection and the Archive collection, the core collections being the historic records of the Royal Mail. As the Post Office was a government department for much of its history, the collection is a Public Record with most items open for consultation after a period of thirty years. The extremely useful document 'An overview of the Royal Mail Archive' (2006) can be downloaded from the BPMA's website. A rapidly expanding proportion of individual files and documents can be identified using the catalogue that can be accessed via the BPMA's website.

Brazil-related documents principally concern 19th-century postal agreements between the UK and Brazil and contracts from this period with shipping companies carrying mail to and from South America. There is also some material relating to early 20th-century telegraph and telephone services linking Britain and Brazil. Examples of such material within the collection include:

- *P 39/07 – Packet Boat Reports, 1813–14*

- *P 29/0096 – Brazil: Postal Agreement, 1853*

- *P 29/0179 – Brazil and River Plate mail: Contract with Royal Mail Steam Packet Co., 1863*

- *P 29/1410 – Brazil: Parcel post service*

- *P 30/6356 – Brazil: Wireless telegraph services, 1906–12*

- *P 33/7277 – Brazil: Telephone service, 1930–39*

◆

GUILDHALL LIBRARY
Manuscripts Section
Aldermanbury
London EC2P 2EJ

ihr.sas.ac.uk/gh/

Tel: (020) 7332 1863/1862 • **Fax:** (020) 7600 3384
E-mail: manuscripts.guildhall@corpoflondon.gov.uk

Open: Mon–Sat 9.30am–4.45pm.
Closed: Public holidays.
Admission: No prior appointment or special permission required although some material must be requested 48 hours in advance of consultation.

Introduction:

The Guildhall Library is primarily a library of London history, although business history generally is an important strength. The Manuscripts Section of the library is the local record office for the City of London, apart from the archives of the Corporation of London, which are separately administered. Reflecting the City of London's development as a national and international commercial centre, the Manuscripts Section has become an important depository for business archives, especially commercial and financial services.

Collections:

Although there are numerous Brazil-related collections, they are disappointing, often featuring little more than minute books of annual general meetings. Some material is listed on the web-accessible electronic catalogue but as not all manuscript collections have been added, researchers are advised also to examine card catalogue entries. The collections listed are those of significant Brazil-related interest. While most material is normally available within fifteen minutes of being requested, some lesser-used items require 24 or 48 hours' advance notice.

Ms. 18506 – **Alliance Life & Fire Assurance**
English
This is an 1885 volume of reports on South American cities examining their fire risk. Of Brazilian cities that were visited, Rio de Janeiro, Salvador and Recife are covered in greatest detail but there are also reports relating to São Paulo, Santos, Porto Alegre, Pelotas and Rio Grande. The reports examine buildings and their methods of construction, emergency access (paying special attention to city layouts and widths of streets), water supply and pressure, the reputation and equipment of local fire brigades, and names of local insurance companies, and they offer sometimes unusual insights into late 19th-century Brazilian urban life. For Rio de Janeiro there is also a list of fires and damage caused between 1882 and 1885.

Mss. 21180 to 21184 – **Alto Paraná Development Co. Ltd**
English
The Alto Paraná Development Co. Ltd was formed in 1912 to acquire and hold the share capital of an existing Argentine company, La Sociedad Anonima Compañia de Maderas del Alto Paraná, established six years previously. The new company's purpose was to exploit and develop the pine, hardwood and erva maté resources of a 600,000-acre property in Brazil on the Paraná River near Sete Quedas (north of Foz do Iguaçu, in the state of Paraná). In 1951 the company changed its name to the Scottish and Mercantile Investment Co. Ltd.

Although substantial in quantity, records are patchy both in terms of the years and the subjects that are covered. Nevertheless, material has been preserved from the establishment of the company to its final winding down in the early 1960s. Included are minute books of meetings of the board of directors (1932–64) and company financial ledgers and journals (1912–54) but these documents offer few clues to the actual company operations on the ground. Only a few manuscripts exist on specific topics of interest to the company, such as the crises in erva maté prices and the possibility of settling Czechoslovakian and Jewish refugees on land belonging to the company. Some printed material has been retained, including copies of memoranda and articles of association and a detailed map of the company's Brazilian property.

Mss. 11216, 11217 and 11224A – Anglican Chaplaincies in the cities of Rio de Janeiro, Bahia and Pernambuco
English
This collection consists of transcripts of baptisms (1821) and burials (1821–22) at Bahia (Salvador), baptisms, marriages and burials (1838–40 and 1842–44) at Pernambuco (Recife) and baptisms, marriages and burials (1840–44) at Rio de Janeiro as reported to the Diocese of London.

Ms. 24531 – Central Bahia Railway Trust
English
The collection is limited to minute books (1909–45) of the trustees of the Central Bahia Railway listing basic financial data such as interest in accounts, dividends due and bonds held by banks. No operational information is included.

Mss. 17981 to 17999 – J.W. Doan & Co.
English
These items are 19th-century business records from the London office of the Rio de Janeiro-based coffee merchant J.W. Doan & Co., including details of the firm's imports into England and the sourcing in Brazil.

Mss. 19075 – Hambros Bank Ltd
French (some English)
The collection is limited to a single bundle of papers discussing a proposed £4 million loan to the Brazilian Government by this

merchant bank. Most of the correspondence is in French to Everard Hambro from the Paris office of the Banque de Paris et des Pays-Bas.

Mss. 22024 and 22047 – **Kleinwort Sons & Co.**
French (some English and Portuguese)
The library holds extensive records of Kleinwort Sons & Co., a London-based merchant bank. There are two volumes [*Ms. 22024*] covering the years 1875 to 1911 of abstracts of correspondence on the credit standing, local reputation and performance of Brazilian clients or prospective clients. The businesses being reported on were mainly locally owned ventures and were located throughout Brazil, with some also operating in Argentina or Uruguay. Most of the Brazil-related correspondence is in French, although some is in English or Portuguese and a few reports are in German. In addition, the collection includes fourteen volumes [*Ms. 22047*] of Brazilian and Argentine client account ledgers covering the years 1866 to 1923.

Ms. 16852 – **Manáos Tramways and Light Company Ltd**
English
Although there is no manuscript material relating to Manáos [*sic*] Tramways and Light Company Ltd., the library holds annual reports to the directors and statements of accounts (1910–73). These do not include, however, insights into the operation of the company, nor are many financial details provided.

Ms. 16860 – **Pará Electric & Pará Gas Companies**
English
The collection is limited to correspondence (approximately one hundred letters) relating to the winding up of the Pará Electric & Pará Gas Companies and the associated Pará Electric Railways and Light Companies and the Northern Tramway Company. The file of correspondence (1954–57) both to and from Brazil includes letters on the valuation of the then relatively few remaining assets and the sale of land owned by the companies.

Mss. 20199 and 20200 – **Rio de Janeiro Lighterage Co.**
English
The collection is limited to minute books (three volumes, 1918–59) and account books (one file, 1949–50) providing basic data on coal shipments to Rio de Janeiro.

*Ms. 21755 – **Stringer & Richardson***
English
This item is a letter copy book for 1827–29 of Stringer & Richardson, a general merchant specialising in coffee, tea and spices. Although most letters are copies of correspondence between London and Trieste and London and Matanzas, there are some letters to agents in Rio de Janeiro and Bahia discussing coffee and sugar prices and demand in Europe.

*Ms. 16517 – **London Chamber of Commerce (Brazilian Section)***
English
Inaugurated in 1922, the London Chamber of Commerce (Brazilian Section) was made up of representatives of shippers, ship-owners and importers in Britain with interests in Brazilian trade. The single bound volume covers the years 1922 to 1969 and consists of copies of minutes of meetings, discussion papers and reports on British trade with Brazil. Material covering the 1920s is especially rich with, for example, some valuable papers concerning the 1929 British trade mission to Argentina and Brazil. There is scant material for the 1930s and 1940s but a clear resurgence in activity took place in the 1950s.

Council for Foreign Bondholders
English (and some Portuguese)
The Council for Foreign Bondholders was formed in 1868 to protect the interests and lobby on behalf of British holders of foreign bonds. There are no surviving manuscript holdings that involve the Council's Brazilian interests.

In the early 1870s the Council's officers began systematically to collect and retain newspaper cuttings, pamphlets, prospectuses, circulars and government reports. This material has been bound in volumes by country, most of which are indexed by subject and can be considered a vital business and financial history resource. Almost all the material is in English with newspaper cuttings (both from British dailies and weeklies and the specialist financial and business press) forming a substantial part of each volume. There are eighteen volumes of Brazil-related cuttings, covering the years 1872 to 1985. The first thirty to forty years are the fullest volumes and include an occasional letter concerning business with Brazil. These volumes may be consulted with 48 hours' advance notice given to the information desk in the library's main reading room.

London Stock Exchange
English
All annual reports issued since 1880 of companies that have been
listed on the London Stock Exchange are available for
consultation. Requests for reports should be made at the
information desk in the library's main reading room.

◆

IMPERIAL WAR MUSEUM
Department of Documents   **www.iwm.org.uk/collections**
Lambeth Road
London SE1 6HZ

Tel: (020) 7416 5221 • **Fax:** (020) 7416 5374
E-mail: docs@iwm.org.uk

Open: Mon–Sat 10am–5pm.
Closed: The Department of Documents is closed on public
holidays, the last two full weeks of November and for a
full week in May.
Admission: By appointment only; proof of identity required.

Introduction:

The Imperial War Museum's interests focus on armed conflicts,
especially those involving Britain and the Commonwealth, from World
War I to the present. Collections include firearms and military equipment, works of art, film, audio and video materials, books, photographs
and documents. The Photograph Archive (photos@iwm.org.uk; tel.
7416 5333) holds some images relating to Brazil. These include photographs of Brazilian army units training in Brazil during World War II
and also of the Brazilian Expeditionary Force in Europe.

Collections:

The Imperial War Museum's Department of Documents includes
extensive holdings of personal letters, diaries, manuscripts and
unpublished memoirs of men and women who served in the armed
forces. Collections also extend to the papers of conscientious objectors,
internees, prisoners of war, refugees and civilians during wartime. No
official records are held by the department – for such documents one
should consult files held by the National Archives (p. 131), especially

amongst Foreign Office, Admiralty, War Office and Air Ministry archives. Very few Brazil-related items are found within the Department of Documents' collection. No documents (other than the photographs mentioned above) are held relating to the activities of the Brazilian Expeditionary Force in Europe during World War II. Moreover, those documents of Brazilian interest in the collection that have been identified only have a marginal relationship to Brazil.

PP/MCR/113 – Sir Henry Beaumont Autobiography
English
This memoir recounts the life of Sir Henry Beaumont (1867–1949), whose Foreign Office career included postings in Europe and South America. Only 26 of the 593 pages are devoted to Beaumont's two years in Brazil (1897–99); they describe his travels and his active social and sporting life.

HBH/1 – Harold Beresford Hope Correspondence
English
Included are three 1914 letters describing Hope's duties as a third secretary at the British Legation in Rio de Janeiro. Other items include a letter (14 Sept 1914) from G.F. Atlee of the British Consulate in São Paulo about a German spy, and a report (11 Sept 1914) on the detention near Rio de Janeiro by the HMS *Bristol* of the Dutch steamer *Kelbergen*, suspected of carrying coal for German ships.

LG/1 – Lycett Gardner Diary (Vol I)
English
This diary (30 July–14 Jan 1915) was kept by a midshipman serving on the HMS *Cornwall*, a guard ship off the Abrolhos Rocks (Arquipélago de Abrolhos), a coaling station some 100 kilometres east of Caravelas (Espírito Santo). Gardner recounts the monotony of life on board the ship and on the Rocks – one marine went insane and a signalman attempted suicide.

OWP/1 – Rear Admiral O.W. Phillips Memoir
English
This memoir (written between 1961 and 1962) recounts the early naval career of O.W. Phillips, especially his experiences on the battleship the HMS *Canopus*. Ordered to the South Atlantic in 1915, the *Canopus* took up position guarding the Abrolhos Rocks and Phillips' memoir includes an account of the harsh conditions endured there.

RTY/1 – Commander Richard Travers Young Memoir
English
This memoir (written between 1965 and 1970) recounts the career
of naval officer Richard Travers Young, born in 1898. In 1915
Young was posted as a midshipman to the HMS *Canopus*, which
proceeded to the Abrolhos Rocks. The memoir includes an account
of guardship duties in relation to the Rocks.

◆

INDIA OFFICE LIBRARY
Oriental and India Office Collections
The British Library
96 Euston Road
London NW1 2DB

www.bl.uk/collections/
orientalandindian

Tel: (020) 7412 7873 • **Fax:** (020) 7412 7641
E-mail: oioc–enquiries@bl.uk

Open: Mon 10am–5pm, Tues–Sat 9.30am–5pm.
Closed: Public holidays.
Admission: Entry with British Library reader's pass (see p. 98).

Introduction:

The India Office Library contains the records of the administration in
London of the pre-1947 government of India. They comprise the archives
of the East India Company (1600–1858), the Board of Control or Board
of Commissioners for the Affairs of India (1784–1858), the India Office
(1858–1947), the Burma Office (1937–48) and a number of other British
agencies overseas. The India Office Library, together with its archival
holdings, is now administered by the British Library (see p. 98) as part
of its Oriental and India Office Collections (OIOC).

Collections:

Brazil does not feature prominently within OIOC records, a reflection
of the limited contacts between the Indian sub-continent and Brazil
prior to Indian independence in 1947. The widely scattered manuscripts
relating to Brazil that have been identified mainly concern shipping
links, trade and migration as well as brief exchanges concerning the
accreditation of Brazilian consuls (or honorary consuls) in India and
Burma. The OIOC's catalogues are very slowly being transferred to

electronic form, with limited access using the *A2A: Access to Archives* search facility (see p. 250). There has been only very limited indexing of material by subject matter in either printed form or as card catalogue – records are catalogued by date and government department alone.

L/MAR – East India Company: Marine Records (1600–1834)
English
Heading to the East Indies and Australia, it was usually necessary to sail as far as the coast of Brazil in order to pick up the southeast trade winds for passage around the Cape of Good Hope. Ships on such journeys would frequently call at Brazil ports for revictualing, repairs or to drop off or take on passengers. The library holds a large collection of East India Company ships' logs, with the ships' names and dates of various ports of call given in the *Catalogue of East India Company Ships' Journals and Logs, 1600–1834* (London, 1999). Ships' journals and logs vary considerably in terms of the detail that is given of a particular voyage but they normally merely provide a ship's day-by-day navigational information.

IOR/G/9 – East India Company: Factory Records: Rio de Janeiro Agents
English
Amongst the volumes of agents' correspondence are scattered and generally brief letters to and from the East India Company's Rio de Janeiro agent. Relevant volumes and folios can be identified using the electronic catalogue. There are a few late 18th-century letters to and from the agent but most correspondence appears to be from the years 1808 and 1811. Letters discuss the agent's activities in Rio de Janeiro, shipping and troop movements and the company's trade with Rio de Janeiro (especially with Southern Africa's Cape of Good Hope but also with the East Indies).

F/4/17/753; F/4/67/1481; F/4/297/6876 – India Office: Board of Control: Cochineal, Importation of Insects and Cultivation
English
These papers (Aug 1795 to Oct 1807) relate to attempts to secure cochineal insects from Brazil and introduce them to India for the production of dye.

F/4/471/11339 – India Office: Board of Control: Brazilian Mariners –
Maldive Islands
English
Correspondence (Aug 1812 to May 1814) between the Board of
Control, the Bengal government and the Sultan of the Maldives
details the Sultan's complaints against João Alwaez [sic], a
Brazilian sea captain of the *Europa*. Alwaez had been shipwrecked
in the Maldive Islands in 1812 and was taken under the wing of the
islanders. The Sultan was offended that Alwaez had repaid his
hospitality with acts of brigandage. The affair concludes with
Alwaez's detention in Bengal and his subsequent deportation to
Portuguese Goa.

L/E/7/1296 – India Office: Industries and Overseas Department: Indian
Immigrants and Brazil (1923–28)
English
This includes correspondence and documents concerning Indian
emigration to Brazil. Just as Japanese immigrants had been
recruited for work in São Paulo coffee plantations, the intention
was that Indian immigrants would settle in Amazonas to work in
the rubber industry and develop rice plantations. In practice, most
Indians (mainly Punjabi Sikhs) were employed as agricultural
labourers or served as herdsmen in the interior of the state of São
Paulo, having travelled to South America with the Brahma cattle
that they were charged with introducing to Brazil.

Material includes dispatches from the British Ambassador in
Rio de Janeiro regarding the attitude of the Brazilian government
towards Indian immigration, correspondence from the Protector of
Emigrants (Bombay), Brazilian immigrant recruitment activities in
India, copies of related newspaper advertisements, and articles,
leaflets and letters relating to the repatriation to India of destitute
immigrants.

L/PJ/6/5, file 232 – India Office: Public and Judicial Department:
Annual Files: Repatriation of Labourers to Mauritius and Seychelles,
1877–81
English
This general series includes responses to a few enquiries in the
1890s concerning the possibility of importing Indian labourers –
'coolies' – into Brazil. The only substantial case that is found within
the files, however, concerns an earlier episode of labour migration.

This case involved an attempt in 1877 to introduce East Indian labourers from the island of Mauritius to a Rio de Janeiro sugar plantation. The first file discusses in some detail the background of the scheme and conditions the labourers experienced in Brazil. The documents in the other files centre on arguments between the India Office, the Colonial Office and the Foreign Office regarding responsibility for covering the costs incurred in repatriating the Indians to Mauritius and to the Seychelles.

[In addition to the above-mentioned file, see also *L/PJ/6/10, file 509; L/PJ/6/19, file 1093; L/PJ/6/27, file 1688; L/PJ/6/34, file 359; L/PJ/6/37, file 562.*]

India Office: Public and Judicial Department (Separate):
L/PJ/12/317 – *Activities of Indians in Brazil (1927–33)*
L/PJ/12/204 – *Activities of Indians in South America (1934–36)*
L/PJ/12/205 – *Activities of Indians in South America (1936–41)*
English

These files are from the Indian political intelligence-gathering wing of the Public and Judicial Department (Separate), a shadowy and formerly non-avowed organisation devoted to the internal and external security of British India. Compared to other communities in the Americas, the activities of the Punjabi Sikhs in Brazil were not considered a security threat. Nevertheless, a watch was placed on Sikhs wishing to travel to Brazil (as entry to Canada and the United States became increasingly restricted) from Shanghai (China), and the possible resurrection of the militantly anti-British Ghadr Party, founded in San Francisco in 1913 by Lala Hardayal. The political tendencies of Indians in São Paulo (many worked as herdsmen and on the São Paulo e Goyaz Railway – with two hundred concentrated in Olympia) were being followed.

● **Private Papers**

Of the collections of private papers (mainly of former diplomats whose careers centred on India or other parts of Asia) that have been deposited in the OIOC in recent years, only two appear to have significant Brazil-related content.

*Mss. Eur F140 – 65 and 66 – **Amherst Collection: Correspondence of William Pitt Amherst, 1st Earl of Amherst***
English

In 1823 Amherst (1773–1857) was sent to Rio de Janeiro, en-route to India (where he was to take up the post of governor general of Bengal), by Foreign Secretary George Canning to report on the Brazilian government's attitude towards the slave trade and to explore terms of the opening of diplomatic relations with the new regime. Papers include copies of 1822 correspondence between Canning and Amherst regarding the independence of Brazil; copies of letters that Amherst was carrying from Canning to the British consul-general in Rio de Janeiro, Henry Chamberlain; and copies of Amherst's reports to Canning dispatched from Brazil between February and May 1823.

Mss. Eur F288 – 78, 79, 186–188 – **Fry Collection**
English
Sir Leslie Fry's early career was spent in the Indian Army and India Political Service; he later transferred to the Foreign Office with the independence of India in 1947. Fry served as British Ambassador to Brazil between 1963 and 1966. His private papers display either the extremely mundane side to Fry's diplomatic position or his lack of insight into Brazil in years of considerable political upheaval, including the establishment of a military dictatorship. They consist of copies of speeches delivered at social functions (for example, 'Ladies Night at the St Andrew's Society, Rio de Janeiro') and records of other non-controversial gatherings. Included in the collection are several photograph albums with images of diplomatic and social events and relating to ambassadorial tours.

◆

INSTITUTION OF MECHANICAL ENGINEERS
Information & Library Service
1 Bird Cage Walk
London SW1H 9JJ

www.imeche.org.uk

Tel: (020) 7973 1265 • **Fax:** (020) 7222 8762
E-mail: ils@imeche.org.uk

Open: Mon–Fri 9.15am–5.30pm.
Closed: Public holidays.
Admission: No appointment is necessary, but preliminary contact
              is advised.

Introduction:

The Institution of Mechanical Engineers (IMechE) is the United Kingdom's qualifying body for mechanical engineers, covering the entire range of technologies and industries in which engineers work. IMechE has one of the most comprehensive engineering libraries in the country, holding books, journals and standards on a broad range of engineering topics.

Collections:

IMechE maintains an archive charting the development of mechanical engineering. Although there are important collections relating to Latin America, especially in the field of railway development, there is little concerning Brazil. An online catalogue of archival holdings is in development – the catalogue of printed works is already online.

IMS 283–320 – Henderson Family Papers, 1865 – c. 1989
English
IMechE holds papers relating to the Henderson family of engineers and to their companies, notably Livesey, Son and Henderson, originally James Livesey and Company (founded 1865). The firm operated as consulting engineers, largely overseas (especially Latin America) and generally on railway construction and operation projects. Apart from the specific Brazil-related files or volumes outlined below, there are many volumes featuring general financial and technical records of both companies, as well as printed maps (1885–1931), some of them of the networks of Brazilian railway companies.

IMS 287 – James Livesey and Company
English
This is a volume of specifications for railway engineering works (1878–82) describing proposed locomotives, rolling stock, track, bridges, buildings and equipment for several South American railway projects, including the Bahia and San Francisco Railway [*IMS 287/1*] and União Mineira Railway [*IMS 287/7*].

IMS 303 and 304 – Witan Investment Company:
Telephone Company of Pernambuco
English
The Witan Investment Company was linked by Henderson family members to Livesey, Son and Henderson and had financial ties to

the Telephone Company of Pernambuco. This collection features trust deeds and lists of shareholders, directors' reports, chairman's speeches to shareholders, memoranda and routine correspondence covering the years 1925–42.

◆

LLOYDS TSB GROUP ARCHIVES
Secretary's Department
71 Lombard Street
London EC3P 3BS

Tel: (020) 7356 1032 • **Fax:** (020) 7929 2901
E-mail: sampsok@lloydstsb.co.uk

Open: Mon–Fri 9.30am–4.30pm.
Closed: Public holidays.
Admission: At the discretion of the company, by application in writing to the Archivist.

Introduction:

The Lloyds TSB Group was created in 1995 when the TSB Group merged with Lloyds Bank. The Lloyds TSB Group Archive holds records of the TSB Group, Lloyds Bank and of many banks that merged with them over the years. Of particular importance was the acquisition in 1971 of the Bank of London & South America (BOLSA). Although only created in 1923, BOLSA had emerged from the amalgamation of several British-registered banks that had been operating in Brazil or elsewhere in South America since the 1860s.

Collections:

All but a few of the records relating to Brazil that are held by the Lloyds TSB Group Archive were created by BOLSA or the banks out of which it emerged or amalgamated. The collection mainly consists of accounts books and ledgers, though other documents are also held. Apart from manuscript records, the collection contains annual reports and printed booklets concerning economic conditions and historical surveys. Brazil-specific documents can be identified with a keyword search on the electronic catalogue (not online).

In addition to the various banking records listed below, London & River Plate Bank minute books, annual reports, and ledgers are held for the years 1862 to 1923; some of these concern business dealings between Brazil and Argentina and Uruguay. Other material relating to the history of BOLSA – most notably head office and Brazilian branch letter books – is held at University College London (see pp. 198–200).

Anglo-Brazilian Commercial Agency
English
The agency was founded in 1918 jointly by the London & Brazilian Bank and the British Trade Corporation in order to win new business in Brazil amongst local merchants. Encountering strong competition, the agency was wound up in 1929. Surviving records are limited to directors' minute books (1918–29).

British Bank of South America
English
Founded in 1863 as the Brazilian and Portuguese Bank Ltd, following a series of amalgamations the bank was renamed the British Bank of South America Ltd in 1891, and was wound up in 1961. Most of the items are staff registers (1868–1936), left service ledgers (1920–36) and annual reports (1863–1936).

London & Brazilian Bank Ltd
English
The London & Brazilian Bank was founded in London in 1862 to finance Brazilian coffee, sugar, hide and cereal exporters. The bank opened a branch in Rio de Janeiro in 1863, followed by branches in Pernambuco later that year and in Bahia and Rio Grande in 1864. The bank amalgamated with the London and River Plate Bank to form the Bank of London & South America.

Records held here relating to the bank include detailed staff registers (1862–1923), annual reports and accounts (1872–1923) and branch journals for Porto Alegre (1872–89), Pelotas (1869–72) and Rio Grande (1867–81).

Bank of London & South America
English
Few items concerning BOLSA are country-specific, although commercial activity in Brazil is easily identifiable within volumes or files. The principal groupings of general records are:

- Summary profit and loss ledgers, 1936–64 – 45 vols.

- Summary balance sheets, 1936–44, 1948–63 – 33 vols.

- Head office and branch accounts, with profit and loss accounts, 1924–33 – 31 vols.

- Board minute books, 1925–74 – 14 vols.

- Chairman's committee minutes, 1959–64 – 6 vols.

- Executive Committee minutes, 1948–55, 1964–71 – 7 vols.

Staff Department

Personnel files are very incomplete. There are three registers listing staff joining the bank covering 1944–58 [*F/2/St/3.1–3*] and two registers listing staff leavers covering 1944–52 [*F/2/St/4.1–2*]. In addition, nineteen sample personnel files [*F/2/St/1.0* and *F/2/St/2.0*] of South American branches have been retained, including confidential reports, personal details, medical reports, career movements, salaries, photographs and disciplinary action.

Directorate Reports (1933–60)

There are ten confidential reports in this series of which nine cover the years 1955–63. These reports discuss 'conditions and prospects' of BOLSA's operations throughout Latin America, including Brazil, in the context of local, national and regional political and economic developments. However, the 1933 report [*F/2/D/Rep./7.0*] – 'Some notes and suggestions arising out of a visit of Sir Alexander R. Murray and Mr F.A. Beane to South America' – is more wide ranging in its content. The Brazilian branches visited were Bahia, Pernambuco, Santos, São Paulo and Rio de Janeiro, with details given of dates of establishment, staff breakdowns, position of premises and comparative statements of results (1923–32) with comments regarding management performance, future banking performance, assets and liabilities.

LONDON

Other business records
English

The archive holds records of many English banks that merged with either TSB or Lloyds in the 19th and 20th centuries. A few files contain usually routine correspondence concerning Brazilian investments or other matters. Files containing 53 items dated 1861–78 that relate to the Recife Drainage Company Ltd [*A/53/9/c/4.0*] and eight items dated 1886–87 relating to the North Brazilian Sugar Factories Ltd offer some insights into debt and other financial management issues. There are also six files [*F/2/Sec/4.0*] of papers dated 1914–38 relating to the Mogyana Railway Company of São Paulo, including reports and accounts, transcripts of annual general meetings and general printed material.

MISSION TO SEAFARERS

St Michael Paternoster Royal
College Hill
London EC4R 2RC

www.missiontoseafarers.org

Tel: (020) 7248 5202 • **Fax:** (020) 7248 4761
E-mail: pr@missiontoseafarers.org

Open: Mon–Fri by appointment.
Closed: Public holidays.
Admission: By appointment only.

Introduction:

The Mission to Seafarers, founded in 1856 as the Mission to Seamen, is a missionary society of the Anglican Church that seeks to care for the spiritual and practical welfare of all seafarers. Since its foundation, a network of chaplains, staff and volunteers has developed in ports throughout the world.

Collections:

Since the 19th century, the mission has maintained a presence in many Brazilian ports, with Santos and Rio de Janeiro being especially important centres. Very little correspondence to or from missions in Brazil survives but complete sets of annual reports (from 1856) and its magazine *The Church and the Sailor* (from 1930) are held; these provide many insights into Brazilian activities.

Santos correspondence
English
Only isolated files survive from the mission's overseas work.
Relating to Brazil, only a 1919 correspondence file discussing the
mission's work in Santos has been retained.

◆

THE NATIONAL ARCHIVES
Kew
Richmond
Surrey TW9 4DU

www.pro.gov.uk

Tel: (020) 8392 5200 • **Fax:** (020) 8392 5286

Open: Mon 9am–5pm, Tues 10am–7pm, Wed 9am–5pm,
            Thurs 9am–7pm, Fri 9am–5pm, Sat 9.30am–5pm.
Closed: Public holidays, Saturdays of bank holiday weekends,
            and first two weeks of December.
Admission: Proof of identity required (non-UK residents
            must produce a passport or, for EU nationals,
            an identification card).

Introduction:

The National Archives (formerly the Public Record Office – the PRO),
located in the London suburb of Kew, is the repository of the national
archives for England, Wales and the United Kingdom. It was founded
by act of Parliament in 1838 to bring together and preserve records of
central government and courts of law and make them available to all
who wish to consult them. The records span an unbroken period from
the 11th century to the present.

Collections:

There is a vast assortment of documentation to be found at the National
Archives, making it the single most important collection of Brazil-
related material in Britain. Documents relating to most of Brazil's
colonial period (16th to 18th centuries) are collected as State Papers
(SP), although a few items are to be found in an early Colonial Office
(CO) class and within the Admiralty (ADM) archive. Later material
(19th and 20th centuries) represents the overwhelming bulk of
documentation relating to Brazil. Although such material is widely

dispersed across archival collections and classes, most papers for the period are found in the Foreign Office (FO) archive but other classes of documents from other government archives should also be considered according to the subject being investigated.

PROCAT: ONLINE CATALOGUE
http://www.nationalarchives.gov.uk/catalogue/search.asp

The online electronic catalogue – PROCAT – is a useful tool for identifying files or other groupings of documents held by the National Archives, especially for post-1940 material. Overall, however, only a very small proportion of documents are individually indexed. Some classes, or particular years, of documents are extremely well indexed, while the descriptions of others offer no information as to the contents of files beyond years covered by documents within a particular volume or file or the general source or subject matter (such as Consular, Trade, Political). This is particularly the case with the key Foreign Office archive, for which very few pre-1940 files can be identified using PROCAT on a subject basis.

Even for files that have been individually listed, PROCAT's word search facility is a blunt instrument. It is important to consider all possible word variations (for example, 'Brazil' and 'Brazilian', 'St Paul' and 'São Paulo') and search combinations of terms (for example, by entering 'Brazil AND coffee'). An assessment of various finding aids (electronic and paper registers and indexes) is provided below with the discussions of the different Brazil-related classes of documents. ▓

● State Papers (SP)

Secretaries of State, State Papers Foreign

State Papers (Foreign) cover England's (and later Britain's) relations with foreign countries from 1500 to 1806. Information was drawn from many sources, including accredited representatives, private individuals, merchants, military or naval officers, consuls and other paid or unpaid agents and informants. By far the greatest number of – and most significant – Brazil-related holdings amongst State Papers are to be found in Portuguese diplomatic correspondence (*SP 89*). There are also more limited Brazil-related documents in other State Papers classes, in particular within Dutch

(*SP 84*) correspondence. Apart from the Portuguese State Papers, identifying subject-relevant State Papers is hampered by the limited indexing of letters and other papers bound within individual volumes or collected in individual boxes.

SP 89 / 3 to 92 – **Portugal, 1598 to 1780**
English and Portuguese (some Latin and French)
This class is almost entirely made up of in-letters, mainly from English (and later British) diplomatic representatives in Lisbon, but also those in Oporto, Madeira and the Azores.

Material relating to Brazil is readily identifiable due to the existence of a number of finding aids (most notably C.R. Boxer, ed., *Descriptive List of the State Papers: Portugal 1661–1780*, Lisbon, 1979) that form the basis of a typescript descriptive list. This list can be accessed electronically via the web using PROCAT. Descriptive lists of documents may be viewed by year or by a keyword search. Linking *SP 89* with the search terms 'Brazil' and 'Brazilian' results in a list of more than five hundred Brazil-related documents, most of which have useful descriptions. The search can be narrowed by adding additional subject terms – for example, 'slaves' or 'slavery', 'trade' or specific names of people, places or commodities.

The volume covering the earlier period [*SP 89 / 3, 1598–1638*] includes little Brazil-related material. Subsequent volumes, however, include many relevant documents but they often form only a small part of a more broad-ranging letter or document on Portuguese trade, political or military matters. Anglo-Portuguese-Brazilian trade relations are most commonly referred to, though many other topics (such as the capture and sale of slaves in Africa and their importation into Brazil, the position of the British community in Brazil, migration from metropolitan Portugal and the Azores to Brazil and contraband flowing between Brazil and Africa) are addressed in varying degrees of detail.

SP 84 / 116 to 160 and 590 – **Holland, 1585 to 1780**
English (some Dutch, French and Latin)
This class consists of the correspondence of English (and later British) diplomats in the Netherlands, the northern part of the Low Countries, including the decades of Dutch domination of northeastern Brazil. The documents are mainly in-letters, mostly to the secretary of state or his assistants in London, from the English ambassadors, envoys or other representatives at The Hague, although there are also some letters or reports (originals or hand-

written contemporary copies) from other sources that were forwarded to London.

There do not appear to be any documents concerning Dutch trading interests in the Amazon earlier in the 17th century. Furthermore, only an extremely small proportion of the documents that are found within the year-specific individual volumes [*SP 84 / 116 to 160* and *590*] relate to the Dutch occupation of northeastern Brazil (1624–54), most being concerned with internal Low Countries affairs or wider European relations.

The descriptive lists relating to *SP 84* volumes are of very limited value as, with few exceptions, they detail only dates and, in some cases, the names of recipients of correspondence or other documents. There are no additional contemporary finding aids (for example, registers of correspondence) to the volumes, nor are there any supplementary descriptive indexes that have been compiled later. As such, it is rarely possible to identify documents that relate to Dutch Brazil. Similarly, PROCAT is of very minor assistance, reproducing as it does the general descriptive handlist: a search linking '*SP 84*' with terms such as 'Brazil', 'Pernambuco' or 'Bahia' leads to only a dozen or so documents. Nevertheless, an examination of the volumes containing these Brazil-related items suggests that other Brazil-relevant documents are to be found within this class of document.

Most of the documents relating to the Dutch period of occupation of northeastern Brazil that are identifiable from the descriptive lists are reports, which range up to forty pages in length, sent from the region to Holland concerning military or trade conditions in the colonies. In addition, there are also brief reports alluding to the 'treasures' arriving in Holland from Brazil. Representative examples of relevant documents are:

- *SP 84 / 117, f. 120* – Albert Koenraat's account of the taking of Bahia, 9 May 1624 (Dutch).

- *SP 84 / 141, f. 94* – Col. Gen. Weerdenbuch (Pernambuco) to States General, 25 Feb 1630 (English).

- *SP 84 / 153, f. 153* – Articles on trade with Brazil, agreed with the Dutch West India Company, Olinda, Pernambuco, 9 April 1638 (English).

- *SP 84 / 590* – Prince Maurice of Nassau's account to States General of the State and Condition of Brazil, 1643–44 (Dutch).

The other main location of material concerning the Dutch in Brazil is the Portuguese diplomatic correspondence [*SP 89*, see p. 133] for the period. It is also possible that other general classes of State Papers feature documents relating to Dutch Brazil. One useful item included within *State Papers Domestic: Supplementary* is:

- *SP 46 / 128, f. 174* – Notes on trade with Brazil, no date, but probably 1653–54 (English).

SP 78 – *France, 1577 to 1780*
335 volumes
English (some French and Latin)
This class consists of the correspondence of English (and later British) diplomats in France. As with the Dutch series [*SP 84*, see p. 133], the chronologically based descriptive lists relating to the French series provide very few indicators as to subject matter of individual volumes. There are no registers of correspondence or additional finding aids, offering readers no alternative but to trawl through the volumes covering the period of interest.

A search with PROCAT produces very few Brazil-related documents. Those documents that do appear are all 18th-century pieces of very slight content concerning trading links and observations regarding Spanish-Portuguese military rivalry in southern Brazil. No documents relating to the French occupation of Brazil in the 16th century have been identified within these papers. It is possible, however, that the series includes more Brazil-related material, not least relating to Franco-Portuguese territorial disputes over northern Brazil.

● Foreign Office (FO)

The Foreign Office was formed in 1782 and the scope of its archival material is vast, covering all aspects of the British-

Brazilian relationship, as well as observations and intelligence generated in and about Brazil for the use of the British government. The Foreign Office archive is, without a doubt, the single largest – and arguably the most significant – collection of documents in Britain relating to Brazil.

During the 19th century the Foreign Office rapidly developed a professionally organised structure, as did the Diplomatic Service abroad. In particular, the 20th-century records of the Foreign Office reflect the growth in complexity of foreign affairs and the communications revolution. One consequence was the huge quantity of records produced. Commercial material relating to Brazil, for example, can be excellent and is often the best source of material on British business in Brazil in the absence of company records. As well as confidential reports relating to specific companies, Foreign Office files often include enclosures of newspaper cuttings and company prospectuses.

*FO 881 – **Confidential Print***
From approximately 1829, important reports, correspondence and other papers on a particular subject were printed for circulation amongst staff in the Foreign Office, the Cabinet Office and other government departments, as well as amongst the staff in legations and consulates abroad. These are found haphazardly in the files and systematically in *FO 881*. Confidential Print volumes are listed by date and title in the relevant class list, and can therefore be searched with PROCAT.

There appear to be 130 items directly relating to Brazil. Some issues (most notably the British Guiana-Brazil territorial dispute) resulted in numerous Confidential Prints being produced over the course of many decades. Lengths vary from a few dozen pages to well over a hundred pages. Examples of Brazil-related Confidential Print papers are:

- *FO 881 / 316* – Brazil: Papers. Slave Trade, Sugar, 1845–46.

- *FO 881 / 4771X* – Brazil: Report on the investigation and collecting of plants and seeds of the india-rubber trees of Pará and Ceará and balsam of Copaiba, 1877.

- *FO 881 / 5886* – Brazil: Claim of the Ceará Water Company, 1887–89.

General Correspondence

The General Correspondence of the Foreign Office contains the most important and extensive documentation of the Foreign Office political departments. These are the papers produced by the Foreign Office itself which have accumulated in London. They include originals and copies of dispatches from representatives abroad, often with enclosures, reports, translations, newspaper cuttings and private letters sent on for the foreign secretary's information.

The volumes (and later files) containing the correspondence include the comments of relevant officials and any correspondence that may have been received from other government departments. Copies of the outgoing telegrams or letters, along with drafts, can also be found in these records.

The General Correspondence also includes other material, such as draft Parliamentary questions for reply on which Foreign Office advice was sought and the records of conversations between senior diplomats or the foreign secretary and visiting officials or foreign envoys resident in London. Correspondence relating to a particular issue or long-term international question may be bound separately and identified by broad topic. Such papers are labelled 'cases', and the volumes are found amongst the General Correspondence at the date at which the issue was finally resolved or when the file was otherwise closed. Very long-term questions where separate volumes were opened (for example, the Slave Trade) were bound up annually and placed at the end of the General Correspondence for that year.

Before 1906 the General Correspondence is arranged chronologically in a separate class or classes for each country, often altering with changes in sovereignty. The most important classes for Brazil are thus Portugal's *FO 63* (of central importance until 1824) and Brazil's own *FO 13* (with independence in 1824). These general classes also contain the Foreign Office consular, commercial and treaty correspondence bound in separate volumes and noted in the class lists. Consular material can also be supplemented using material in *FO 83* and *FO 84* (see p. 143).

Note: Portuguese (for the pre-Independence period) and Brazilian classes of General Correspondence are described in chronological order of significance, followed by other classes of General Correspondence that include Brazil-related material.

FO 63 – Foreign Office: Political and Other Departments: General Correspondence, Portugal, 1781 to 1905

English (some Portuguese and French)

This class contains general correspondence accumulated in London relating to Portugal. For the period 1781 to 1824, this is the main class of documents featuring Brazil-related correspondence. Especially vital are the volumes covering the years 1808 to 1824 (the period from the arrival in Rio de Janeiro of the Portuguese royal family until Independence), during which the formal British diplomatic presence in Brazil was established.

For 1808–24 the volumes that are devoted to correspondence to and from Brazil are identified in the class descriptive lists. There is no register of correspondence by subject, making identification of specific material a time-consuming, and often unproductive, process.

FO 13 – Foreign Office: Political and Other Departments: General Correspondence, Brazil, 1824 to 1905

865 volumes (on microfilm)

English (some Portuguese and French)

Note: As these volumes are stored in Cheshire, orders must be placed a minimum of three working days in advance.

This class of volumes and files contains general correspondence accumulated in London relating to Brazil. The class is generally considered the most important source of documentation on British-Brazilian political and commercial relations. As well as political and commercial bilateral relations, the material includes often very detailed coverage of Brazilian internal politics and Brazil's relations with other countries. Many volumes and files include correspondence between British and Brazilian officials and reports supplied by Brazilian non-governmental sources. While undoubtedly important, *FO 13* is best used in conjunction with other classes – for example, *FO 128* (see p. 144).

From approximately 1870, individual volumes with groups of files and individual documents on particular ongoing political, diplomatic, consular or commercial topics or cases were created

and placed in sequence according to the year the item was closed.
Examples of these are:

- *FO 13 / 49–50* – British mediation between Argentina
  and Brazil over Uruguay, 1828.

- *FO 13 / 506* – Alleged murders of 'negroes' at Rio by
  marines of HMS *Reindeer*, 1871–74.

- *FO 13 / 560* – Emigration of 'coolies' from Mauritius
  to Brazil, 1877–79.

- *FO 13 / 824* – Great Northern Railway of Brazil,
  1893–1901.

- *FO 13 / 832* – Naturalisation Law, 1891–1902.

- *FO 13 / 862* – State of Counani, 1903–05.

References to papers contained in this class can be found in
indexes and registers of correspondence (for 1824 to 1890,
see *FO 605*; then *FO 662* and *FO 409*). There is both a general
index and separate registers for particular areas (e.g. 'Commercial',
'Diplomatic', 'Consular'). PROCAT is only of value in identifying
the volume numbers for particular years, areas of interest, and
names of individual consuls and ministers.

FO 371 – Foreign Office: Political Departments: General Correspondence, 1906 to 1966
English (some Portuguese)
This class contains the correspondence, policy papers, memoranda
and minutes of the Political Departments of the Foreign Office.
The Political Departments were divided on a geographical basis,
with Brazil handled by the Americas Department. Also amongst the
Political Departments were the War Department (1914 to 1920) and
the Political Intelligence Department (1939 to 1946), the latter
including Brazilian material. Brazil-related records for the Political
Departments before 1906 are in *FO 13* (see p. 138).

FO 371 represents the most important series of PRO documents
for diplomatic and political historians for the 1906 to 1966 period,
but all subjects of interest to the Foreign Office are included. The

files are the main source showing how Foreign Office officials reached a policy position and what action resulted. Files often include notes of Cabinet ministers' opinions on a particular issue and might include Cabinet papers, intelligence reports and correspondence from British and foreign official or private sources. Files vary hugely in terms of their quantity and quality of material, however – they may include a single brief letter or weighty reports, commentaries and enclosures.

Especially valuable are the annual files (in some cases several files for a year) which contain general reports on internal and external political, economic or diplomatic situations relating to Brazil, along with supplementary material such as newspaper clippings and letters from local informants. The files include annotations made by Foreign Office staff that can be helpful for understanding how the reports were acted on in London. The reports were generally compiled by the appropriate first secretary at the embassy and are found in the files entitled *Economic Situation in Brazil* or *Political Situation in Brazil*, or in those with titles concerning Brazilian relations with the UK, US or other named countries. Additionally, files were opened for specific topics or cases concerning Brazil's internal political or economic conditions or external relations. Examples of such annual files include:

- *FO 371 / 51923* – Affairs of the Leopoldina Railway Co. Ltd in Brazil.

- *FO 371 / 51942* – Affairs of the Rio de Janeiro City Improvements Co. Ltd.

- *FO 371 / 74554* – Communism in Brazil, 1949.

'Country Tour' files can offer illuminating insights into parts of the country beyond the Rio de Janeiro or Brasilia Embassy precincts, especially with the post-1945 running down of Britain's once extensive network of consulates and vice-consulates. Such reports, however, frequently amount to no more than poor travelogues and can say more about the attitudes and prejudices of individual diplomats than about the area of the country that they are visiting.

The class is arranged by year and then by department and by region and country. Material relating to Brazil is usually found in files listed under 'Latin America: General' (for example, *FO 371 / 25969 – German Activities in Latin America, 1941*). Similarly, Brazilian relations with other countries are detailed from a non-Brazilian perspective in other country files, especially those for Latin American neighbours (for example, *FO 371 / 2155 – Venezuela: Frontier with Brazil, 1938*).

From 1938 a file-based system replaced the bound volumes, with descriptive titles to the individual files given in the class list. It is not possible to calculate how many volumes and files relate entirely or partly to Brazil, but a word search on 'Brazil' with PROCAT suggests that there are over 1,275. Reference is by means of the card index and registers in *FO 566* and *FO 662* for the years up to 1920 and thereafter in the indexes in *FO 409*. PROCAT is a useful tool for post-1938 files.

FO 368 – Foreign Office: Commercial and Sanitary: General Correspondence, 1906 to 1920
English (some Portuguese)

There are 46 volumes of specifically Brazilian commercial and sanitary correspondence for this period. Volumes include both in-letters and drafts or replies and are listed by year in the class handlist though no description of the contents is given. Reference is by the card index and registers in *FO 566* and *FO 662*.

Much of the correspondence is routine queries from British companies concerning Brazilian rates of duties and telegrams informing the Foreign Office of outbreaks of infectious diseases and quarantine regulations in often outlying parts of Brazil. There are also more detailed reports, often grouped together within the volumes, discussing Brazilian commercial conditions generally or those of individual companies (for example, assessments of the Manaus to Boa Vista railway concession in 1911 [*FO 368 / 515*]), or describing prospects for Brazil-bound emigrants.

The records for the Commercial Department before 1906 are in *FO 13* (see p. 138) and are bound in volumes described by the wording 'Commercial'. After 1920 commercial correspondence is found in a combination of the consular, political and treaty correspondence.

FO 369 – Foreign Office: Consular Department: General Correspondence, 1906 to 1966

5,961 files and volumes

English

This series contains correspondence, policy papers, etc., of the Consular Department in London. The records of the Consular Department before 1906 are in the *FO 13* series of General Correspondence (see p. 138), where they are usually bound separately and are distinguished in the catalogue by the description 'Consular' for the relevant pieces.

There is considerable Brazil-related correspondence including many enclosures, complementing (and occasionally duplicating) material in the Consular Archives (*FO 128*, see p. 144). The normal range of consular duties is discussed, such as disputes relating to property belonging to members of the British community (individuals, businesses and community institutions such as churches and cemeteries) and appeals relating to distressed British subjects. There are also regular detailed reports on the position of British communities throughout Brazil.

Reference is through the card index and registers in *FO 566* and *FO 662* to 1920, and thereafter by the indexes in *FO 409*. Descriptive file titles are given in the class handlist for post-1940 files.

FO 370 – Foreign Office: Library and the Research Department: General Correspondence, 1906 to 1965

2,929 files and volumes

English

This series contains correspondence of the Library (1906–64) and the Research Department (from 1946). These sections received requests for information or publications from other departments and from abroad, with a result that the records contain information on a vast variety of topics, but rarely are they unique to this particular class. Typical of Brazil-related material are [*FO 370 / 891*] details of a 1944 cultural agreement between Brazil and Canada and [*FO 370 / 1353*] arrangements for a British delegation to study the total eclipse of the sun in Brazil in 1947.

Papers up to 1951 are indexed in *FO 409*. For later Foreign Office and also Foreign and Commonwealth Office Library files see *FCO 12*. For later Foreign Office and also Foreign and Commonwealth Office Research Department files see *FCO 51*. For records of the British Council Section after it became the Cultural Relations Department see *FO 924* (p. 171).

FO 372 – **Foreign Office: Treaty Department and successors:**
General Correspondence, 1906 to 1965
English
The few files that relate to Brazil in this class concern disputes,
enquiries and bilateral agreements regarding marriages, extradition
treaties, diplomatic privilege, nationality and military service.
Some files also discuss arrangements for issuing British visas to
Brazilians and citizens of third countries.

FO 83 – **Foreign Office, General Correspondence, Great Britain**
and General, 1745 to 1967
English
This class contains miscellaneous collections of correspondence,
both to home departments and to diplomats abroad, and numerous
case papers. Brazil-related material mainly concerns disputes
regarding shipping and is found in:

- *FO 83 / 2236–2241* – Law Officers Reports: Brazil:
  Legal Cases, 1823–76

FO 84 – **Slave Trade Department, 1816 to 1892**
2,276 volumes (on microfilm)
English and Portuguese
This is the correspondence of the Slave Trade and African Departments
of the Foreign Office, including many volumes exclusively or
partially devoted to Brazil between 1822 and 1888. It includes
considerable material relating to fugitive slaves, the position of
British subjects in Brazil relative to slave ownership, the interception
of slaving vessels, and proceedings in the Vice-Admiralty court at
St Helena against slave ships, many of which were Brazilian.

Other Brazil-related material may be found in *FO 315*, the
archives of the Sierra Leone Slave Trade Commission (1819–68).
These include records of the Commission – specifically original
correspondence, letter books and registers of emancipated slaves,
and papers concerning ships' adjudications.

References to papers contained in this class can be found on
microfilm in *FO 605*.

FO 610 – Foreign Office: Passport Office, 1795 to 1948
410 volumes
English
There are few means of identifying emigrants and others departing
from British ports. Passport applications are one such possibility,
but 19th-century emigrants departing to foreign countries,
including Brazil, rarely travelled on British passports and instead
often travelled on passports issued by a consulate of the country
of destination. This series contains chronological registers of
passports issued, showing the intended destination and personal
details (including occupation) of the applicant. Brazil rarely
features as a destination. Indexes of names [*FO 611*] give the date
of issue and serial number of each passport in the years 1851–62
and 1874–98.

Embassy and Consular Archives

British legations, embassies and consulates kept their own archives
until they were normally returned to the Foreign Office in London
and eventually transferred to the PRO. However, with the notable
exception of the consulate in Bahia [*FO 268*], the consular archives
that found their way to the PRO are, at best, patchy, suggesting the
deliberate or unintended destruction or disposal of collections
while still in Brazil. Such consular collections that have survived
can be supplemented by exploring the important 'Consular'
volumes and files in *FO 128* (see below) as well as those in *FO 13*
(see p. 138) and, post-1905, in *FO 369* (see p. 142). Using both the
General Correspondence and Embassy and Consular classes will
not only bridge possible gaps in documentation, but will often give
different interpretations of events.

Note: General embassy and consular classes are described first,
followed, in alphabetical order according to place names, by
classes for individual consular districts and classes for special
commissions.

FO 128 – Foreign Office: Embassy and Consular: General Correspondence,
Brazil, 1821 to 1956 *(no correspondence survives 1914 to 1931)*
481 volumes and files
English (some Portuguese)
This series contains papers produced by the staff of the British
Embassy and consulates in Brazil. The series represents the most
extensive – and for many posts the most important – source of

consular records relating to Brazil. It is also important for the range of material generated from local contacts of the embassy and consulates, instructions from London and copies or drafts of replies. Subjects covered are extremely diverse but the files are especially valuable for their discussions and descriptions of events beyond Rio de Janeiro. For example, many of the reports of provincial rebellions and slave revolts of the 1830s make fascinating reading, as do the many reports on British communities and British commercial interests in often remote parts of the country. These documents are especially important where business or other specialist records are unavailable for topics as diverse as the construction of the Madeira-Mamoré Railway in western Amazon and the settlement of English immigrants in Paraná. In broad terms, the collection consists of:

- Dispatches and telegrams received by the embassy in Rio de Janeiro from the Foreign Office in London, and draft dispatches (or copies) for reply.

- Correspondence from and to British consulates and vice-consulates throughout Brazil.

- Correspondence with the Brazilian Foreign Ministry.

- Correspondence with individuals and agencies in Brazil, including Brazilian officials, representatives of British or other business interests in the country, and distressed or other British subjects seeking assistance or advice.

- Correspondence with individuals and agencies abroad seeking advice or assistance regarding individuals in Brazil or economic conditions of the country.

Until 1940, most documents were placed in annual volumes marked 'To Embassy', 'From Embassy', 'Brazilian Government', 'Commercial and Treaty', 'Consuls' and 'Miscellanea'. Some ongoing files were also maintained and bound with a number of others in volumes marked simply as 'Cases' (generally claims by British subjects or companies against the Brazilian authorities).

A few long-running claims generated sufficient documentation for separately marked volumes such as *Porto Alegre and New Hamburg (Brazilian) Railway Co. Ltd, 1906 to 1913* [*FO 128 / 312*].

From 1940 files were kept separately, and their subjects are clearly identifiable in the class handlists and accessible with a PROCAT search. Some of these files are extremely weighty, including correspondence and enclosures from diplomatic staff and local contacts, while others contain no more than a brief letter. Examples of files are:

- *FO 128 / 387–390 and 395* – Enemy Activities (German) in Brazil, 1940–41.

- *FO 128 / 402* – Brazil–Russia: Political Relations, 1942.

- *FO 128 / 433* – Brazilian Expeditionary Forces, 1944.

- *FO 128 / 463* – Political Exiles in Brazil, 1947.

- *FO 128 / 478–480* – Brazil: Internal Political Situation, 1956

FO 129 – **Foreign Office: Consulates: Letter Books, Brazil, 1828 to 1863**
17 volumes
English
These are copies of out-letters from British consulates throughout Brazil and are best used in conjunction with the coinciding years' volumes of *FO 128*.

FO 130 – **Foreign Office: Consulates: Register of Correspondence, Brazil, 1828 to 1912**
15 volumes
English
These are registers of incoming and outgoing consular letters contained within *FO 128*. *FO 130 / 9* is an index of the British Claims correspondence in *FO 306* (see p. 150).

FO 131 – Foreign Office: Consulates: Miscellanea, Brazil, 1820 to 1885
18 volumes (on microfilm)
English
Dispatches, drafts and miscellaneous papers relating to the slave
trade (1820–81), commercial treaty negotiations (1842–45), a
special mission to Argentina and Uruguay (1847) and other papers,
accounts, etc.

FO 268 – Foreign Office: Consulates: Bahia: General Correspondence,
1812 to 1905
50 volumes
English and Portuguese
Bahia (Salvador) was an important consular office and the only
one for which an archive survives that stretches over a long period.
The files include in-letters and supplementary material arriving at
the consulate. In addition to copies of dispatches from the
consulate to London, the files feature Foreign Office dispatches
and correspondence from Ascension Island (a key British naval
base for the interception of slave ships) and other posts.
Correspondence includes prices of slaves.

    Volumes are not indexed but are identifiable by date and
broad source of documents ('From Presidents and Captains
General', 'From Foreign Office', 'From British Legation, Rio de
Janeiro', 'From Brazilian Authorities', 'From Board of Trade',
'From Various'). The latter includes correspondence to and from
individuals and businesses in Britain and Brazil. Apart from the
file 'From Foreign Office (Slave Trade)', there are no subject-
specific volumes. Reference is with FO 270.

FO 269 – Foreign Office: Consulates: Bahia: Letter Books,
1853 to 1906
13 volumes
English
These include copies of out-letters from the consulate in Bahia.
The individual volumes (identifiable by year) are divided into
sections: 'To Legation, Rio de Janeiro', 'To Presidents',
'To Foreign Office', 'To Board of Trade' and 'To Various'.
The latter includes correspondence to and from individuals and
businesses in Britain and Brazil.

FO 270 – Foreign Office: Consulates: Bahia:
Register of Correspondence, 1891 to 1909
1 volume
English
This volume is the register of correspondence from the British
Consulate in Bahia.

FO 271 – Foreign Office: Consulates: Bahia:
Shipping Records and Naval Court Proceedings, 1853 to 1915
33 volumes
English
This series features shipping records and Naval Court proceedings
of the British Consulate in Bahia. The volumes are registers of
shipping movements, protests to and from the local authorities, and
orders for and reports of surveys and Naval Court proceedings.

FO 272 – Foreign Office: Consulates: Bahia: Miscellanea, 1875 to 1915
6 volumes
English (some Portuguese)
These volumes include accounts, papers relating to the property of
deceased British subjects, returns, certificates, etc.

FO 843 – Foreign Office: Consulates: Pernambuco:
General Correspondence, 1821 to 1912
20 volumes (no correspondence 1824–63)
English
Mainly copies of out-letters to the British Legation in Rio de
Janeiro concerning the local economy, trade, shipping, politics and
concerns relating to resident and visiting British subjects. There are
also some in-letters, mainly from the British Legation but also
from bodies in London such as the Board of Trade and from the
local Brazilian authorities. See also *FO 865* below.

FO 865 – Foreign Office: Consulates: Recife (Pernambuco):
Various Papers, 1927 to 1948
7 files
English
Extremely limited in scope, the surviving files relate to the
inspection of the consulate (1927–31) and matters relating to the
Anglican Church and cemetery. See also *FO 843* above.

FO 587 – **Foreign Office: Consulates: Porto Alegre:**
Letter Books, 1868 to 1900
3 volumes
English
These are entry books of copies of out-letters and related
dispatches covering the usual range of consular business. Included
also are regular returns listing ships' arrivals and departures, trade
figures and slave prices.

FO 588 – **Foreign Office: Consulates: Porto Alegre:**
Register of Correspondence, 1881 to 1935
6 volumes
English
These are entry books of in- and out-letters of the British Consulate.
The actual correspondence has not been preserved. The value,
therefore, is limited to identifying the main concerns occupying the
consulate during this period and the names of correspondents.

FO 589 – **Foreign Office: Consulates: Porto Alegre:**
Miscellanea, 1881 to 1916
1 volume
English
This entry book of miscellaneous proceedings contains copies of out-
letters and notes of consular actions. Shipping movements and routine
consular duties (such as registering British subjects and issuing
passports) form the bulk of the volume.

F0 743 – **Foreign Office: Embassy and Legation, Rio de Janeiro:**
General Correspondence and Registers of Births, 1815 to 1950
41 volumes and files.
English
The first ten volumes in the class [*FO 743 / 1–10*] are Registers of
Correspondence for the Rio de Janeiro consulate for 1897–1934 –
in- and out-letters are listed giving subject, date and name of
correspondent. Letter copy books have not been retained. The
remaining volumes and, for the most part, files in the class feature
both material generated by the Rio de Janeiro consular district
itself and inherited from the Pará and Maranhão consular districts.
Especially noteworthy are 1930s files [*FO 743 / 16–18*] concerning
the disappearance of the British explorer Colonel Percy Fawcett
in Mato Grosso; files [*FO 743 / 22–27*] outlining the British

Community Council activities in support of the Allies in World War II and the local recruitment of British volunteers; and committee files [*FO 743 / 12–13*].

FO 863 – Foreign Office: Consulates: São Paulo: Register of Births and Marriages and Correspondence, 1919 to 1948
13 files
English
These files include register of births, 1932; register of marriages, 1933; correspondence relating to the Foreigners' Cemetery, Santos, 1919 and 1936; and correspondence relating to nationality, 1943.

FO 306 – Foreign Office: Archives of the British and Brazilian Claims Commission, 1858 to 1877
9 boxes
English and Portuguese
These are papers of successful and unsuccessful claims against the Brazilian authorities for losses incurred by British subjects, especially during periods of war or insurrection in Brazil. Claims relate to the early decades of the 19th century and include compensation claimed for 'illegal imprisonment' of British subjects, for losses incurred while the Banda Oriental (Uruguay) was a part of Brazil (1827–28) and for the 'forced and irregular payments of duties' made by British businesses in Maranhão.

The index to this Claims Commission (including dates and basic details of the nature of claims) is found in *FO 130 / 9* (see p. 146).

FO 308 – Foreign Office: Archives of Commissions and Delegations: British and Portuguese Mixed Commission, 1817
English and Portuguese
These are papers concerning successful and unsuccessful claims against the Portuguese authorities for losses and expenses incurred by British subjects. Brazil-related material concerns the interception of Portuguese ships carrying slaves from Africa to Bahia.

Other Foreign Office Classes
Depending on a researcher's subject and period of interest, non-Brazilian classes might contain relevant material and so should be explored. For the early 19th century, Portuguese papers are an obvious source, although they are likely to be disappointing. For example, no Brazil-related documents have been identified

amongst the extensive records of the British Consulate in Lisbon, 1809–1949 [*FO 173*]. Similarly, there does not appear to be relevant material amongst the 1807–67 British consular records of Ponta Delgado (Azores) [*FO 559*]. However, the various classes for the United Provinces of the Rio de la Plata (e.g. *FO 505*) can be helpful for some early 19th-century subjects. Document classes for European or Latin American countries regularly feature files discussing aspects of their relations with Brazil. *FO 63* (Foreign Office: Political and Other Departments: General Correspondence, Portugal, 1781–1905) has been outlined above, but other classes worth considering are described below.

*FO 505 – **Foreign Office: United Provinces of Rio de la Plata***
English
This class includes some files [e.g. *FO 505 / 2*] concerning Brazilian blockades of Buenos Aires, 1826–28.

*FO 811 – **Foreign Office, British Consulate, Funchal, Madeira, c. 1750 io 1931***
61 volumes and files
English
This includes very few identifiable Brazil-related documents. However, *FO 811 / 42* contains a brief 1851 letter concerning the refitting of Brazilian slave ships in Madeira, while *FO 811 / 43* discusses the intentions and wishes of the Dowager Empress of Brazil regarding her departure from Madeira in 1853.

Foreign Office Private Papers
Until well into the 20th century, foreign secretaries and diplomats took away as their own property unregistered papers relating to their official business. Many such papers are described elsewhere in the guide, but it is suggested that, where names of individuals are known, a National Register of Archives (NRA) web search is carried out (see p. 251). Some collections of so-called private papers were, however, returned to the Foreign Office before being transferred to the PRO. Some such collections are, however, disappointing. For example, the papers of George Villiers, 4th Earl of Clarendon (foreign secretary Feb 1853–Feb 1858, Nov 1865–July 1866 and Dec 1868–June 1870), in *FO 361* do not contain any Brazil-related material.

FO 355 / 1 and 6 – Aston Papers
English

Sir Arthur Aston (1798–1859) served as secretary and chargé d'affaires of the British Legation in Rio de Janeiro between 1826 and 1833. *FO 355 / 1* contains drafts of correspondence from Rio de Janeiro (1827–32), while *FO 355 / 6* covers a longer period (1827–43), including some Brazilian correspondence. War between Brazil and Argentina is a frequent topic, and correspondents include Woodbine Parish (of the British Legation in Buenos Aires; see *FO 354 / 7–9*, below) and Lords Granville and Palmerston.

FO 954 – Avon Papers
English

These are microfilm copies of the private papers of Anthony Eden (1899–1977) accumulated while foreign secretary (1936–38 and 1940–45). The original papers are held by the University of Birmingham Library, where access is restricted (see p. 11). Few items relate to Brazil – limited to a few letters discussing Brazilian views of the political situation in France and Italy in 1943 and mentions of Brazilian military operations in North Africa and Italy.

FO 353 / 96 – Jackson Papers
English

Sir George Jackson was a diplomat whose later career was closely connected with the abolition of the slave trade. In 1828 he was appointed 1st commissary judge of the Mixed Commission Court at Sierra Leone. In 1832–41 he was chief commissioner under the Convention for the Abolition of the African Slave Trade at Rio de Janeiro. He held the same position at Suriname (1841–45) and Luanda (1845–59). Reports from Jackson recounting his Rio de Janeiro activities are contained within a single volume.

FO 354 / 7 to 9 – Parish Papers
English

Sir Woodbine Parish (1796–1882) was a diplomat who served both in Europe and South America. In 1823 he was appointed as British consul-general at Buenos Aires, and in 1828 he was closely involved in ending the war between Argentina and Brazil and establishing Uruguay as an independent state. Included is correspondence with both the Foreign Office in London and the British Legation in Rio de Janeiro.

PRO 30 / 22 – **Russell Papers**
English
The career of Lord John Russell (1792–1878) included twice
holding the position of prime minister (1846–52 and 1865–66) and
twice foreign secretary (a three-month period in 1852–53 and
1859–65).

Papers of Brazilian interest are mainly letters received during
Russell's second term as foreign secretary, especially slave trade
related. It was under Russell that the so-called 'Christie Affair'
occurred. William Dougal Christie, the British minister to Brazil
in the early 1860s, infuriated the authorities in Rio de Janeiro by
pressuring Brazil to undertake measures to end slavery. In 1863
he ordered the seizure by British ships of several Brazilian
vessels outside the port of Rio de Janeiro to suggest British
willingness to apply force with regard to slavery. This led to
Brazil suspending diplomatic relations with Britain. There is
considerable correspondence relating to this episode – from
Christie's acceptance of his Brazilian appointment [*PRO 30 / 22 / 48*]
in August 1859 to the reinstatement of diplomatic relations in 1865
with the arrival in Rio de Janeiro of the new minister, Edward
Thornton [*PRO 30 / 22 / 33*]. (See also Layard Papers under
British Library, p. 110.)

FO 933 – **Thornton Papers**
English
Sir Edward Thornton (1766–1852) served as British minister to the
Portuguese Court in Brazil between 1819 and 1821 [see *FO 933 /
78–86*] and subsequently as minister in Lisbon in 1823 and 1824
[see *FO 933 / 87–91*]. Correspondence mainly duplicates material
found in other Foreign Office classes but can be useful for filling
gaps in files. Subjects are wide-ranging with much material on
Brazil's relations with Buenos Aires and concerning the detention
of the property of British merchants in Pernambuco. Thornton's
son, Sir Edward Thornton the younger (1817–1906), served as
minister to Brazil between 1865 and 1867 [see *FO 933 / 93*].
The only Brazil-related documents concern a dispute about the
salvaging of a United States whaling ship, the *Canada*, wrecked
off Pernambuco in 1856.

• Colonial Office (CO)

Generally British colonial administrations did not enter into direct contact with Brazil; there were virtually no direct contacts with the Brazilian government or its agencies. Instead, representations were generally made by the British Embassy or consulates in Brazil through the Foreign Office in London. Most such documents are held within Foreign Office files. Occasionally colonial administrations and individual residents in British colonies requested advice or information directly from British representatives in Brazil. It should be noted that Indian affairs were at no time handled by the Colonial Office. For relations between India and Brazil one should consult Foreign Office (see p. 135) and India Office records (see p. 121); from 1907, relations between Brazil and the British dominions were handled by the Foreign Office and the Dominions Office (see p. 156).

Trade and other links between British colonies and Brazil were limited, a fact that is reflected in the lack of Colonial Office records. The one major area of interest linking Brazil and British overseas possessions is the long-lasting territorial dispute concerning British Guiana, for which numerous FO and CO files and volumes were created. Such files that exist on other topics and places are widely scattered; readers should consult the class list appropriate to the colony or possession of interest. Some Brazil-related material is certainly found amongst *CO 733* Palestine department files, while the important Newfoundland–Brazil salt cod trade is covered in *CO 194* (pre-1922) and *DO 35* (1922–49); and there are records scattered between several Admiralty (ADM), CO and FO classes concerning the mid-Atlantic island of St Helena for its role in the interception of slave ships. The Board of Trade (BT) archive (see p. 162) includes some files relating to trade agreements between British colonies and dominions and Brazil and agreements for the export to Brazil of specific Empire products, such as jute.

*CO 1 / 1 and 2 – **Colonial Office: America and West Indies, colonial papers, 1574 to 1623***
2 volumes
English
Although these volumes cover the period of the Amazon Company's short-lived (1619–21) efforts to establish trading posts and settlements in the Amazon delta region, only a few passing mentions to the venture feature in these documents. See also under British Library, pp. 102, 104 and 107 and National Library of Ireland, p. 38.

CO 111 – Colonial Office: British Guiana: Original Correspondence, 1781 to 1951
825 volumes
English

British Guiana was the only British territory sharing a frontier with Brazil, and parts of the south were subject to a long-standing territorial dispute. Although the exploration and demarcation of limits in the disputed Rio Branco region are reported to have been made by Brazil between 1754 and 1823, the conflicting claim was first brought to a head in about 1838.

There are many dozens of files devoted to the long-lasting territorial dispute. Material includes correspondence between the British and Brazilian governments, documents relating to the work of the various border commissions (for example, detailed reports on the recruitment of local staff and other operational details on the ground), maps, sketches and photographs. Haphazard indexing makes identification a painstaking process.

Beyond the territorial dispute, there were very few points of political or economic contact between Brazil and British Guiana. During the 1920s, however, plans were put forward to construct a railway connecting British Guiana and Manaus, documented within several detailed files.

Printed descriptive class lists and PROCAT enable Brazil-related material to be identified. Later Colonial Office records concerning British Guiana are in *CO 1031* (see below). Other correspondence concerning the British Guiana–Brazil frontier dispute may be found in the FO series, in particular *FO 13* (see p. 138) and *FO 371* (see p. 139), and much of the correspondence was brought together for distribution as Confidential Print (see *FO 881*, p. 136). (See also British Guiana Papers under British Library, p. 105.)

CO 1031 – Colonial Office: West Indian Department: Original Correspondence, 1947 to 1966
English

This class of documents includes all British West Indies territories, including British Guiana, for which there is a four-year overlap with *CO 111* (see above). There are several files relating to the British Guiana–Brazil boundary [*C0 1031 / 114; C0 1031 / 115; C0 1031 / 1852*] covering the years 1950–56. Otherwise, there appears to be only one file on a separate subject, a 1953 plan concerning the migration of British West Indians to Brazil [*CO 1031 / 1137*].

Nothing became of the plan, mainly due to the Brazilian authorities' racial concerns. Other West Indies-related correspondence (generally concerning individuals seeking advice regarding trade possibilities or concerning the British Guiana frontier dispute) may be found in various FO series, in particular *FO 128* and *FO 371*.

• Dominions Office (DO)

In 1907 the Colonial Office was divided into a Crown Colonies Division and a Dominions Division. In 1925 the Dominions Division became independent of the Colonial Office as the Dominions Office. In addition to the self-governing Dominions (Australia, Canada, New Zealand and South Africa), the office was responsible for Bechuanaland, Basutoland and Swaziland, Southern Rhodesia, the Irish Free State (Eire), Newfoundland and Nauru.

CO 532 – Dominions Office: Original Correspondence, 1907 to 1925
325 volumes
English
Although originally a Colonial Office (CO) class, these documents feature Dominions Office correspondence for 1907–25.

DO 35 – Dominions Office and Commonwealth Relations Office: Original Correspondence, 1915 to 1971
10,914 volumes and files
English
General correspondence of the Dominions Office (1925–47), including correspondence concerning the dominions' relationship with Brazil, falls within this class. Although relations were extremely limited, there are some files for the 1930s covering Brazilian trade with Eire (Ireland), Australia, New Zealand, South Africa, Canada and, especially, Newfoundland. Only with the latter were trade relations significant, and there are several detailed files containing letters and other documents discussing issues surrounding Newfoundland's important salt cod exports, supplying northern Brazil in particular. (*Note:* Pre-1922 Newfoundland files are in *CO 194*.) Other files detail discussions concerning the opening of direct political relations between Brazil and the dominions (i.e. bypassing London), especially relations with Canada. The *DO 35* class list includes brief subject descriptions of individual files and batches of small files that have been tagged together.

● Foreign and Commonwealth Office (FCO)

Records are kept of the Foreign and Commonwealth Office and the Foreign Office, the Commonwealth Office and the Diplomatic Service Administration Office during the period in which they operated a common registry scheme. Files are described by date and subject matter; some files contain just a single letter, while others are much more weighty, including correspondence to and from the embassy and/or Foreign Office, background reports, newspaper cuttings, photographs, etc. All descriptions may be accessed electronically via a subject word search using PROCAT.

FCO 7 – Foreign Office and Foreign and Commonwealth Office: American and Latin American Files, January 1967 to October 1968
English
This class includes all countries in the Americas, although files for individual countries are grouped and listed together for each year.

- ● *FCO 7 / 1–118* – Files relate to individual Latin American countries and regional issues, especially concerning trade and political relations and observations. The class also includes reports of country tours by resident British diplomats and official and semi-official visits from Britain, such as Queen Elizabeth II's 1968 tour of Brazil and Chile.

- ● *FCO 7 / 275–336* – Files include assessments of the political affairs in Brazil, anti-US sentiment, border disputes (involving Guyana and Venezuela), trade (British and non-British), claims concerning formerly British-owned infrastructure (including ports and railways), Queen Elizabeth's state visit, and British scientific expeditions in the Amazon basin. Relationships between Brazil and other countries are sometimes discussed in the dispatches from other embassies (for example, Argentine/Brazilian relations are detailed in *FCO 7 / 134*; Chilean/Brazilian relations are detailed in *FCO 7 / 353*; Venezuelan/Brazilian relations in *FCO 7 / 899*; a 1971 file considering Paraguayan/Brazilian relations in *FCO 7 / 2136*). Any discussion with non-American countries is usually found outside these classes (for example, Danish/Brazilian relations in *FCO 9 / 275*; Portuguese/Brazilian relations in *FCO 9 / 360*).

- *FCO 7 / 322 and 1120* – Papers (1967–69) relate to outstanding claims concerning the São Paulo Railway Company (Santos–Jundaí Railway), including a document charting a history of the financial dispute.

FCO 4 – Foreign Office and Foreign and Commonwealth Office: Consular Department: Registered Files, 1963 to 1973
501 files
English
This series consists of registered files of the Foreign Office Consular Department (January to March 1967), the Joint Foreign Office/Commonwealth Office Consular Department (March 1967 to October 1968), and the Foreign and Commonwealth Office Consular Department (October 1968 onwards). They are the London headquarters end of correspondence with UK consular representatives overseas. Brazilian correspondence is extremely limited, containing very few case files of the kind found in the earlier Foreign Office Consular Department records [see *FO 13* and *FO 369*]. There are, however, general reports on the status of the British community in Brazil [*FCO 47 / 368*] and a report on the state of British cemeteries in Brazil [*FCO 47 / 367*]. Reference is by the class list or with PROCAT.

• Admiralty (ADM)

The ADM archive contains the records of the Admiralty, Naval forces, the Royal Marines, the Coastguard and related bodies. During times of war the Admiralty oversaw merchant shipping. Although some ships' logs are held within this class, others are held by the National Maritime Museum (see p. 172).

ADM 1 / 19–53 – Admiralty and Ministry of Defence, Navy Department: Correspondence and Papers: Brazil Station, 1807 to 1839
34 volumes
English
ADM 1 is official correspondence directed to the secretary of the admiralty for the information of the lord admiral or the lords commissioners. In time the series developed into a collection of correspondence to, from and within all departments of the

admiralty. *ADM 1 / 19–53* consists of correspondence concerning the Brazil Station.

The Brazil (or South America) Station for the years 1807 to 1839 covered both the east and west coasts of South and Central America outside the Caribbean. The station owed its inception to the flight of the Portuguese royal family to Brazil in advance of Napoleon's invading armies. The first reports (see especially *ADM 1 / 19*) are from the squadron escorting the Portuguese royal family to Brazil and were sent from Lisbon, the Azores and Brazil.

The geographic coverage of the squadron was broad, but the largest number of documents were dispatched from Brazil, in particular Rio de Janeiro and Bahia. Apart from the reports on the flight of the royal family, other important subjects relate to conflicts with the United Provinces of the River Plate and the slave trade. A large proportion of the documents is routine, however, with discussions of supplies, shipping movements, and the plight of British mariners held in Brazilian prisons.

Reference to the Brazil Station volumes are found in the Admiralty Index and Digest in the PRO's main Reference Room. These volumes provide subject and nominal indexes to the letters in *ADM 1* together with a summary of their contents. *ADM 12 / 55* serves as a subject index from 1808.

ADM 123 / 177 and 182 – Admiralty: Africa Station: Correspondence, Southern Division, Cape Verde, Brazil, Cuba and Native Chiefs, 1857 to 1860
English
These reports relate to the interception and freeing of slaves, although few documents feature more than passing and indirect mentions of Brazil. Of particular value, however, are tables listing numbers of slaves disembarking at the port of Bahia and of slave interceptions on the high seas. The Index to Correspondence (1845–1918) is found in the fourteen volumes of *ADM 124*.

ADM 53 – Admiralty, and Ministry of Defence, Navy Department: Ships' Logs, 1799 to 1972
English
These logs were books maintained by the Officer of the Watch for every ship of the Royal Navy in commission. They provide a permanent and consecutive daily record of the ships' movements and position, recording all wheel and telegraph orders, weather

encountered and other events, such as the employment of the ship's company, any deaths on board, disciplinary action (i.e. the reading of punishment warrants), loss or damage to stores and any other items of interest, such as visits by dignitaries or foreign officers.

The lists are maintained on an annual basis where possible and under each ship alphabetically by month. These may be searched with PROCAT. Although ships would have regularly sailed into Brazilian ports, it is not possible to identify ships' movements using the catalogue.

● High Court of the Admiralty (HCA)

The High Court of the Admiralty was originally (in the 16th century) concerned mainly with cases of piracy. It later took on a wider role, dealing with privateering and other matters that would warrant the arrest of ships and cargoes, and occasionally of masters and owners.

HCA / 6 – High Court of Admiralty: Instance Court: Assignation Books, Series II, 1767 to 1810
English
These two large boxes of unindexed case papers concern 28 selected Brazilian claims arising out of British actions in connection with the suppression of the slave trade.

HCA / 36 – High Court of Admiralty: Slave Trade: Additional Papers, 1837 to 1876
English
These eight bundles of papers include drafts, accounts and original correspondence used to prepare reports sanctioning the capture of vessels engaged in the slave trade. Correspondence includes that with Edward Thornton and George Buckley Mathew of the British Legation, Rio de Janeiro (1865–71), case papers concerning Brazilian claims, and a memorandum on relations with Brazil (1865).

● Supreme Court of Judicature (J)

During the 19th century a series of legal reforms was instituted affecting the court jurisdiction for handling bankruptcies and other company winding-up procedures. This led to a Companies Court being established in 1890 as part of the High Court. Cases are listed chronologically and listed alphabetically within each year of proceedings, under the initial letter of the company concerned. Cases may be identified through the class list or using PROCAT, searching by name of company (if known) or keywords such as 'Brazil' or 'Brazilian'. Cases fall within the years 1886 to 1945. The following classes all include cases involving British-registered companies operating in Brazil:

- *J 13* – Supreme Court of Judicature: High Court of Justice, Companies Court: Companies (Winding-up) Proceedings, 1883–1995.

- *J 90* – Supreme Court of Judicature and former Superior Courts: Central Office: Documents Exhibited or Deposited in Court, c. 1700–1953.

- *J 10* – Supreme Court of Judicature: High Court of Justice, Companies Court: Registrars' Notes, 1893–1948.

Documents found in the files typically include copies of summonses, affidavits, judge's notes, maps, plans, catalogues or prospectuses, and share certificates. The contents rarely offer any insights into the workings of a company, only occasionally offering more than what is immediately relevant to the narrow administrative concern of winding up a company.

• *Treasury (T)*

The Treasury was and is responsible for the control and management of the British government's entire public revenue and expenditure. Brazil-related material is diverse, with files listed by name and date in the class lists and identifiable with PROCAT. Over 130 files directly relate to Brazil; most such files are found in *T 160* and concern currency and financial transactions between Brazil and Britain during World War II. Other files relate to financial disputes between different British government departments – for example, between the Foreign Office and the Colonial Office over responsibility for repatriation costs of distressed British subjects. In some cases the Treasury found itself responsible for pursuing the Brazilian authorities on behalf of British companies. Examples of files of this type are:

- *T 1 / 12754* – Violating slave trade acts by the St John d'El Rey Mining Co.; freedom of the Cata Branca slaves, 1880.

- *T 190 / 128* – Lazard Bros., Ltd (São Paulo Water Service), 1925–26.

- *T 236 / 4087 and 4089* – São Paulo Railway Co. Ltd: payment of compensation by the Brazilian government due to expropriation, 1947–49.

● Board of Trade (BT)

The Board of Trade was responsible for many aspects of Britain's overseas trade, also having responsibility for trade agreements with foreign countries involving British colonies and dominions. Shipping and air travel have been major areas of responsibility, including overseeing the movement of goods and passengers and investigating shipwrecks and air crashes. Much Board of Trade correspondence is also found with FO classes, often filed separately.

BT 11– Board of Trade and successors: Commercial Relations and Exports Department and predecessors, 1866 to 1975
English
Most material in this class is from the 20th century, with Brazil-related files mainly of the 1920s–40s. Files mainly relate to general trade agreements between Britain and Brazil (and also between the dominions and Brazil), but some concern individual specific transport services or industrial or agricultural products. Included in the class, for example, are some very substantial files (*BT 11 / 1432* and *BT 11 / 1654*) concerning the winding up of the financial affairs of the Brazil Railway Company in the 1940s.

BT 2 – Board of Trade: Seagoing Passenger Lists, Outwards, 1890 to 1960
English
These lists contain the names, ages, occupations and sometimes addresses of people leaving United Kingdom ports for final destinations outside of Europe. Vessels picking up passengers in European ports en route to their final destination would report details of these additional passengers. As ships sailing from

Liverpool and elsewhere in the United Kingdom frequently stopped off in Vigo (and occasionally Oporto or Lisbon), these records can be useful for tracing Iberian immigrants to Brazil. The purpose or length of the intended stay in the travellers' final destinations are not recorded, however. The lists are copies provided by ships' masters, as required by law, to port officers. Lists are arranged under the names of the ports of departure. Although this class basically covers the period 1890–1960, a few earlier lists are included. Searching the lists can be very time-consuming as there are no indexes of names and most lists are not alphabetical. If searching for an individual, without the approximate date of departure and name of the port one cannot realistically hope to find the passenger's name.

BT 31 – Board of Trade: Files for Dissolved Companies, 1856 to 1948
English

This contains files of dissolved British joint stock companies of all kinds incorporated between 1856 and 1931 and mainly dissolved before 1932 (although some files concern companies dissolved between 1933 and 1948). Examples of Brazil-related case files are:

- *BT 31 / 993 / 1508C* – Ceará (North Brazil) Water Company Ltd, 1864.

- *BT 31 / 13177 / 108727* – Rubber Corporation of Brazil Ltd, 1910.

Files usually include memorandum and articles of association containing particulars of the company's constitution, copy of the certificate of incorporation, statement of nominal share capital and list of the shareholders and liquidation and dissolution documents. Although there are files relating to numerous dissolved British-registered companies (especially railways) operating in Brazil, few insights into their operation can be gleaned beyond mere financially technical aspects of their launch and dissolution.

BT 4 – Board of Trade: Companies Registration Office: Files of Joint Stock Companies Registered under the 1844 and 1856 Acts, 1844 to c. 1860
English

This is similar in general content to material found in *BT 31* files, but it covers joint stock companies registered between 1844 and approximately 1860.

● Home Office (HO)

Most of the limited foreign-related Home Office material is found within the *HO 45* class of document. Some of the documents are merely copies of Foreign Office files but most of the Brazil-related material (such as there is) appears to have been generated by, or under the direction of, the Home Office itself. Although the files are few in number, they are often quite substantial and valuable.

HO 28 / 1 to 63 – Home Office: Admiralty Correspondence
English
These volumes, covering the years 1762 to 1840, consist of original letters from the Lords of the Admiralty to the Home Office and draft out-letters from the Home Office to the Admiralty. Brazil related material is limited and scattered, but some exists. For example, *HO 28 / 2* includes correspondence from 1782 concerning attempts by Britain to annex the island of Trinidade. Related documents can be found in *ADM 1 / 54*.

HO 45 / 4565 – Recruitment to Brazilian Navy
English
The file relates to the 'scandalous treatment' of boys recruited in 1852 in Liverpool for the Brazilian Navy and the eventual repatriation to England of some of the survivors.

HO 45 / 10502 / 123556 – Foreign: Free State of Counani, and its self-styled President
English and French
This very substantial file relates to the activities in 1904–15 of Adolph Brezet, the self-styled 'President' of the so-called 'Free State of Counani', a disputed territory located in present-day Amapá, bordering French Guiana. Included within the file are Brazilian and British diplomatic documents and correspondence, Metropolitan Police reports and British newspaper clippings detailing the activities of Counani's 'emissaries' and of Brezet (described in one report as 'an adventurer and a foreign swindler') in 'exile' in London. Other important PRO files on Counani are *FO 13 / 862* and *MEDPOL 2 / 776*. The FO file contains 1903–5 material. The MEDPOL (London's Metropolitan Police) file

centres on detailed intelligence reports on Brezet and his entourage in London, and also includes newspaper clippings.

HO 161 – Diaries of Sir Roger Casement, 1901 to 1911
5 volumes (on microfilm)
English
Roger Casement (1864–1916) was a career diplomat who served as British consul at Santos (1906–8), Pará (Belém; 1908–9) and Rio de Janeiro (1909–13). Casement's investigations into the abuses against indigenous peoples in the Belgian Congo and Peru were rewarded with a knighthood in 1911. Casement was executed in England in 1916 for high treason due to an alleged plot to assist a German invasion of Ireland.

The Casement Diaries consist of three private diaries, a notebook and a ledger that were seized by the police in London. In addition to notes on the slave-like conditions of native peoples in Congo and workers in Peruvian rubber estates, the diaries contained graphic details of homosexual encounters, including many entries in Brazil. The diaries were not shown in court but were used to blacken Casement's character in the face of a campaign for a reprieve. (See also under National Library of Ireland, p. 39.)

HO 294 / 133 and 134 – Czechoslovak Refugee Trust: Records – Brazil, 1940 to 1948
English (some Portuguese and German)
The Czechoslovak Refugee Trust was established on 21 July 1939 jointly by the British government and the trust's voluntary predecessor, the British Committee for Refugees from Czechoslovakia. The trust aimed to assist people fleeing persecution in Nazi-occupied Czechoslovakia and, where appropriate, assist refugees to find permanent settlement.

There are several hundred Czechoslovak Refugee Trust files, many of them case files relating to individual refugees and their families. Two large files concern the resettlement of refugees from Czechoslovakia (Czechs, Slovaks, Jews and Sudeten Germans) in Brazil between 1940 and 1948. Letters and other documents discuss settlement possibilities in rural São Paulo and Paraná, but possibilities for tradesmen and industrial workers are also considered. There are lists of some of the individuals applying for settlement in Brazil and some background information on them.

*HO 213 / 759 – **Polish ex-servicemen***
English
The file centres on the issuing of travel documents to Polish
ex-servicemen demobilised in Britain and seeking to settle in
Brazil, 1946–48.

• Ministry of Labour (LAB)

The Ministry of Labour was established in 1916 to extend the work
of the Labour Departments of the Board of Trade. In 1920 the
International Labour Division was created and was renamed the
Overseas Department in 1942. In the same year the Labour Attaché's
Service was created, with the appointment in Washington, D.C. of
its first attaché. Immediately after World War II, Labour attachés
were appointed to British embassies in many parts of the world,
including those in Mexico City, Buenos Aires and Rio de Janeiro.
The role of the attachés was primarily political and involved
establishing and maintaining close working relationships with
industrial leaders and managers, with trade union leaders and their
members, and with government employment specialists.

*LAB 13 – **Ministry of Labour: International Labour Division and
Overseas Department: Registered Files, 1923 to 1979***
English (some Portuguese)
There are at least fourteen files from British Labour attachés in
Brazil, spanning the years 1946 to 1974. The files are generally
substantial and contain a mimeo of the attaché's report that was
produced for limited circulation within the Ministry of Labour,
Foreign Office and British government circles. Files also include
Labour attachés' correspondence, newspaper clippings,
photographs and other material not reproduced in actual reports.
Duplicate copies of some of the reports – including some missing
from *LAB 13* itself – can be found listed in *FO 371* (see p. 139)
often with Foreign Office annotations.

   The biannual reports generally feature statistical tables
detailing the cost of living and wages in Brazil and discuss such
issues as labour conditions, internal and international migration and
labour legislation. Special attention is paid to British-owned firms
(such as gold mines in Minas Gerais), but labour relations
generally are considered, in particular the activities of Brazilian
trade unions, and assessments are made of key figures in Brazil's

Ministry of Labour, the trade unions and employers' organisations. Although the views expressed are generally focused on Rio de Janeiro, attachés frequently travelled to other parts of Brazil, filing reports based on their tours.

● War Office (WO) and Air Ministry (AIR)

The War Office was originally the office of the secretary-at-war. These archives include the records created or inherited by the War Office, Armed Forces and related bodies, 1568–1990. There appears to be little Brazil-related material amongst the various WO and AIR classes. Material relating to Brazilian interest in Britain's military forces is, instead, mainly confined to Admiralty (ADM) files (see p. 158). Nevertheless, some files covering the Brazilian Expeditionary Force's participation in World War II are to be found.

WO 32 – War Office and successors: Registered Files (General Series)
English
Brazil-related files are limited to the awarding of Allied military decorations to members of the Brazilian Expeditionary Force serving in Europe during World War II.

WO 204 – War Office: Allied Forces, Mediterranean Theatre: Military Headquarters Papers, Second World War, 1941 to 1947
English
There are some 23 Brazil-related files scattered within this class of documents emanating from the Allied Forces Headquarters Liaison Section. Most of the files (some slim, some substantial) concern operational details of the activities of the Brazilian Expeditionary Force in Italy in 1943–45. *WO 204 / 2332* includes a detailed history of the Brazilian Liaison Detachment, closely related to the history of the Brazilian Expeditionary Force itself.

AIR 50 – Air Ministry: Combat Reports, Second World War
AIR 51 – Mediterranean Allied Air Forces: Microfilmed Files 1941 to 1945
English
These include several files discussing at length operational details of the Brazilian Fighter Squadron serving in Italy, 1944–45.

● **Security Services (KV)**

The Security Service's files relating to the World War II years are only gradually being opened. KV2 (Personal Files) appear to offer the greatest Brazil-related scope and should be searched with PROCAT. One such open file is:

> ● *KV2 / 285* – Albrecht Gustav Engels, alias Alfredo Reis and Walter Goldermann, Abwehr representative in Brazil – This file covers the period 31 Dec 1941 to 14 May 1946 and contains detailed reports (in English) on Engels' and other German agents' activities in Brazil.

● **Government Communications Headquarters (HW)**

This archive contains records of the Government Communications Headquarters (GCHQ), the intelligence-gathering arm of the Home Office. The GCHQ was established as the Government Code and Cypher School (GCCS) in 1919. Later, signal intelligence was to expand greatly with the outbreak of World War II in 1939. It is in this area that Brazil-related HW records are found.

HW 1 – Government Code and Cypher School:
Signals Intelligence Passed to the Prime Minister,
Messages and Correspondence, 1940 to 1945
English
Approximately one hundred Brazil-related files are found within this class of documents, which contains summaries of selected signals intelligence intercepts, translated where appropriate into English.

The files are all readily identifiable using PROCAT. The intercepts cover the years both before and after Brazil joined the war effort against Germany, Italy and Japan. Each file generally includes a cover note along with actual documents (usually telegraphic messages or reports) and annotated minutes that were issued by the Government Code and Cypher School and sent by the head of MI6 to Churchill (or in his absence the Lord Privy Seal or deputy prime minister). Many of the messages were intercepted in neutral territories (e.g. concerning the views or activities of

Brazilians in Switzerland) or created by neutral powers in Brazil (e.g. reports sent from the Spanish ambassador in Rio de Janeiro to Madrid). Some intercepts concern specific war plans (e.g. in particular relating to Brazil's perception of Vichy control over West African and other French colonial territories).

- ## Captured Records of the German, Italian and Japanese Governments (GFM)

This archive contains copies of documents seized by British and American forces with most having a bearing on World War II. The original German documents were returned to the Federal Republic between 1950 and 1958, and Italian records were returned to Italy in 1947. The only Brazil-related material appears to be found within the German Foreign Ministry (GFM) material. As the original documents contained within the GFM files can be found in other archives, only very general information concerning their scope will be covered here.

GFM 33 – German Foreign Ministry Archives: Photostat copies, 1867 to 1945
German
There appear to be 79 files relating directly to Brazil, mainly covering the years 1936–56, although a few contain material relating to the 1920s. Most files concern German–Brazilian commercial and political relations but other subjects are also covered. Approximately ten files deal with Brazil's position regarding Germany's conflicts with the League of Nations; two files examine Brazilian–US relations and one covers Germany's cultural relations with the German–Brazilian community. File titles and years can be identified with PROCAT, searching under 'Brazil'. Two days' advanced notice is required to produce a file.

- ## United Kingdom Atomic Energy Authority and its Predecessors (AB)

Only two files deal with UK–Brazilian exchanges relating to atomic energy. Material mainly concerns visits and exchanges of personnel. The files are:

- *AB 38 / 767* – Brazil: nuclear development, correspondence, 1969–82.

- *AB 57 / 117* – Brazil: political relations concerning atomic energy, 1968–71.

- **Ministry of Agriculture and Food / Ministry of Agriculture and Fisheries (MAF)**

There are some 24 specifically Brazil-related files in the MAF archive, with those that are of particular importance concerning the procurement of food supplies by Britain during and immediately after World War II and also the monitoring of Brazilian sales to other countries, especially the Soviet Union. Examples of files are:

- *MAF 74 / 349* – Trade with Brazil, 1939–40.

- *MAF 74 / 112–113* – Purchases of meat from various countries: Brazil, 1939–40.

- *MAF 83 / 2121–2122* – Brazil: supplies of coffee, 1945–46.

- *MAF 88 / 88–93* – Bulk purchase of canned meat from Brazil, 1940–1952.

- *MAF 86 / 158 and 161* – Oranges from Brazil, 1940–45.

- **British Council (BW and various)**

On the instruction of the Foreign Office, a British Committee for Relations with Other Countries was established in 1934. Soon after, 'Committee' was replaced by 'Council' and in 1936 the organisation became known as simply the 'British Council'. Records of activities of the British Council, and related bodies, in Brazil are extremely limited in extent and scope due to internal weeding and the terms of transfer to the PRO. Most records are found in the British Council's dedicated *BW* class, but *FO 370*, *FO 924* and *FCO 13* (pp. 162, 171 and 172) should also be investigated.

*BW 16 – **British Council: Registered Files, Brazil 1935 to 1967***
English
This category includes some ten files of correspondence from Brazil. Discussions relating to the British contributions to the São Paulo Bienal (1950–67) represent most of the files. In addition there are individual files concerning St Paul's School (the British school in São Paulo) covering the years 1937–46 and on the activities of the Sociedade Paulista de Cultura Anglo Brasileira for the years 1935–45.

*BW 2 – **British Council: Registered Files, GB Series, 1942 to 1986***
English
These six files on administrative concerns relate to the selection and shipping of British exhibits for the São Paulo Bienal in the 1950s and early 1960s.

*FO 924 – **Foreign Office: Cultural Relations Department: Correspondence and Papers, 1944 to 1966***
English
This series contains correspondence and papers of the Cultural Relations Department, relating mainly to the activities of the British Council and British relations with the United Nations Educational, Scientific, and Cultural Organization (UNESCO). There are several annual country files documenting British Council activities in Brazil, but otherwise files are of minor importance, containing a single piece of correspondence on a particular issue. Examples of files are:

- *FO 924 / 178* – British Council activities in Brazil, 1945.

- *FO 924 / 1606* – Brazil: UK participation in the International Festival of Popular Song, Rio de Janeiro, 1966.

- *FO 924 / 967* – Brazil: Notes on Brazilian educational systems; offer to create Brazilian studies chair at London University.

Reference is by class handlist and PROCAT.

*FCO 13 – **Foreign and Commonwealth Office: Cultural Relations Departments: Registered Files, 1967 to 1971***
English

- *FCO 13 / 36* – Educational television in Brazil, 1967.

- *FCO 13 / 55* – Brazil: conversion of British Residence at Petrópolis into teacher training college, 1967.

- *FCO 13 / 157* – Music festivals in Brazil: British participation, 1967–68.

◆

NATIONAL MARITIME MUSEUM
Caird Library
Greenwich
London SE10 9NF

www.nmm.ac.uk

Tel: (020) 8312 6691 (Manuscripts) • (020) 8312 6528 (General Library)
E-mail: manuscripts@nmm.ac.uk

Open: Mon–Fri 10am–4.45pm.
Closed: Public holidays and third week of February.
Admission: By appointment only; proof of identity required. Note that one collection described below requires two weeks' notice for ordering documents.

Introduction:

The National Maritime Museum's archive is a non-official depository of maritime-related records. Official Admiralty records are found at the National Archives (p. 158), with other significant depositories of marine records being the Merseyside Maritime Museum (see p. 85), the Royal Naval Museum (p. 223) and, for the East India Company, the India Office Library (p. 121). The museum has a separate Picture Library (picturelibrary@nmm.ac.uk; tel. 8312 6631) which has access to one of the world's largest collections of maritime art. Amongst the many thousands of photographs, lithographs, watercolours and oil paintings are several hundred images relating to Brazil.

Collections:

The National Maritime Museum (NMM) has a scattered yet still substantial manuscript collection relating to Brazil with holdings dating from the early 16th century into the 20th century. The collection includes isolated holdings linked to early voyages of exploration, with the suppression of the slave trade, international migration, business history and general travelogues being particular strengths.

The collection is accessible via the NMM's online catalogue for both printed and manuscript holdings. Many logs and journals that are held by the archive will have some bearing on Brazil but only samples that are considered to be especially significant are described here. In addition, there is a separate online catalogue listing to part of the NMM's holdings of pictures, including a few watercolours and many prints of Brazil-related subjects.

DEY – D'Eyncourt Papers
English
Sir Eustace Tennyson D'Eyncourt (1868–1951) was an engineer who became director of naval construction in England. Brazil-related material includes papers relating to his work for Armstrong Whitworth (Elswick) between 1902 and 1912, especially the design of warships for the Brazilian Navy [*DEY/9*] and visits to Brazil in 1910 and 1911 to secure and revise the contract for the battleships the *Rio de Janeiro* and the *Minas Gerais* [*DRY/10*]. There are also pocket-book plans of the *Minas Gerais* [*DRY/90* and *99*] and a report of a 1928 visit to Brazil [*DRY/63*].

HAM – Hammond Papers
English
The long career of the naval officer Sir Graham Eden Hammond took him to Brazil on many occasions. In 1823 he escorted the diplomat Sir Charles Stuart to Rio de Janeiro on his mission to mediate the terms of Brazilian independence. While in Brazil Hammond was promoted to rear-admiral and ordered home. On the way back to England he delivered to the king of Portugal the Treaty of Separation between Brazil and Portugal. Between 1834 and 1838 Hammond served as commander-in-chief of the Navy's South America Station. Although the collection includes considerable correspondence covering the years 1834–46 [*HAM/19*], Brazil-related content is slight.

ELL – Minto Papers
English

These are the papers of Gilbert Elliot, 2nd Earl Minto (1782–1849), whose diplomatic and political career culminated with the position of First Lord of the Admiralty. Brazil-related documents in the collection appear to be limited to the following items:

- *ELL / 263* – Recruiting for the Brazilian Navy in Orkney and Shetland, 1836 – This slim file consists of two notices and three letters detailing terms of recruitment in the Orkney Islands and, especially, the Shetland Islands, of men for the Brazilian Navy – officially travelling to Brazil to establish a sperm whale industry on the Island of Santa Catarina. (See also under Shetland Archives, p. 81.)

- *ELL / 264* – Slavery Reports, 1839 – This file contains copies of letters from Lord Minto to Palmerston (foreign secretary) and copies of letters from various officers describing the action of HMS *Columbine* in the sinking of two Brazilian slave vessels sailing under Portuguese colours in the Congo.

RMS – Royal Mail Steam Packet Company (1839–1932) and Royal Mail Line Ltd (1932–69)
English

In 1850 the Royal Mail Steam Packet Company (RMSPC) inaugurated a monthly service between England and Rio de Janeiro from where passengers and cargo were transhipped to a branch line steamer to Montevideo and Buenos Aires. In 1878 the RMSPC added Vigo (Galicia, northwest Spain) to its South American route, gaining Spanish and Portuguese emigrants and other passengers and cargo. As the principal shipping line serving the east coast of South America, the Rio de Janeiro service was extremely important to the company's development.

The archive includes a continuous set of minute books of director's meetings (1839–1934, 3 vols) and of general meetings (1842–1933) and a less complete set of director's reports (1850–1902). Mail contracts, general correspondence concerning the carriage of mail and passengers, publicity material and newspaper clippings are included in the collection, much of which relates directly or indirectly to Brazil.

Note: This material is stored in an outhouse and at least two weeks' notice is required for ordering documents. The collection is well indexed by subject – consult the website for call numbers.

TAI – Tait Papers
English

The papers of Admiral Sir William Eric Campbell Tait (1886–1946) include a file featuring notes by him regarding the Brazilian Navy generally, individual Brazilian naval officers and those of the United States Naval Mission in Brazil, whom he met during port visits to Bahia and Rio de Janeiro in 1930 [*TAI/6*]. Tait was unimpressed by the Brazilians due to their 'indolence and dislike of a lengthy cruise' but found that the US officers did their utmost to work effectively with them.

HIS/38 – Vernon Narrative

'Narrative of a voyage by Captain George Vernon (born c. 1787), Commander of the Alert *of Liverpool, Privateer, to Pernambuco and the Brazils and the Mediterranean, 26 December 1806 to June 1810.'*
English

Although not contemporaneously transcribed, the narrative takes the form of a series of letters sent 'at every opportunity' by Captain Vernon to his father in England. The loading of the merchant vessel in Liverpool is described in detail, and there are some fine descriptions concerning business and social life of British and Irish merchants in the city and province of Pernambuco ('In most houses the walls are hung with English landscapes and everything is contrived to keep in mind that happy country') and observations on Pernambuco society (the slaves are said to be 'very humanely treated').

● Ships' Logs and Journals

The NMM has several hundred logs and journals, usually those kept by ships' captains and lieutenants. Some of these items have been indexed but most have not, making it difficult to identify logs or journals featuring entries relating to Brazilian ports. Furthermore, logs and journals usually contain little apart from navigational information.

JOD/4 – Edward Barlow's Journal
English

Edward Barlow (born in 1642 in 'some village near Manchester')

kept a journal of his Atlantic and East Indies voyages between
1659 and 1703. Barlow's journal is extremely detailed and most
pages are illustrated with watercolours depicting sea creatures,
ships, landscapes or urban scenes. In 1663 Barlow's ship called
in at Rio de Janeiro; his journal is the earliest manuscript
in the NMM's collection to include a description of the town.
Accompanying the written account is a two-page watercolour of
'the manner of the town and harbour of Regeneire [*sic*] in Brazil
in America'. There is also a brief note on Fernando de Noronha,
with an illustration of the island depicting three Dutch ships
sailing offshore. The journal was published as *Barlow's Journal:
of his life in King's ships, East and West Indiamen and other
merchantmen from 1659 to 1703* (London, 1934).

DRY/11 – HMS Dryad, HMS Narcissus, HMS Spiteful and HMS Brecon
English
These are the logs (1864–70) of four ships serving in Brazilian,
Argentine and Paraguayan waters as part of the Royal Navy's
South America Station. Of particular note are the watercolour
inserts depicting Brazilian (and also Uruguayan and Falkland
Island) coastal and urban scenes and a list of Brazilian warships
engaged in the Paraguayan War.

MCL – McClintock Papers
English
Amongst the papers documenting Admiral Sir Leopold
McClintock's long career in the Royal Navy are only a few Brazil-
related items. An envelope [*MCL/2*] contains miscellaneous maps,
pen-and-ink sketches of ports and other coastal features of the
1830s and 1840s. There are few such images of Brazil – limited to
poor-quality views of Alagoas (Maceió) and Bahia (Salvador).
The collection also include logs [*MCL/6*] for 1843–44 of the HMS
Gorgon, which served in the South America Station. Typical of
other such logs, virtually all information noted is navigational data.

MLN – Milne Papers
English
In these papers of Admiral of the Fleet Sir Alexander Milne
(1806–96), Brazil-related material is limited to two files.
MLN/101/2 contains a log of the HMS *Conway*, a watch bill and
signal books of the HMS *Cadmus* for the early 1820s, while

MLN/179/7 includes a manuscript track chart of the *Cadmus* on the Brazilian coast, 1827–29.

RCE/4 – Rice Papers
English
The journal of William McPerson Rice, shipwright, includes a good description of Rio de Janeiro in 1824–25.

SIS/4 – Sison Papers
English
Lieutenant James Sison kept this journal while serving on the HMS *Peterad*. Included are some fine descriptions of the city of Rio de Janeiro in 1872.

◆

NATURAL HISTORY MUSEUM
Cromwell Road
London SW7 5BD

www.nhm.ac.uk

Tel: (020) 7942 5207 • **Fax:** (020) 7942 5559
E-mail: genlib@nhm.ac.uk

Open: Mon–Fri 10am–4pm.
Closed: Public holidays.
Admission: Appointment and proof of identity required.

Introduction:

The Natural History Museum traces its origins to 1753, the year the British Museum was founded. Not until the following century, however, was a dedicated building for its rapidly growing collections erected; it opened in 1880 in South Kensington.

The museum has five libraries, each with separate premises though working closely together (except the Picture Library, which operates as a private company). Each has substantial Brazil-related collections of books, scientific reports and journal articles, with considerable pre-20th-century holdings. Apart from the Picture Library, the collections are divided among the General Library, the Zoology Library, the Tring Library (including ornithological material, pre-1940 travel and general natural history) and the Botany Library.

Collections:

Manuscript holdings of natural historians who travelled to Brazil to collect specimens or as part of expeditions of wider scientific interest are disappointing, rarely even venturing into the field of economic botany (see Royal Botanic Gardens, p. 186). Items deposited in the museum provide little beyond specialised scientific interest, lacking ethnographic or topographic insights into the usually remote parts of Brazil where the natural historians ventured. Manuscript holdings may be searched via the libraries' joint online catalogue. For a more detailed survey of the museum's manuscripts, see Gavin D.R. Bridson, et al., *Natural History Manuscript Resources in the British Isles* (London, 1980).

Elizabeth Agassiz
English
These are letters (1865–72) from Elizabeth (née Cary) Agassiz to Ida Higginson, written while accompanying her husband, the naturalist Louis Agassiz, in Brazil. A naturalist in her own right, Elizabeth Agassiz writes of the work she and her husband did but she also offers some sense of the hardships of travel and life in the Amazon.

Henry Walter Bates
English
In April 1845 Henry Walter Bates (1825–92) and Alfred Russel Wallace (see p. 179) departed for Pará in Brazil to collect insects and other natural history specimens. Bates – who became well known for his book *The Naturalist on the River Amazons* (London, 1863) – lived in a very frugal way, having to sell his specimens in Europe in order to survive. He collected many new species, and his contribution to the taxonomy of Lepidoptera was enormous. He also developed important ideas on the theory of mimicry.
The manuscript collection of Bates comprises two small notebooks containing important observations and notes made as he travelled on the Amazon between 1851 and 1859. The notebooks are illustrated with many watercolour drawings of Lepidoptera and Coleoptera. (See also British Library, p. 113.)

John Miers
English
This catalogue of the woods of Brazil, compiled by John Miers (1789–1879), is arranged alphabetically by the Brazilian names of the woods and lists native localities, their dimensions, colours and

special markings, hardness, specific gravity, the purposes to which they are applied and their botanical names.

Alfred Russel Wallace
English

Alfred Russel Wallace (1823–1913) was a biologist and traveller whose work is considered vital for the understanding of the development of Charles Darwin's theory of natural selection.
In 1848 Wallace set off to Brazil with his friend and collaborator Henry Walter Bates (see p. 178) to explore the Amazon and Negro rivers and to collect natural history specimens. To cover more territory, the two men split up, with Wallace sending his specimens to Pará (Belém) for storage. On his way back to England in 1852, disaster struck: Wallace's ship caught fire and had to be abandoned, losing his entire collection and most of his notes.

The Wallace collection – personal and scientific – is a large one but little survives relating to Brazil apart from a series of pencil drawings of fish of the Rio Negro, made in 1850–52. Wallace's personal library is held, including copies of his own books – which include *Narrative of Travels on the Amazon and Rio Negro* (London, 1852) as well as works on Malaya and other parts of east Asia – with annotations giving further insights into the development of his ideas. Although many manuscripts are held, these relate to Wallace's later travels and family life in England.

POLISH INSTITUTE AND SIKORSKI MUSEUM
Archive Department
20 Princes Gate
London SW7 1PT

www.sikorskimuseum.co.uk

Tel: (020) 7589 9249

Open: Tues–Fri 9.30am–4pm.
Closed: Public holidays and over Christmas and New Year.
Admission: No appointment necessary.

Introduction:

The Polish Institute was founded in 1945 and its archives are the largest outside Poland of primary sources concerning that country, with a particular emphasis on World War II and the activities of the Polish government-in-exile, 1945–90.

Collections:

Collections with Brazil-related material are the records of embassies, legations and consulates (1939–49) and demobilisation records of Polish soldiers and airmen moving to Brazil after World War II. There is a general index to all collections and a register of subject files to most collections.

KOL. 48 – Maj. Gen. Francizek Arciszewski
Polish (some Portuguese)
Francizek Arciszewski (1890–1969) was an officer in the Polish Army whose service included the position of Chief of the Military Mission at the Polish Embassy in Rio de Janeiro, 1944–46. Included in Arciszewski's personal, military and diplomatic papers are press cuttings, correspondence and other documentation relating to his activities in Brazil. Especially significant were Arciszewski's activities while in South America, recruiting expatriate Poles into the Polish armed forces for active service in Europe during World War II.

A. 11 – Polish Ministry of Foreign Affairs
(Ministerstwo spraw Zagranicznych)
Polish
These are fragmentary records of the Polish Ministry of Foreign Affairs covering the years 1918–44 and complete records for the year 1945. Included are reports and letters regarding all aspects of Polish foreign relations, with much material on Polish communities abroad, including Brazil. Records concerning the foreign relations of the Polish government-in-exile (1939–90) are also held; the main Brazilian content regards negotiations and arrangements for the transfer to third countries of Polish soldiers and airmen and their families who were in Britain at the end of World War II – Brazil, Argentina and the USA were the main countries of settlement. Reference is by means of a chronological subject inventory.

Note: The records of the Polish Legation in Rio de Janeiro (1920–38) are held by the Pilsudski Institute of America, New York [http://dione.ids.pl/~ijp/].

*A. 17 – Switpol – Swiatowy Zwiazek Polaków z Zagraniy
(World Association of Poles Abroad)*
Polish
Fragmentary records for Switpol are held for the years 1940–46,
a period when the association was being reconstituted in exile in
London. Also held are files (1940–55) concerning contacts
amongst Polish expatriates in South America, including Brazil.
Switpol records for 1923 and 1925–39 are held by the State
Archives (Archiwum Panstwowe) in Warsaw [www.archiwa.gov.pl].

◆

THE ROTHSCHILD ARCHIVE
New Court
St Swithin's Lane
London EC4P 4DU

www.rothschildarchive.org

Tel: (020) 7280 5874 • **Fax:** (020) 7980 5657
E-mail: info@rothschildarchive.org

Open: Mon–Fri 10am–4.15pm.
Closed: Public holidays.
Admission: By appointment only. Two letters of recommendation
             must be received in advance of a visit.

Introduction:

The Rothschild Archive was established in 1978 to preserve and arrange
the record of one of the historically most influential banking families in
the world. The London-based merchant bank N.M. Rothschild dates
back to the beginning of the 19th century, with close historical connections with many parts of the world.

The bank began its relationship with Brazil in 1824 with a five
percent loan issued to the government of newly independent Brazil. For
most of the subsequent decades of the 19th century, Rothschild was the
major banker to the Brazilian government. In 1855, Rothschild was
appointed as Brazil's financial agent in England and had a monopoly of
flotation of Brazilian central government loans until 1907. In addition
to government loans, the bank issued most public utility (notably
railway) loans, from the São Paulo Railway loan of 1859 to the issue of
the Brazilian Railways four percent rescission bonds in 1901 to finance
the purchase of the Bahia and San Francisco Railway Company, the

Conde Deu Railway Company and the Recife and San Francisco (Pernambuco) Railway Company.

During the 20th century Rothschild maintained strong business links with Brazil, helping to finance the country's coffee valorisation initiative and major bond issues.

Collections:

There is an electronic catalogue (searchable via the web) with the contents of the archive listed series by series. There is also an excellent printed version of the catalogue, *The Rothschild Archive: A Guide to the Collection* (London, 2000), although the web version is more detailed. Brazil-related material can generally be identified with both the electronic and printed catalogues, while most collections of individual letters or other documents can be identified using the indexes to volumes of correspondence or other finding aids of names or places. Also valuable is Caroline Shaw's article, 'Rothschilds and Brazil: An introduction to sources in The Rothschild Archive', *Latin American Research Review*, 40/1 2005.

Manuscript holdings directly and indirectly relating to Brazil are well represented in the archive but 19th-century material largely takes the form of ledgers of various kind, offering few insights into the often murky world of government financing. Although throughout the century Rothschild's primary and best-known area of business was issuing of bonds as a means of raising loans for governments, researchers have been frustrated by the very limited correspondence between the bank, its Brazilian agents and the government of Brazil that might have a bearing on certain extremely sensitive and costly episodes – not least the Paraguayan War of 1864–70, during which time Rothschild raised several major loans. Of much greater practical use are the bank's records for early 20th-century business dealings involving Brazil.

Accounts Current Department: Government Accounts
English
Rothschild handled a large number of accounts on behalf of the Brazilian government. Records of these take the form of ledgers containing details of monthly interest rates, balances and payments on orders. Examples of such account records are:

- *I/26/1–5 – Brazilian Agency Balances, 1895–1916 –* Monthly balances of the Brazilian government current account with Rothschild.

- *I/25/1–2 – Brazilian Agency Cargo (Brazilwood), 1855–58* – A record of shipments and sales of brazilwood, two volumes.

- *I/62/1–7 – Bahia & Timbo Railway Co., Bahia and San Francisco Railway Co. and São Paulo Railway Co. accounts, 1858–1918 –* Ledgers containing general, capital and advance accounts, seven volumes.

Correspondence: Banks and Governments
English and Portuguese
These boxes contain routine records with respect to the authorisation of payments on behalf of clients (banks and governments). These include the Banco da Republica dos Estados Unidos do Brasil, 1892–1906 [*XI/43/0–3*] – renamed the Banco do Brasil, 1907–16 [*XI/44/0–5*], the Banco Internacional do Brazil, 1886–88 [*XI/38/25*] and others.

There are 32 boxes of documentation of the Brazilian government's account, 1825–1919 [*XI/65/0–13*] with Rothschild. This material is divided into two sections. The first (1825–34) consists of letters from members of the Brazilian Legation in London instructing that bonds should be sent to them for signature, and drawing on the Brazilian government's account with Rothschild. The second (1840–1919) consists of letters from the Finance Ministry in Rio de Janeiro and concerns the management of the government's London account. There are also thirteen boxes [*XI/66/0–5*] of correspondence regarding the separate account of the Brazilian Legation in London, 1855–1918, consisting of routine requests for payments.

Sundry Correspondence (incoming)
English (some French and other languages)
This series consists of more than a thousand boxes of in-letters covering 1802–34 [*XI/112*] and 1835–1918 [*XI/113–129*]. Letters to Rothschild from private individuals are found here and are usually

brief instructions relating to an account, but small pieces of business – such as support to a particular firm by way of a loan – are also recorded here. A separate name and place index has been combined (not available online), allowing the identification of correspondence originating in Brazil.

Outgoing Correspondence
English
There are several Brazil-related categories of outgoing correspondence, though legibility can be extremely difficult and the content, even when the subjects are loans to the Brazilian government or shipping of goods, is generally routine. The most extensive series of outgoing correspondence is the Brazilian Agency Letter Copy Books, 1855–1918 [*XI/142/0–13*], mainly addressed to the Brazilian minister or ambassador in London or to the minister of finance in Rio de Janeiro.

Special Subject Correspondence
English
Brazil-related files in this series mainly concern individual businesses being financed by Rothschild or political and economic intelligence on a particular part of the country or sector of the economy. Although only *Series XI* [*XI/111/103–435*] includes Brazil-related files (some sixty in total, covering the years c. 1918–30), many of them include reports, letters and other documentation of general, rather than very narrowly financial, interest. Examples of files are:

- *XI/111/103* – Correspondence concerning political instability, 'a misleading nature of the prospectus of the Rio de Janeiro Harbour & Dock Co. Ltd to the granting of a 7.5% coffee security loan to the Brazilian Government'. Also correspondence concerning harbour improvements in Brazil and requests for funding, 1914–23'.

- *XI/111/168* – Reports on wheat production in Rio Grande do Sul, the financial situation in Brazil, currency exchanges and British-owned railways, 1921–22.

- *XI/111/204* – Correspondence from Sir Henry Lynch (Rio de Janeiro) regarding the state of the Brazilian coffee, sugar and cotton crops, the political situation in Rio de Janeiro and Rio Grande do Sul and Brazilian centenary celebrations, 1921–23.

- *XI/111/285* – Correspondence regarding railway finances and proposals for the protection of Jewish agricultural colonies in Rio Grande do Sul 'due to violent civil disturbances', 1926.

- *XI/111/307* – Reports, balance sheets and agreements concerning the Brazil Victoria Minas Railway and Itabira Iron Ore Co., 1918–26.

- *XI/111/401* – Correspondence concerning the D'Abernon Mission to Argentina, Brazil and Uruguay, 1929.

Major Correspondents

English and French

Rothschild operated with the assistance of an extensive network of official, semi-official or informal correspondent banks or agents throughout the world. Collections of material relating to collaborators in Brazil is very limited, with no separate holdings relating to Sir Henry Lynch – member of a long-established Anglo-Brazilian family, the partner of an import/export firm and often close to Rothschild and to ministers of the Brazilian government during the late 19th and early 20th centuries. Collections concerning the activities of correspondents in Brazil are limited to the following:

- *XI/38/167, 3 boxes – Leuzinger & Co., 1830–40* – Based in Rio de Janeiro, Leuzinger provided many services for Rothschild including accepting bills and purchasing commodities to be sent for sale in Europe. Rothschild was also provided with detailed information on local commodity, money and bullion markets, the political situation, and coffee, sugar and other crop production, all of which is reflected in the collection.

- *XI/38/215, 2 boxes – Samuel, Phillips & Co., 1815–16, 1819–33, 1841–43* – Based in Rio de Janeiro, the company operated in much the same way in relation to Rothschild as did Leuzinger & Co. and also Finnie Bros & Co. The collection contains very detailed assessments of the Brazilian economy and observations regarding political developments, most significantly concerning moves towards independence from Portugal.

◆

ROYAL BOTANIC GARDENS, KEW
The Library and Archives
Richmond
Surrey TW9 3AE

**www.rbgkew.org.uk/
collections/archives**

Tel: (020) 8332 5417 • **Fax:** (020) 8332 5430
E-mail: archives@rbgkew.org.uk

Open: Tues–Thurs 10am–1pm and 2–5pm.
Closed: Public holidays.
Admission: By appointment only. Contact as early in advance as possible and confirm appointment in writing.

Introduction:

The Royal Botanic Gardens is located in Kew, a southwest London suburb. Although Kew Gardens, as it is commonly referred to, dates back to the early 18th century, it was not until the end of that century that it gradually developed a formal scientific purpose. A rich variety of Brazilian plants, acquired since the early 19th century, are to be found growing within the grounds and glasshouses of Kew Gardens, and seeds, bulbs and pressings are stored in the Herbarium.

The archives' manuscript holdings are wide-ranging and include material on the exploration, discovery and investigation of the world's plants and fungi, particularly in the 19th and 20th centuries. Botanic drawings and paintings are held at Kew, including important Brazilian Amazon-related works by Marianne North (1830–90) and Margaret Mee (1909–88).

Collections:

The archive holds many field notebooks, including some which were kept by 19th-century plant collectors who travelled through the Amazon and other parts of Brazil in collaboration with the Royal Botanic Gardens. Although of continuing importance to professional botanists endeavouring to identify plants, these volumes feature little or no text that is likely to be of interest to non-specialists. The notebooks tend to be catalogue listings of plants collected, with identification by a combination of number code, place where collected, colour or other descriptives. Especially important are the plant catalogues of botanists William Burchell, Charles Carlisle, George Gardner and Richard Spruce.

Sir William Hooker Correspondence and Directors' Letter Books
English (some German, French and Portuguese)
Very little official Kew correspondence dating before about 1840 survives in the archive. During the 19th century, Kew Gardens' first official directors, Sir William Hooker (1785–1865), followed by his son Sir Joseph Hooker (1817–1911), did most of the administrative work themselves, and their correspondence forms the basis of the archives today.

Correspondence is contained in bound letter books of Sir William Hooker and includes letters received while serving as professor of botany at the University of Glasgow and also later as director at Kew (1841–65). Letters to Sir Joseph Hooker, who succeeded his father as director (1865–85) and, following his retirement, to his son-in-law, William Thiselton-Dyer (1843–1928), continue this series.

Mainly containing in-letters and enclosures, the Directors' Letter Books are arranged by region and date, although some Brazil-related material is found in other volumes. There is a card index to the correspondence, and the location of letters in individual volumes may be identified by their originator (e.g. Wickham, Henry).

Most significant 19th-century botanists would have engaged in correspondence with Sir William (or his successors) at some point. Many of these letters include accounts of the travels of plant collectors or relate to economic botany. There is also considerable correspondence giving insights into Kew's links with Brazilian institutions during the 19th and early 20th centuries, such as the Jardim Botânico in Rio de Janeiro and the Museu Goeldi in Belém.

The earliest surviving letter sent from Brazil to Sir William appears to be an account by William Burchell (1781–1863) in Goiás dated 25 April 1828 [*Vol. 66*]; Burchell was a botanist who

travelled widely in the country between 1825 and 1829. Other
Brazil-related letters to Hooker include ones from George Gardner
(1812–49) writing between 1836 and 1841 from the Serra dos
Órgãos in Rio de Janeiro and from Minas Gerais, and from Richard
Spruce (1817–93), who travelled widely collecting plants in South
America (especially Brazil) between 1849 and 1864. Later
correspondence within the Directors' Letter Books includes
detailed botanical and general topographical accounts by Robert
Cunningham writing from Patagonia and Rio de Janeiro (1867) and
by Charles Carlisle, who collected rubber plants in the Amazon
(1897). Letters from significant non-British botanists are also
found, including 1860s correspondence (in English) from the
Germans Fritz Müller and Victor Gärtner, who lived and worked in
Blumenau and Itajaí in the province of Santa Catarina.

● Sir Henry Alexander Wickham

Letters from Henry Alexander Wickham (1846–1928) – best
known for smuggling rubber seeds (*Hevea brasiliensis*) from Brazil
to Kew and his subsequent involvement in the foundation of rubber
plantations in Ceylon and Malaya – are found within the Directors'
Correspondence and can be identified by the index. The first such
letter appears to be one dated 22 March 1872 [*Vol. 215*] in which
Wickham, writing from Fazenda Piquiatuba (his sugar plantation
near Santarém), introduces himself and offers his services to collect
and send rubber seeds to Kew. Other Wickham letters amongst the
Directors' Correspondence concern the selection and shipment of
seeds and plants and their introduction to Asia. In addition,
Wickham and rubber-related correspondence is found within the
two volumes described below. (See also under Wolverhampton
Archives, p. 239.)

India Office – Caoutchouc: Misc. Reports (1873–1901)
English
This is correspondence between Henry Wickham and the Royal
Botanic Gardens respecting the shipment of rubber seeds from
Brazil to Kew and the introduction of rubber to Ceylon. The
correspondence includes letters dated 1873 from Wickham stating
his financial terms, and letters and other documents commenting
on the results of the experimental cultivation of rubber in Asia.

Brazil – Balata Gum & Rubber: Correspondence (1877–1900)
English

This contains letters, printed reports, and newspaper and other articles discussing the collection, cultivation and use of rubber, especially in Brazil.

● Other Economic Botany

Economic botany has always been an important concern of the Royal Botanic Gardens. In addition to rubber (see above), other Brazilian plants attracted the interest of Kew. Contacts between botanic gardens throughout the world have traditionally been close; the relationship between Kew and the Jardim Botânico in Rio de Janeiro is no exception and has resulted in copious correspondence.

3/Braz/M – Brazil – Miscellaneous (1928–44)
3/Braz/Ma – Brazil – Miscellaneous (1945–54)
English

These files consist predominantly of letters from individuals or institutions in Brazil either seeking, or making available, plants or seeds.

3/Braz/2 – Brazil – Coroa coffee (1932–33)
English

These letters concern the identification in Espírito Santo of what was believed to have been a new genus of coffee tree. The correspondents conclude that the tree was in fact merely an abnormal form of Arabian coffee.

Brazil Misc. Reports – Cultural products (1852–1908)
English

This volume contains articles, letters and reports on exchanges between British colonies and Brazil of plants with economic value or potential such as guaraná and bamboo. Letters also discuss diseases affecting coffee and sugar cane. Most items are dated after c. 1880.

Brazil Misc. Reports – Jequié Maniçoba and general (1879–1912)
English

This volume contains articles, letters and reports relating to various Brazilian plants and their potential commercial and industrial uses. Most of the volume is devoted to Jequié Maniçoba (a rubber tree

indigenous to the state of Bahia) and the possible supply of plants to Jamaica or India. Also discussed at length are *Canhamo Braziliensis Perini* (Brazilian linen) as well as other plants.

Brazil – Miscellaneous Correspondence, etc. (1909–28)
English
This volume contains articles, letters and reports on the economic potential of Brazilian plants including rubber, araroba, jabuticaba, passion fruit and orchids.

● **Jardim Botânico, Rio de Janeiro**

In addition to the Directors' Correspondence (see p. 187), there are two files that document Kew's 20th-century links with the Jardim Botânico in Rio de Janeiro.

*3/Braz/1 – **Brazil – Jardim Botânico, Rio de Janeiro (1928–39)***
*3/Braz/1A – **Brazil – Jardim Botânico, Rio de Janeiro (1940–54)***
English
These files contain correspondence relating to the exchange of bulbs and plants for the gardens and herbariums and also requests for help with the identification of plants.

ROYAL GEOGRAPHIC SOCIETY ARCHIVES
1 Kensington Gore   **www.rgs.org**
London SW7 2AR

Tel: (020) 7591 3000 • **Fax:** (020) 7591 3001
E-mail: archives@rgs.org

Open: Mon and Tues 10am–5pm.
Closed: Public holidays and Christmas to New Year.
Admission: No appointment required but photo identification and proof of address needed.

Introduction:

The Royal Geographic Society (RGS) was founded in 1830 for the advancement of geographical science. Since that time the RGS has supported research, education and training. One important aspect of its work has been organising or sponsoring research expeditions.

The RGS's archives consist of material arising out of the conduct of its business and manuscripts relating to persons or subjects of special interest. There are few papers that date from prior to the RGS's foundation. Although individual collections are rarely comprehensive, they usefully complement those in other establishments. The archival holdings are especially useful to biographers of 19th- and early 20th-century travellers, social historians and historical geographers.

The RGS also has a picture library (tel: 7591 3060; e-mail: pictures@rgs.org). There are several hundred Brazil-related images, with a particular strength being photographs (c. 1900–30) relating to the Amazon, Mato Grosso and railways.

Collections:

Brazil-related material is scattered widely throughout the RGS's archival collections. A major project is underway to make available on the web the catalogue of all RGS archival and library holdings. Until the completion of this project, a steadily increasing proportion of the RGS holdings may be searched using *A2A: Access to Archives* (see p. 250).

The RGS's Brazilian holdings pale in importance compared to those concerning other countries or regions, such as Africa. Nevertheless, the collection is especially valuable for insights into the British contribution to the scientific exploration of Brazil, especially during the 19th and early 20th centuries. The RGS's archival holdings are divided among seven broad groups of papers. The RGS's *Administrative Papers* and the *Institute of British Geographers Records* contain only passing references but other groups feature some items of significant interest.

Correspondence Files
English
These files contain letters from 1830 to the officers of the RGS requesting or offering advice or information. While the letters are generally brief and contain little in the way of substantive insights, Brazil-related items sometimes contain inserts or refer to manuscripts or projects in preparation that may prove worth pursuing. Typical of Brazil-related correspondence are the following:

- *CB2/342* – King of Bavaria is sending an atlas of Bavaria; he explains that he is preparing a publication on medicinal plants of Brazil and asks about the use of some Brazilian maps, 9 Nov 1840.

- *CB6/891* – Gibbs, Antony and Sons, sending information from the Peruvian Ambassador about plans of Colonel Church to develop a railway link between Brazil and Bolivia, 4 Oct 1871.

- *CB6/1598* – Juan B. Minchin (La Paz) seeking aid or advice on his proposal for exploring and mapping rivers between Bolivia and Brazil, 11 May 1876.

- *CB6/2430* – Thomas Bigg-Wither offering a paper on his explorations in Paraná, 30 June 1877.

Journal Manuscripts
English

These items are published, part-published and unpublished manuscripts submitted for publication in the RGS's *Journal* or *Proceedings* from 1830. The earliest Brazil-related submission appears to be an 1831 table outlining Pará's trade [*JMS/6/7*]. The Amazon region (especially concerning international frontiers) continued to be the focus of many of the submissions, such as Dr Jules Crévaux's 1880 article on the French Guiana–Brazil border dispute [*JMS/6/125*] and several short manuscripts by the naturalist Richard Spruce. Other submissions take more of a travelogue approach (e.g. an 1894 submission of random notes on a journey in northern Brazil [*JMS/6/148*]) or examine aspects of economic geography (e.g. an 1850 description of diamond mining at Santa Isabel de Paraguassa in the interior of the province of Bahia).

Library Manuscripts
English

Library manuscripts are miscellaneous small groups of papers, diaries, log books and letters which do not necessarily have any connection to the RGS but which are of potential interest to historians of geography. Brazil-related material may take the form of a single folio within a larger holding or it may be the focus of the entire collection. There are some important manuscripts that, while focusing on British Guiana, have a bearing on the frontier dispute with Brazil (most notably Robert H. Schomburgk's 'Reports from a journey into Guyana, 1836–40'; see also under University of Birmingham, p. 11 and British Library, p. 106). Cataloguing is incomplete but examples of Library Manuscripts of more specific Brazilian interest are:

- Navarro y Campos – Account of a journey from Bahia to Rio de Janeiro, 1808.

- *LMS/W/11* – Capt. W. Wellesley – Out-letter book of HMS *Sapphire* on voyage England–Brazil–Nova Scotia; included are an account of the India rubber tree and a description of the north coast of Brazil, 1830–33.

- Lieut. William Smyth – An account of the Amazon and Negro rivers, 1835.

- F.C.P. Vereker (Commander) – Journals and logs relating to service on Royal Navy survey ships, including many entries on Brazil, 1865–86.

- Dr Hamilton Rice – Notes on the Brazilian Amazon and the Venezuela–Guyana expedition, 1925.

- *LMS/W/15* – J.J. Whitehead – Diary kept during the abortive search for the explorer Colonel Percy Fawcett, who went missing in the Mato Grosso (see p. 194 under 'Special Collections'), 18 Feb–19 Sept 1928.

Special Collections
English

The Special Collections are the correspondence, diaries or other papers of named individuals who were associated with the RGS. Perhaps historically the most important collections concern 19th-century British explorers of Africa such as David Livingstone and H.M. Stanley. With the odd exception, Brazil-related material within collections is limited to the following:

- *Barclay Collection* – Included within this collection are several unrelated items concerning Brazil, including a 1912 report by F.D. Cardoso on railways in the state of Ceará, a 1919 report by Dr M. de Souza Bandeira on Brazilian ports and a 1919 report by R.C. Simonson on the meat and cattle industry in Brazil.

- *Burton Collection* – Minimal manuscript material survives of the explorer, translator and diplomat Sir Richard Burton (1821–90) as following his death most was destroyed by his wife. A log is held that was kept by Burton from March to October 1868, a short period of the time he served as British consul in Santos (1865–69).

- *Fawcett Collection* – Correspondence between the explorer Colonel Percy Harrison Fawcett (1867–1925), the RGS and his wife; eighteen folders of letters and other material concerning the search for Fawcett, who went missing in the Mato Grosso, 1921–51. There are also many other letters (1906–39) in the Correspondence Collection that relate to Fawcett.

Observations Files
English

These files contain reports of a technical nature detailing astronomical, meteorological and topographical notes of a particular area. Brazilian localities are well represented, with the 1908–10 file entitled 'Astronomical observations, Brazilian/Bolivian border' [*PHF/25*] being a typical example.

SCHOOL OF ORIENTAL AND AFRICAN STUDIES LIBRARY
www.soas.ac.uk/Archives/home

Archives and Special Collections
University of London
Thornhaugh Street
Russell Square
London WC1H 0XG

Tel: (020) 7898 4180 • **Fax:** (020) 7436 2388
E-mail: docenquiry@soas.ac.uk

Open: Mon–Thurs 9am–7pm, Fri 9am–5pm (summer vacation Mon–Fri 9am–5pm).

Closed: Public holidays and for a week in June.

Admission: United Kingdom university staff or student identification or letter of introduction required.

Introduction:

Collecting materials since 1917, the School of Oriental and African Studies (SOAS) Library holds over one million items relating to the study of Asia, Africa and the Middle East. Brazil-related books and periodicals are held where there is a direct relationship to SOAS interests, for example African slavery or Japanese international migration.

Collections:

SOAS Library has important holdings of papers of Christian mission and aid organisations, businesses, diplomats and colonial administrators, scholars and travellers. Two collections suggest Brazil-related content, but on examination only one has any relevant material.

PP MS 14 – *Sir Charles Stewart Addis Papers*
English

Charles Stewart Addis (1861–1945) was a banker whose early years were spent working in, or in relation to, China. In December 1923 he travelled to Brazil with a mission of British bankers led by the British former Cabinet minister Edwin Montagu for visits to the Treasury and banks and to report on trade and finance. The documents on his stay in Brazil (Jan–Feb 1924) consist of Addis' private diaries and letters to family members in which he records his meetings with Brazilian bankers and politicians, discusses his report on the Brazilian internal debt and describes sightseeing excursions and the hospitality that he and the other members of the mission received. Other letters and reports relating to the Montagu Mission are in the 1923–24 files at the Bank of England Archive (see p. 94).

PP MS 1/CORR1/104 (Box 26) – *Captain J.M. Lachlan Letters*
English

Amongst the papers of Sir William Mackinnon (co-founder of the British India Steam Navigation Company in 1862 and chairman of the Imperial British East Africa Company from 1883 to 1895) are twelve letters (46 folios) dated 1888–91 from Captain Lachlan (general manager of the U.S. & Brazil Mail Steamship Company). The only operational details of the steamship company that are referred to in the letters are some engineering details of ships being ordered and mentions of purchases of British coal.

◆

UNIVERSITY COLLEGE LONDON LIBRARY

Special Collections
140 Hampstead Road
London NW1 2BX

www.ucl.ac.uk/Library/
special-coll

Tel: (020) 7679 5197 • **Fax:** (020) 7679 5157
E-mail: spec.coll@ucl.ac.uk

Open: Mon–Thurs 9am–5pm, Fri 9am–4.45pm.
Closed: Public holidays and between Christmas and New Year.
Admission: By appointment only.

Introduction:

The Special Collections of the University College London Library is an important centre for the deposit of archives relating to Latin America, especially business history records. Although banking records are a particular strength, the records of other companies and of some individuals with interests in Latin America are also held.

Collections:

There are substantial holdings relating to Chile, Peru and Argentina, with smaller yet still significant collections of manuscripts relating to Brazil, Cuba, Mexico and Uruguay. Especially important are the archives of the Bank of London & South America (BOLSA), of which a substantial proportion of material is deposited here, including some of the records of the individual banks that were eventually to amalgamate to form BOLSA.

Two catalogue files of Latin American business record holdings are available for consultation in the library – one for the Latin American collection generally and one for the BOLSA archive. Although there is no subject index, individual volumes of bound correspondence or other manuscript material can usually be identified by year and place.

Bahia and San Francisco Railway Co. Ltd
English

The collection is limited to 1901 liquidation papers that offer minimal insights into the operation (technical or financial) of the railway company.

Brougham Manuscripts
English

This collection is based on the correspondence (1809–65) of Henry Peter Brougham, 1st Baron Brougham and Vaux (1778–1868), sometime member of Parliament and an active supporter of the anti-slavery movement. Brougham corresponded with many of the leading British politicians and anti-slavery campaigners of his time. Although the manuscripts (approximately 60,000 letters, some with enclosures such as business prospectuses) reflect Brougham's varied interests, most of the letters relating to Brazil concern slavery and commercial and general relations and were written between approximately 1830 and 1866. The collection is indexed under the name of the sender.

Edward Johnston & Co. Ltd
English

In 1827 Edward Johnston went out to Rio de Janeiro from England, and in 1842 he established a coffee-exporting business there. In 1881 his sons opened a coffee-exporting house in Santos under the name Edward Johnston & Sons. The collection consists of two volumes of copy books of private letters sent from Santos to London between 1892 and 1904. Letters refer to all aspects of the coffee business, although they concentrate on the affairs of Edward Johnston & Co. Business results are discussed in detail, as are the purchase in Brazil, and shipment abroad, of coffee. Especially interesting are reports from the interior of the state of São Paulo and discussions concerning the establishment by the company of its own buying centres.

Western Telegraph Co. Ltd
English

The Western Telegraph Co. Ltd emerged in 1884, having developed cable links with Brazil since 1873 under the name of the Brazilian Submarine Telegraph Co. In 1929 the Western Telegraph Co. amalgamated with the Eastern Telegraph Co. to form Cable & Wireless Ltd.

The collection consists of fourteen boxes of letter books covering the years 1883 to 1947. The correspondence is both from the Brazilian headquarters in Rio de Janeiro to offices throughout Brazil (from Maranhão to Rio Grande do Sul) and also from London to Brazil (mainly instructions to Rio de Janeiro, but also direct to agencies elsewhere in the country). Although there is no index to the correspondence, the material is divided by date and place of origin of the correspondence.

The subjects dealt with in the correspondence are for the most part domestic in nature – very little technical or even financial information is given. Typical are discussions of Western Telegraph properties (both offices and staff accommodation), the design of counters, and supplies – from stationery to spoons. Some staffing information (both Brazilian and expatriate) can be found scattered within the correspondence – details of salaries, requests for permission to marry, health and discipline (mainly alcohol related). Inspection reports on Western Telegraph buildings and instructions on their maintenance are detailed down to the level of responsibility for methods concerning the correct way to clean lavatory seats.

See also Cable & Wireless Archive (p. 221) for considerable additional Brazil-related material concerning Western Telegraph and related companies.

● *Bank of London & South America (BOLSA) Business Archive*

The Bank of London & South America was formed in 1923 as an amalgamation of the London & Brazilian Bank and the London & River Plate Bank, with the absorption of other British-owned banks operating in Latin America over the course of later years. The archive includes material from many of BOLSA's constituent banks. Brazilian holdings are well represented, with the greatest strength being the letter books, with correspondence concerning staffing issues, local and national business conditions and information on clients. Additional records concerning BOLSA and its constituents are held by the Lloyds TSB Group Archives (see p. 127).

London & Brazilian Bank (1862–1923)
English
Founded in London in 1862 to finance Brazilian coffee, sugar, hide

and cereal exporters, the bank opened a branch in Rio de Janeiro in 1863 followed by branches in Pernambuco (Recife) later that year and in Bahia (Salvador) and Rio Grande in 1864. In 1923 the bank amalgamated with the London & River Plate Bank to form the Bank of London & South America (BOLSA). The bank went on to become, for a time, the largest and most highly respected bank in Brazil. Surviving letter books include correspondence from the London head office to Rio de Janeiro (1868–1923) and also from the Brazilian branches to London (1876–1923).

Brazilian and Portuguese Bank Ltd (1863–66)
English
Founded in London in 1863, a year later the bank opened a branch in Rio de Janeiro and an agency in Oporto (which was closed in 1866). In 1867 a branch was opened in Pernambuco (Recife). Only a very few documents survive and those that do are virtually illegible.

English Bank of Rio de Janeiro (1866–91)
English
With the closure of its Oporto agency in 1866, the Brazilian and Portuguese Bank changed its name to English Bank of Rio de Janeiro. This archive largely consists of letters from London to Rio de Janeiro concerning business loans and the financial position of the bank and letters from Brazil (both head office in Rio de Janeiro and branches). The documents are difficult and in many cases almost impossible to read, with the earliest not available for view due to their fragile condition.

British Bank of South America (1891–1920)
English
This was the successor of the English Bank of Rio de Janeiro, and the archive contains correspondence from branches of the bank throughout Brazil, as well as letter books and packets (São Paulo to London, Rio de Janeiro and branches, 1886–88 and 1890–1927 and from London and branches to São Paulo, 1892–1913). The letters include often detailed assessments of the prospects of local economic conditions, of local business and of the bank's clients. Staffing matters are also discussed, including the problems of individuals such as tendencies towards 'intemperance'. Control of the bank was passed to Anglo-South American Bank in 1920.

London & River Plate Bank (1865–1923)
English
Amongst the many surviving Brazil-related letter books in this series are volumes of correspondence from Buenos Aires to Brazil (1869–1924), from Rio de Janeiro to Brazilian branches (1893–1930), from Rio de Janeiro to London (1891–1922), and from Bahia to London (1913–21); general letters to Rio de Janeiro (1891–1930) and from London to Brazilian branches (1919–22).

Bank of London & South America – BOLSA (1923–37)
English
Brazil-related records specific to BOLSA from its creation in 1923 are limited to letter books and letter files. These include volumes of correspondence from Rio de Janeiro to London and elsewhere (1922–33), from Brazilian branches to and from London (1923–33), from Bahia (Salvador) to Rio de Janeiro and London (1926–35), from Pará (Belém) to London, Rio de Janeiro and Brazilian branches (1919–37), from Porto Alegre to Rio de Janeiro (1923–30), from São Paulo to Rio de Janeiro, London and Brazilian branches (1919–30), and from Vitória to London (1931–33).

◆

THE WIENER LIBRARY
Institute of Contemporary History
4 Devonshire Street
London W1W 5BH

www.wienerlibrary.co.uk

Tel: (020) 7636 7247 • **Fax:** (020) 7436 6428
E-mail: library@wienerlibrary.co.uk

Open: Mon–Fri 10am–5.30pm.
Closed: Public holidays.
Admission: Although appointments are not necessary, first-time visitors must show photo identification and proof of address.

Introduction:

The Wiener Library is the world's oldest Holocaust memorial institution, tracing its history back to 1933. Alfred Wiener, a German Jew who worked in the Central Verein deutscher Staatsbürger jüdischen Glaubens, fled Germany in 1933 for Amsterdam. Together with David Cohen, he set up the Jewish Central Information Office, collecting and disseminating information about events in Nazi Germany. The collection was transferred to London in 1939 with Wiener making the resources available to British government intelligence departments. After the war the Library's academic reputation increased and the collecting policies were broadened to include material related to the Holocaust, its causes and legacies.

Collections:

The Wiener Library attempts to collect comprehensively in the following areas: historiography and documentation of the Holocaust; Jewish refugees and exiles in Great Britain; and resistance against the persecution of Jews by Nazis and collaborators. Over seven hundred document collections have been catalogued and there are several hundred additional collections waiting to be processed. The collections vary in size from a single letter to many boxes, and exist in original manuscript form, microfilm, bound volume and loose folder.

The material relating to Brazil that has been identified amongst the Library's holdings principally concerns the situation of Jewish refugees during the 1930s.

949 / 1–6 – Reports on South America as a haven for refugees from Nazi Germany, 1937
English
This collection of reports focuses on South America (specifically Argentina, Brazil and Uruguay) as a refuge for German Jewish emigrants. The reports, which were published in the United States, were produced by Bruno Weil, vice-president of the *Central Verein*, who toured South America on behalf of the organisation. The first three reports *[949 / 1–3]* cover Brazil and discuss climate, geography, population and politics and prospects for Jewish settlement.

1532 / 3 – The present status of Jewish settlement and Jewish migration to Brazil and the Argentine
English
This 70-page report (c. 1930s) on the situation of German Jewish immigrants in Brazil and Argentina was written by Cecilia Razovsky Davidson for the Central British Fund for the Relief of German Jewry. Shorter reports in this series cover the position of German Jews in Venezuela *[1532 / 1]* and in Colombia *[1532 / 2]*.

915 – Olga Benario
German (some in Portuguese)
Olga Benario (1911–42) was a German Jew and Communist Party militant. In 1928 she went to Moscow where she met the Brazilian revolutionary Carlos Prestes and in 1934 she accompanied him to Brazil. This collection of Belnario family genealogical papers, copies of official documents and a letter from Carlos Prestes explores the life of Olga until her expulsion from Brazil in 1936 and her eventual death in a concentration camp in Germany in 1942.

1411 – Reg Freeson: Correspondence and cuttings re. the death of Josef Mengele
English, German and Portuguese
Reg Freeson (1926–2006) was a journalist and member of parliament for the Labour Party who developed a keen interest in the fate of Josef Mengele (1911–79), the notorious SS doctor who was responsible for the deaths of thousands of prisoners at Auschwitz. This folder details Freeson's attempts to confirm whether a body exhumed in 1985 from a grave in Embu, São Paulo, was that of Mengele. The documents, which cover the years 1985–91, include copies of Brazilian police forensic reports and correspondence between Freeson and the Brazilian, German, Israeli and US authorities.

1366 – Kaye Family Documents
English
The papers in this collection document the lives of an Austrian Jewish family – Walter and Hansi Finkler and their daughter Eveleyn Kaye – who had managed to escape the Nazis and came to England in 1939. Included is correspondence (late 1930s) from Walter's brother Max in Brazil describing his arrival and life in Brazil and his attempts to secure immigration permits for Walter and Hansi for Brazil [*1366 / 7* and *1366 / 11*].

MANCHESTER

JOHN RYLANDS UNIVERSITY LIBRARY
OF MANCHESTER

rylibweb.man.ac.uk/spcoll

Special Collections
University of Manchester
150 Deansgate
Manchester M3 3EH

Tel: (0161) 834 5343 • **Fax:** (0161) 834 5574
E-mail: jrul.special-collections@manchester.ac.uk

Open: Mon–Fri 10am–5.30pm, Sat 10am–1pm.
Closed: Public holidays and Christmas to New Year.
Admission: Advance contact advisable.

Introduction:

The Special Collections of the John Rylands University Library of Manchester (JRULM) are housed in the former John Rylands Library in Manchester's city centre. The subject and period range of the manuscript collections is vast, including the records of Manchester University itself, papers of local families and businesses, and archives of social, religious and business organisations of national significance.

Collections:

With few exceptions, Brazil-related items within JRULM collections are difficult to identify, the general catalogue being of very limited assistance. Given the importance of Manchester's exports (not least to South America) in the 19th century, and with so many archives of local and regional textile manufacturers and traders being held by the library, it would be surprising not to find Brazil-related material. For example, evidence of exports to Brazil, especially between 1805 and 1829, can be found within the ledgers and amongst other papers of the cotton spinners McConnel & Kennedy.

Hodgson, Robinson and Co.
English
The South American links of the Manchester-based import/export house Hodgson, Robinson and Co. were mainly with Argentina,

where it had considerable ranching interests. The archive includes correspondence, personal notebooks, sales books and other financial records, the Brazil-related content being especially for the 1820s and 1830s. A detailed handlist is available.

Owen Owens and Son
English

The firm of Owen Owens and Son emerged in Manchester in the 1790s, initially manufacturing and selling hat linings and trimmings. From around 1810 the company diversified into the production of umbrellas, and from 1815 exports became increasingly important, with the company sending consignments of hats, textiles and umbrellas to agents in North and South America. During the 1830s and 1840s the firm's most profitable business was with Argentina, Uruguay and, increasingly, Brazil. Agents in Bahia (Salvador) and Pernambuco (Recife) were particularly important, with payments often made in goods such as sugar or coffee. Records of the company's Brazilian business dealings survive in general outgoing letter books from 1820 onwards and loose incoming letters from 1838, as well as in various financial and accounting ledgers for which there is a detailed handlist.

LABOUR HISTORY ARCHIVES AND STUDY CENTRE

www.nmlhweb.org/archive.htm

National Museum of Labour History
103 Princess Street
Manchester M1 6DD

Tel: (0161) 228 7212 • **Fax:** (0161) 237 5965
E-mail: archives@nmlhweb.org

Open: Mon–Fri 10am–5pm.
Closed: Public holidays.
Admission: By appointment only.

Introduction:

The Labour History Archives and Study Centre is Britain's only specialist repository for manuscripts and other documents relating to the political wing of the labour movement. The archival collections complement the objects, photographs and banners found in the National Museum of Labour History's collections.

Collections:

The archive holds an extensive and rapidly growing collection of political pamphlets, journals, press cuttings and manuscript records on working-class political organisations from the Chartists to the present day. Brazil-related material is extremely limited.

CP/CENT/INT/32/02 – **Communist Party of Great Britain: International Department**
English
This collection includes reports and correspondence relating to the Communist Party of Brazil and to repression of communists in Brazil between 1946 and 1980.

Judith Hart Papers
English
Judith Hart (1924–91) was a Labour member of Parliament, campaigner, and minister for overseas development. Her personal papers include several files [see especially *LP/HART/05/20* and *LP/HART/05/24*] containing material on Brazilian political developments between 1964 and 1985.

NORTHALLERTON

NORTH YORKSHIRE COUNTY RECORD OFFICE

www.northyorks.gov.uk/archives

County Hall
Northallerton
North Yorkshire DL7 8AF

Tel: (01609) 777585 • **Fax:** (01609) 777078
E-mail: archives@northyorks.gov.uk

Open: Mon, Tues, Thurs 9am–4.45pm, Wed 9am–8.45pm,
             Fri 9am–4.15pm.
Closed: Public holidays.
Admission: Appointment required.

Introduction:

The North Yorkshire County Record Office is an archive holding local government, church and business records, as well as the private papers of individuals and of families with a close connection to the county.

Collections:

The only collection that appears to contain Brazil-related manuscripts is the Beresford-Peirse family records.

*ZBA 21/8, MIC 586 – **Admiral Sir John Poo Beresford Papers***
English (some French and Portuguese)
The career of Sir John Poo Beresford (1766–1844) is documented by his private papers, covering the years 1781 to 1844. Brazil-related papers include an eighteen-page document written by Rear Admiral Beresford entitled 'Private Remarks Rio de Janeiro', an account (dated 28 December 1814 to 9 April 1815) of his unsuccessful mission to induce the Portuguese prince regent, Dom João, to return to Lisbon from Brazil, placing his ship, the HMS *Achilles*, at his disposal. Other documents are five drafts of letters from Beresford to Dom João, attempting to persuade him to return to Europe. One draft refers to the prince's desire to use Portuguese soldiers to strengthen Brazil's southern (Rio Grande) frontier.

NORWICH

NORFOLK RECORD OFFICE

Anglia Square
Upper Green Lane
Norwich NR3 1AX

archives.norfolk.gov.uk

Tel: (01603) 761349 • **Fax:** (01603) 761885
E-mail: norfree.nro@norfolk.gov.uk

Open: Mon–Fri 9am–5pm, Sat 9am–noon.
Closed: Public holidays and two weeks over late November
and early December.
Admission: Appointment advisable.

Introduction:

The Norfolk Record Office documents the history of the county and people of the county of Norfolk. Material relating to foreign countries is usually held only if the creator of a manuscript has a link with Norfolk.

Collections:

Only one collection appears to contain any material of Brazilian interest, and this is limited to a single document within the Walsingham (Merton) collection of family and estate papers, an otherwise large and varied series.

> *WLS/LXX/112/481 x 8 – **Southern Gold Trust Ltd***
> *· English*
> A typescript report produced in 1902 by Augusto Federico de Svacerdo discusses in some detail the gold-mining properties located in the district of Minas do Rio de Contas, state of Bahia, belonging to the Southern Gold Trust Ltd.

NOTTINGHAM

UNIVERSITY OF NOTTINGHAM

Hallward Library
Department of Manuscripts and
Special Collections
University Park
Nottingham NG7 2RD

www.nottingham.ac.uk/mss

Tel: (0115) 951 4565 • **Fax:** (0115) 951 4558
E-mail: mss–library@nottingham.ac.uk

Open: Mon–Fri 9am–5pm.
Closed: Public holidays and Christmas to New Year.
Admission: Proof of identity required.

Introduction:

The University of Nottingham's Hallward Library concentrates on collecting manuscripts documenting the history of Nottingham and the wider East Midlands. Included are family and estate papers, letters and journals of local individuals, ecclesiastical records, records of local business and official bodies, literary papers and hospital records. With few exceptions, manuscripts in the collection concerning other countries have a direct bearing on industry and trade with the East Midlands.

Collections:

Nottingham was once famous for lacemaking, and by the 19th century the town had become important for the manufacture of hosiery. Brazil-related material within the library's business collections appears to be extremely limited but provides evidence of some trading ties.

J & H Hadden & Co. Ltd (Nottingham Hosiers, 1685–1915)
English
Amongst the small collection of documents are two exceptionally well-kept and informative ledgers detailing the long-established company's exports. These are:

- *Ledger, 1805–17* – Export figures showing that Hadden's overseas trade was primarily with Brazil, Portugal and Germany.

- *Ledger, 1851–66* – Export figures showing Hadden's continued concentration of exports to Latin America, including Brazil, but also to Australia.

*MS 428 – **A Ransome & Co. Ltd***
English

Records and correspondence of A. Ransome & Co. Ltd, saw-mill engineers and iron founders of Newark, Nottinghamshire. Included within this collection is 1921–30 correspondence with Brazilian clients (*MS 428 / 11 / 1 and 2*) discussing the provision of hardware.

*Pw F 4895 – **Affidavit of Capt. William Robertson, 2 August 1770***
English

Affadavit relating to the seizure of the ship *Argyle* by Portuguese forces at Rio de Janeiro in 1770. Captain Robertson gives details of his ship's cargo, where it was destined for and explains the circumstances which led him to Rio where the cargo was to be confiscated and he and his crew imprisoned. Captain Robertson accused the Portuguese of piracy and reported that he sent a written protest to the Viceroy of Brazil but this was not accepted as it was submitted in English.

OXFORD

ALL SOULS COLLEGE

The Codrington Library
High Street
Oxford OX1 4AL

www.all-souls.ox.ac.uk/library/

Tel: (01865) 279299 • **Fax:** (01865) 279299
E-mail: codrington.library@all-souls.oxford.ac.uk

Open: By arrangement only.
Closed: Public holidays.
Admission: Contact in advance for identification requirements
             and for booking.

Introduction:

Founded in 1438, All Souls College is primarily a research institution
and forms part of the University of Oxford. The Codrington Library is
for the use of fellows of the college, though external readers may gain
access by special arrangement.

Collections:

One manuscript collection of 19th-century diplomatic papers that is
held by the Codrington Library appears to have some Brazil-related
content.

Sir Charles Richard Vaughan Papers (1804–48)

English
These are the private and semi-private correspondence of Sir
Charles Richard Vaughan (1774–1849), a British diplomat who
served in Spain, France, Switzerland and the United States.
Brazil-related correspondence in the collection appears largely to
have been generated during and immediately following Vaughan's
tenure as British minister in Washington (1825–26). The papers are
catalogued and arranged by diplomatic mission and date, with
identification by subject difficult. Access to the very few Brazil-
related manuscripts (mainly concerning early diplomatic relations
between the United States and Brazil) is most easily accomplished

with the listing in Peter Walne, *A Guide to Manuscript Sources for the History of Latin America and the Caribbean in the British Isles* (London, 1973).

◆

BODLEIAN LIBRARY

Department of Special Collections
and Western Manuscripts
University of Oxford
Broad Street
Oxford OX1 3BG

www.bodley.ox.ac.uk

Tel: (01865) 277158 • **Fax:** (01865) 277182
E-mail: western.manuscripts@bodley.ox.ac.uk

Open: Mon–Fri 9am–10pm (vacation until 7pm), Sat 9am–1pm.
Closed: Christmas to New Year (inclusive); Easter long weekend; August bank holiday (the last Monday in the month).
Admission: Those without direct connections to the university normally require a letter of reference confirming the need for admission. The Admissions Office is in the Clarendon Building, on the corner of Broad Street and Catte Street, and is open Mon–Fri 9.30am–4.30pm and Sat 9.30am–12.30pm. Further information regarding admission and application procedures can be obtained from the Admissions Office, tel: (01865) 277180 and e-mail: admissions@bodley.ox.ac.uk.

Introduction:

The Bodleian Library is the principal library of the University of Oxford. It has been collecting printed works since 1602 and became a national legal deposit library in 1610.

Collections:

As one of Britain's largest libraries, the Bodleian undoubtedly features one of the most extensive and most important collections of Brazil-related books, many of which are of antiquarian interest. There is also a large collection of official publications, including what are said to be some remarkable Brazilian congressional holdings. The Bodleian's map collection is one of the world's largest, including many important antiquarian items, some of which relate to Brazil.

There has never been anything close to a systematic search of the Bodleian's Brazilian holdings of books, maps and manuscripts, in part due to the cataloguing difficulties and confusions. There are four general catalogues of western manuscripts held by the Bodleian and many specialised catalogues, both published and unpublished. While the catalogues of books are now accessible online, the process of producing an electronic version of the manuscript catalogues is only in the very early stages of development. Nevertheless, the various manuscript subject catalogues permit some identification of Brazil-related material, although many of the documents are merely isolated letters found within a wider series. Some important documents have, however, been identified, most notably some mid-17th-century letters discussing English trading privileges and settlement prospects in northern Brazil.

Ashmole Manuscripts
English
Amongst the manuscripts bequeathed to the University of Oxford by the 17th-century court official and collector Elias Ashmole are several items relating to Dutch and English interest in the Guianas, including contemporary accounts of Sir Walter Raleigh's and Sir Francis Drake's voyages to the region. A separate catalogue and index allows identification of such documents. One item that specifically refers to what is now Brazilian territory is:

- *MS Ashmole 749, no. II* – A narrative of a projected colony in Guiana or the Amazons, signed by Richard Thornton, 1629.

Clarendon Manuscripts (1st Earl)
English (some Spanish)
The Clarendon Manuscripts [*MSS. Clar.*], the state papers of the historian and statesman Edward Hyde, 1st Earl of Clarendon (1609–74), are perhaps the most important single body of material for the study of 17th-century English domestic and foreign policy.

Although the papers are catalogued in O. Ogle, W.H. Bliss et al. (1869–1970), *Calendar of the Clarendon State Papers Preserved in the Bodleian Library*, 5 vols (Oxford), access to the widely scattered Brazil-related manuscripts is best accomplished with the listing in Peter Walne, ed. (1973), *A Guide to Manuscript Sources for the*

History of Latin America and the Caribbean in the British Isles (London). There appear to be approximately twenty letters and other papers of Brazilian interest within the collection, covering the years from c. 1614 to 1661 (and especially from 1635), focusing on trade and European rivalries in northern and northeastern Brazil. Representative examples of Brazil-related Clarendon Manuscripts are:

- *Clar. MS 18, ff. 206–7: Cal. I, 199* – Letter, Sir Arthur Hopton (Madrid) to Sir Francis Windebank, reporting news of the destruction of Spanish sugar-works in Brazil by the Dutch, 15/25 June 1640.

- *Clar. MS 73, ff. 247–48: Cal. V, 56* – Draft letter from King Charles II of England to Queen of Portugal, asking to redress grievances of British subjects voyaging to Brazil and delayed in São Miguel, Oct 1660.

- *Clar. MS 76, ff. 93–94: Cal. V, 153* – Letter, Bishop Russell to Clarendon about trading with Brazil under Anglo-Portuguese treaty of 1654, ?Oct 1661.

- *Clar. MS 92, ff. 177–79: Cal. V, 91–92* – Account by Sir Balthazar Gerbier Douilly of the profit to be obtained from the silver mines at 'Chiara near Pernambuco in Brazil' (presumably Ceará), with accompanying map, ?March 1660/1.

Clarendon Papers (4th Earl)
English
These are the private and semi-official papers of George Villiers, 4th Earl of Clarendon (1800–70), a professional diplomat who went on to serve three periods as foreign secretary (1853–58, 1865–66 and 1868–70). The papers are bound by country or groups of countries and year of correspondence, and are further divided between incoming or outgoing letters. There is no subject or person index to the papers but there is a separate catalogue listing volumes by year and country or region. Only for the years 1853 and 1856–58 is there substantial correspondence relating to Brazil, although very limited material for other years is bound in general 'South America' volumes.

De Bunsen Papers

English

Maurice William Ernest De Bunsen (1852–1932) was a British career diplomat who was dispatched on a special mission to South America between 12 April and 30 September 1919. This mission is documented in 45 letters and a journal and includes only limited Brazil-related material. The collection has not yet been fully catalogued and there are no accession numbers.

Kimberley Papers

English

This collection is based on the correspondence of John Wodehouse, 1st Earl of Kimberley (1826–1902). Kimberley's long political career included a brief period serving as foreign secretary (1894–95). The papers are indexed and include some correspondence with the British Legation in Rio de Janeiro [*MS Eng. c. 4392, ff. 71–76*] concerning Brazil's territorial dispute with France over the French Guiana border region.

Rawlinson Papers

English

The Rawlinson Papers [*MSS Rawl. A. 1–73*] are papers accumulated by John Thurloe (1616–68), secretary to the Council of State under Oliver Cromwell. A detailed catalogue is *A Collection of the State Papers of John Thurloe*, edited by Thomas Birch (London, 1742, 7 vols). The catalogue features an index, but relevant papers from the collection are listed in Peter Walne *A Guide to Manuscript Sources for the History of Latin America and the Caribbean in the British Isles* (London, 1973). Among the many documents relating to the military and commercial affairs of South America and, especially, the West Indies, Brazil is the subject of very few items. One notable example of Brazil-related documents in the collection is:

- *MS Rawl. A. 176, f. 355* – 'A historical and geographical description of the great river of the Amazons, and of the several great rivers that pay tribute of their waters to her, and of the several nations inhabiting that famous country' by Colonel J. Scott, c. 1670s.

OXFAM ARCHIVE

Oxfam GB
274 Banbury Road
Oxford OX2 7DZ

www.oxfam.org.uk/atwork/history/archive

Tel: (01865) 312610
E-mail: rdodd@oxfam.org.uk

Open: Mon–Fri 10am–5pm.
Closed: Public holidays.
Admission: By appointment only. Apply in writing to the archivist at the above postal or e-mail address. The archive is located at Bicester, Oxfordshire, but material can be made available for consultation in Oxford.

Introduction:

The international campaigning and development organisation Oxfam traces its origins to 1942 and the setting up of the Oxford Committee for Famine Relief. The committee sought to raise funds and political awareness for refugees and displaced persons in Greece and elsewhere in wartorn Europe. In the 1960s Oxfam (as the committee was informally called, officially adopting the name in 1965) switched its focus of activity to Africa, Asia and Latin America and developed into one of Britain's best-known charities.

Oxfam has worked with Brazilian partner organisations since 1968, maintaining an office in Recife. Although the priority area for Oxfam's Brazilian programme has been the Northeast and Amazon regions, projects in other parts of the country have received support. Oxfam works with the most vulnerable groups in Brazil, including Indians, the urban poor (including women and street children), the landless and other rural poor.

Note: A full guide to using the archive may be downloaded in .rtf format from the website.

Collections:

Although records from Oxfam's early years are limited, the archive holds historic records from its foundation. Minutes of meetings of the governing body and subsidiary committees are relatively complete for the entire period of Oxfam's history. Over 21,000 project files, relating to grants made to project partners, form the bulk of the archival holdings. Some project files date back to 1954, but the series is more complete from the early 1960s.

Files have been kept on almost all Oxfam's Brazilian programmes. Records (for which there is usually no closure period) concern many areas of activity and include support for campaigns of indigenous peoples (both Indians and the descendants of escaped slaves) for the demarcation of their traditional land and to defend their cultural rights, languages and resources, and for drought relief projects, urban sanitation measures and popular education.

◆

RHODES HOUSE LIBRARY
University of Oxford
South Parks Road
Oxford OX1 3RG

www.bodley.ox.ac.uk/dept/rhl/

Tel: (01865) 270909 • **Fax:** (01865) 270912
E-mail: rhodes.house.library@bodley.ox.ac.uk

Open: *Term time:* Mon–Fri 9am–7pm, Sat 9am–1pm.
          Easter and summer vacations: Mon–Thurs 9am–7pm, Fri 9am–5pm, Sat 9am–1pm.
          Christmas vacation: Mon–Fri 9am–5pm, Sat 9am–1pm.

Closed: Closed on Sundays, the Easter long weekend, between Christmas and New Year, and the Saturday preceding and the week following August bank holiday (the last Monday of the month). The library closes at 5pm on the two bank holidays in May (which fall on the first and last Mondays of the month).

Admission: Short-term reader's tickets, valid for two consecutive days, are issued at Rhodes House Library on production of suitable academic credentials. For a longer admission period, apply for a Bodleian reader's ticket, available from the Admissions Office in the Clarendon Building in Broad Street (see under Bodleian Library, p. 211).

Introduction:

Rhodes House Library, which opened in 1929, is a dependent library of the University of Oxford's Bodleian Library, specialising in the history and current affairs of the Commonwealth as well as other parts of sub-Saharan Africa. Previously, the library also covered the USA, but this material has been transferred to the new Vere Harmsworth Library of the University of Oxford's Rothermere American Institute.

Collections:

The library has more than 4,000 manuscript collections and is particularly strong in material relating to the history of British colonial administration. Although Brazil falls outside of the library's normal areas of interest, there are two important slavery-related manuscript collections featuring correspondence and other documents discussing the country.

- **Anti-Slavery Society**
  (The British and Foreign Anti-Slavery and Aborigines Protection Society)

In 1823 a number of men – led by William Wilberforce and Sir Thomas Fowell Buxton (see p. 219) – began to meet regularly in London to discuss the slave trade and slavery in British possessions. From these meetings a number of informal committees and societies were formed before, in 1835, the Anti-Slavery Society was set up.

The society initially concentrated its attentions on the conditions of the recently emancipated slaves in British possessions, the Atlantic slave trade and the continuance of slavery in Africa and the Americas. In later years, the society altered its focus of attention to areas such as bonded labour, prostitution and the defence of aboriginal people, campaigns that still continue.

There is a list of files according to broad topic and/or dates but there is no subject or name index to individual documents contained within the files. Brazil receives passing mentions in many early letters and other documents (such as minute and letter books), and there are four files specifically devoted to Brazilian material.

E2/1–20 – Minute books of the Society, 1823–1935
English
These minutes of committee meetings include brief outlines of the discussions and actions ordered. There is considerable Brazil-related content to the proceedings but no subject index.

*E3/1–10 – **Letter Books of the Society, 1869–99***
English
The volumes contain copies of outgoing letters. There is a subject index but little in the way of Brazil-related content.

*G79 – **Brazil: 1840–83***
*G80a – **Brazil: 1888 and after***
English
These files contain miscellaneous 19th-century Brazil-related letters, reports and memorandum concerning the slave trade, conditions endured by slaves and proposed schemes to introduce indentured labour. Although the dates given for the *G80a* file are '1888 and after', the documents cover the years 1881–88 with no divisions in terms of their subject. Topics dealt with and types of documents include:

- Several detailed statements outlining the terms of reference of a proposed mission to Brazil (undated, but probably 1840s) to investigate conditions of slaves, free people of colour and native Amerindians.

- Statements of defence by the Brazilian Mining Association (1840) and the Imperial Brazilian Mining Association (1847 and 1851) of their treatment of slaves.

- Notes concerning German immigrants and their sufferings in Bahia (undated, but apparently 1872–73).

- Approximately fifteen letters and several other documents discussing the proposed introduction of Chinese 'coolies' to Brazil (1881 and 1883).

- Letters (1887) from Rio de Janeiro discussing the demise of slavery.

- Reports (1888) from the Brazilian Emancipation Committee in Lagos, Nigeria on the celebrations of 'repatriates' to mark the end of slavery in Brazil.

G80b – Brazil: 33 letters by or about Joaquim Nabuco, 1880–1900
English

Thirty of the items are letters, all in English, from Joaquim Nabuco (1849–1910), a leading Brazilian abolitionist, liberal politician and diplomat, to Charles Allen, who served as secretary of the Anti-Slavery Society from 1879 to 1898. All written in English, the often lengthy letters from Rio de Janeiro, Pernambuco, London and France discuss the efforts of abolitionists in Brazil, political machinations in Pernambuco and Nabuco's travel plans. Nabuco extends his thanks to the Anti-Slavery Society for their support, and some of the letters include enclosures of his articles that he wanted placed in British newspapers.

G944 – Brazil: 1969–74
English

Correspondence and enclosures from Brazilian anthropologists, clerics and others concerning the conditions of, and government policy towards, Amerindians.

Sir Thomas Fowell Buxton
English

Together with William Wilberforce, Sir Thomas Fowell Buxton (1786–1845) was a leading campaigner in England for the abolition of slavery and a founder of the Anti-Slavery Society (see p. 217). Although Wilberforce's activities were concentrated almost entirely on the British Empire and the United States, Buxton's campaigning activities were broader. In the years after the abolition of slavery in British dominions and the prohibition on the transportation of slaves by British ships, Buxton focused his attention on the wider African slave trade – both internal and the continued traffic across the Atlantic, especially to the United States, Cuba and Brazil.

The manuscripts (mainly letters – some with enclosures – to Buxton, with notes or copies of some outgoing letters) are in 46 bound volumes and record Buxton's life from a student in Dublin in 1804 to his death in 1845. There is a thorough index (by name and subject) of the papers, and each item is provided with a detailed synopsis.

Brazil-related correspondence, found in volume 29, represents only a very small proportion of the Buxton collection and mainly covers the mid-1830s. Examples of documents are:

- Lists Brazilian and Portuguese slave ships intercepted and taken to Sierra Leone, 1828–38.

- List Brazilian and Portuguese slave ships arriving or departing Bahia (Salvador) to or from Africa, 1838.

- Letters and enclosures detailing the bad character of Sir George Jackson, the British representative on the Mixed Commission, with respect to his treatment of servants employed in his home in Rio de Janeiro, 1835.

- Correspondence with accounts of the cruelty inflicted by British and Brazilian slave owners in Rio de Janeiro, 1830s.

PORTHCURNO

CABLE & WIRELESS ARCHIVE

Museum of Submarine Telegraphy
Eastern House
Porthcurno
Cornwall TR19 6JX

www.porthcurno.org.uk

Tel: (01736) 810811 • **Fax:** (01736) 810640
E-mail: archive@tunnels.demon.co.uk

Open: Access by advance arrangement.
Closed: Public holidays.
Admission: By appointment only.

Introduction:

The Cable & Wireless Archive is located in Porthcurno, near Land's End in Cornwall, an important location in the history of telecommunications. In 1870 the first international telegraph cable was laid from the beach at Porthcurno, and a cable station was opened there by the Falmouth, Gibraltar and Malta Telegraph Company (FGMTC). It was at this station where company 'probationers' were sent to learn telegraphy skills in readiness for postings overseas. In 1870 the FGMTC won a concession to establish and work a telegraph between Porthcurno, Carcavellos (Portugal) and Gibraltar. This in turn led to the opening in 1874 by the Brazilian Submarine Telegraph Company of a cable between Portugal and Brazil, via Madeira and São Vicente (Cape Verde), linking with the Carcavellos–Porthcurno cable. During the remainder of the 19th century, the cable system expanded to include cables extending from Pará (Belém) to Chuy in Rio Grande do Sul, with connections south into Uruguay and Argentina, west along the Amazon and north through the West Indies to the United States. The early operators developed into the Western Telegraph Co.; in 1929 this amalgamated with the Eastern Telegraph Co. to form Cable & Wireless Ltd.

Collections:

The Cable & Wireless Archive includes a wide range of historic material relating to the development of international communications business and technology. While the archive includes material from the 1850s to the present day, the main period covered by the collection is between c. 1870 and c. 1970. Over the course of this period there were many changes in the names of the cable companies, and their subsidiaries and documents survive from most of them. The collection includes directors' minute books (and indexes), ledgers and leases, as well as printed ephemera (such as promotional literature, commemorative publications and annual reports), newspaper cuttings dating back to the 1850s, photographs, maps and charts. A complete run of *The Zodiac*, the staff magazine started in 1906, and its successor magazines are also held. All these catagories of material include significant references to Brazilian operations and are best used with the Western Telegraph Co. archival holdings of University College London (see pp. 197–98).

The archive's catalogue is fully accessible online: text searches with keywords such as 'Brazil', 'Brazilian' and 'Amazon' result in over 130 document or file matches, all in English. Representative examples of items held by the archive are:

- *DOC/WTC/12/3/* – Western Telegraph Co. – *History of the Company in Brazil*, nd.

- *DOC/BZSTC/6/1/* – Brazilian Submarine Telegraph Co. Ltd – Correspondence with Western Telegraph Co. including copy of inaugural message of Queen Victoria to the emperor of Brazil, 1873–74.

- *DOC/BZSTC/1/1/* – Brazilian Submarine Telegraph Co. – Board minutes, 1873–78. [*Note:* Minute books and index survive for this company for 1873–1903.]

- *DOC/BZSTC/2/1/* – Brazilian Submarine Telegraph Co. – Balance sheets with supporting accounts, 1873–82. [*Note:* Balance sheets survive for 1873–99.]

- *DOC/AZTC/1/2/* – Amazon Telegraph Co. Ltd – Annual reports, 1896–1929.

- *PHO/WTC/9/1* – Western Telegraph Co. – Photographs of the Western Telegraph Co.'s quarters in Rio de Janeiro and architectural drawings of the mess, reading and billiards rooms building, 1923.

- *DOC/WTC/4/1* – Western Telegraph Co. – Specification for construction of a new building, Rio de Janeiro, c. 1930.

PORTSMOUTH

ROYAL NAVAL MUSEUM

HM Naval Base (PP66)
Portsmouth PO1 3NH

www.royalnavalmuseum.org

Tel: (023) 9272 7562 • **Fax:** (023) 9272 7575
E-mail: library@royalnavalmuseum.org

Open: Mon–Fri 10am–4pm.
Closed: Public holidays.
Admission: By appointment. Proof of identity required.

Introduction:

The Royal Naval Museum's manuscript department concentrates on the collection of documents that are a source for a social and operational history of the Navy rather than a history of technological development. Descriptions of manuscripts that are held by the museum are given in M. Sheldon's *Guide to the Manuscript Collections of the Royal Naval Museum* (Portsmouth, 1997) and in the Manuscript Catalogue Database which can be accessed via the Museum's website.

The museum is particularly strong on personal diaries, memoirs, journals and collections of letters since around 1780, some of which were previously held by the Admiralty Library. Apart from a few stray items of official material, the museum's archival collections do not include official Admiralty records – these are mainly held by the National Archives (see pp. 158–60).

Collections:

Brazil-related material forms only a very small portion of the Museum's archival holdings. There are numerous charts of the east coast of South America, including Brazil, and several 18th-century maps and plans of the islands of Fernando de Noronha, Trinidade and Martín Vaz. Only one substantial Brazil-related manuscript collection has been identified but the museum holds a large collection of original 19th- and early 20th-century diaries and logs, some of which relate to voyages to South America and can be found by searching 'South America' using the Manuscript Catalogue Database.

Letters of the Admiral Sir Thomas Masterman Hardy
English

Sir Thomas Masterman Hardy (1769–1839) was an officer in the Royal Navy who served in many parts of the world during his career. The collection consists of nineteen letters sent by Hardy to Henry Chamberlain between 1820 and 1823. Seventeen of the letters are dated 1822–23 while Hardy was commander-in-chief of the Navy's South America Station and Chamberlain was serving as British consul-general in Rio de Janeiro. The letters are mainly dispatches and reports relating to moves towards Brazilian independence.

PRESTON

LANCASHIRE RECORD OFFICE

Bow Lane
Preston
Lancashire PR1 2RE

www.archives.lancashire.gov.uk

Tel: (01772) 263039 • **Fax:** (01772) 263050
E-mail: record.office@ed.lancscc.gov.uk

Open: Mon, Wed and Thurs 9am–5pm, Tues 9am–8.30pm,
Fri 9am–6pm.
Closed: First full week each calendar month and public holidays.
Admission: Proof of identity required.

Introduction:

The Lancashire Record Office collects and preserves documents relating to the county of Lancashire. Local administration, church and private (individuals, businesses or societies) records are all held. Documents concerning other parts of England or other countries are held only where the creator or, in the case of letters, recipient has a close link to Lancashire.

Collections:

Although several collections have been identified that include documents relating to Brazil, most are isolated letters concerning the export of textiles from Lancashire's important textile mills or business ledgers. A handlist (number 17) is available that lists some of the documents Record Office staff have found among the collections which relate to the West Indies and South America, including several references to Rio de Janeiro and other places in Brazil. Only two collections appear to include significant Brazil-related content.

DDX 503/1 – *John Cottam Letters*
English
This letter book consists of the correspondence of John Cottam, covering the period 17 January 1856 to 7 January 1869. A draper from Fleetwood, Lancashire, Cottam was also employed as a railway clerk in Brazil, where many of the letters were written.

DDPSL – Platt Saco Lowell
English
Dating back to the early 19th century, the Saco-Lowell corporation developed into Britain's most important producers of equipment for the manufacture of textiles. From factories across Lancashire, machines and machine-parts were dispatched throughout the world. In 1973 the US-owned Platt International acquired Saco-Lowell and created Platt Saco Lowell.

The collection includes records created by the various manufacturers of machinery that were absorbed into Saco-Lowell. Records that specifically relate to Brazil have been identified as:

- *DDPSL 5/2/5 Tweedales & Smalley Ltd of Castleton –* Orders and prices books, including brief descriptions, Brazil, 1899–1937.

- *DDPSL 13/5/1 & 13/2/28 – Textile Machinery Makers Ltd of Helmshore –* Correspondence concerning Brazilian exports, 1953–58.

SOUTHAMPTON

SOUTHAMPTON CITY ARCHIVES

South Block
Civic Centre
Southampton SO14 7LY

www.southampton.gov.uk/
leisure/history/archives

Tel: (023) 8083 2251 • **Fax:** (023) 8083 2156
E-mail: city.archives@southampton.gov.uk

Open: Tues–Fri 9.30am–4.30pm.
Closed: Public holidays.
Admission: Appointment advisable.

Introduction:

The Southampton City Archives is a municipal repository collecting material relating to the city and port of Southampton. It holds documents that relate to other parts of the United Kingdom or to overseas countries only where there is a close connection to Southampton.

Collections:

Despite Southampton's status of having been one of Britain's most important ports, few Brazil-related records have been identified. One general port-related source held by the city archives are the crew lists for Southampton-registered vessels covering 1863–1913, a number of which record voyages to Brazil during the period. Another source relating to the Merchant Navy is the Central Index of Merchant Seamen 1913–41. In addition to lists of British merchant seamen, there are records for foreign nationals and possibly service records for Brazilians if they served on board a British-registered vessel between those years. The Central Index is alphabetically arranged, so unless particular surnames are known it would be difficult to extract cards for Brazilian seafarers.

*SC/AG 14/15 – **Board of Guardians' Records: 'German Russens'***
English
In June 1878 a group of Russians of German descent emigrated to Paraná. Soon disillusioned with local conditions, many of the

newly arrived immigrants resolved to leave Brazil. On 9 December 1879 a group of ninety destitute returnees arrived in Southampton from Rio de Janeiro on the RMS *Minho*. The Russian government was initially reluctant to take the group back but eventually it was persuaded to accept them and they were dispatched on 3 January 1880. The papers concern the attempts of Southampton Corporation and the Board of Guardians to recover the costs incurred in supporting the emigrants. Included is official correspondence (December 1879–January 1880) between the Southampton Corporation, the Local Government Board, the Foreign Office and the Russian Embassy. There are also lists of the quantities of provisions consumed by the emigrants, a detailed report of the conveyance of the emigrants from Southampton to Russia and a letter of thanks to the people of England and Southampton signed by six 'poor German Russen Emigrants'.

D/VT 10 – *Thornycroft (Brazil) Ltd*
English
Amongst the papers of the shipbuilders John I. Thornycroft & Co. Ltd are records (mainly financial) relating to Thornycroft (Brazil) Ltd. These include annual accounts (1927–57), annual general balances (1938–63), a report on a visit from head office to Rio de Janeiro offices and stores (1948) and plans, photographs of buildings, offices and other premises in Rio de Janeiro and São Paulo (1943–48).

UNIVERSITY OF SOUTHAMPTON
Hartley Library
Archive and Special Collections
Highfield
Southampton SO17 1BJ

www.archives.lib.soton.ac.uk

Tel: (023) 8059 2721 • **Fax:** (023) 8059 3007
E-mail: archives@soton.ac.uk

Open: Mon–Fri 9am–5pm (Wed 10am–5pm).
Closed: Public holidays.
Admission: By appointment only. Apply in writing at least one week prior to first visit.

Introduction:

The manuscript collections at the University of Southampton's Hartley Library focus on political and military topics, on Jewish communities in England, maritime history and on the university itself. Amongst the archival holdings are private papers of several prominent 19th-century figures who had strong interests in Brazilian affairs. The catalogue is being developed to include an online search facility.

Collections:

Without a doubt, the most significant manuscript collections held by the Hartley Library that feature Brazil-related material are the Palmerston Papers and Wellington Papers, two extremely important series of private political papers. The library also holds the papers of Richard Wellesley, 1st Marquis (1760–1842), who served as foreign secretary between December 1809 and 1812; no papers relating to Brazil have been identified in the collection [*MS 63*], however. Brazil-related material in other collections tends to reflect Southampton's maritime heritage.

MS 62 – *Palmerston Papers*
English
The Palmerston Papers mainly relate to Henry John Temple, 3rd Viscount Palmerston (1784–1865). As secretary of war (1809–28), foreign secretary (1830–34, 1835–41 and 1846–51) and prime minister (1855–58 and 1859–65), Palmerston's political career spanned an important period in Anglo-Brazilian relations, including the Independence era, war with Argentina, and the abolition and suppression of the transatlantic slave trade.

Some three-quarters of this semi-official correspondence consists of Palmerston's papers as foreign secretary and is largely composed of his private correspondence, including with British diplomats in Brazil and with Brazilian and Portuguese diplomats in London. Material from Palmerston's years as secretary of war and as prime minister are extremely fragmentary. The printed catalogues indicate the basic descriptions of correspondence (incoming or outgoing, name and position of correspondent, date; the subject matter is not always indicated). Material relating to Brazil is largely scattered and perhaps largely disappointing in quantity and scope.

The Palmerston Papers are divided into four overlapping classes – *General Correspondence [GC]*, *Slave Trade [SLT]*, *Dispatches [BD]* and *Memoranda [MM]*, the latter two classes including virtually nothing relating to Brazil. The material highlighted below indicates the range of Brazil-related correspondence.

GC – *General Correspondence*

General correspondence is considerable, with the slave trade being the focus of discussion of the in-letters, mainly written by British diplomats. The following are the main Brazil-related correspondents and groupings of papers but there are also some individual letters. In addition, consideration should be given to correspondence from British diplomats in Uruguay and Argentina, some of which will have a bearing on Brazil.

- *GC/BA/264–306 – Barry* – Letters from Sir Francis Thornhill Barry, first lord of the admiralty, to Palmerston concerning the suppression of the South American slave trade, 1849–51.

- *GC/F/27 – Forster* – Letter from Palmerston to William Forster (philanthropist) concerning the abolition of slavery in Portuguese Africa, 1849.

- *GC/FO/162–170 – Fox* – Correspondence between Palmerston and Henry Stephen Fox (British minister to Brazil) concerning the slave trade, 1833–36.

- *GC/HO/147–89 – Hoppner* – Correspondence from Richard Belgrave Hoppner, acting British consul-general, Portugal, including observations on Dom Pedro's abdication of the Brazilian imperial crown, 1831–33.

- *GC/HU/1–52 – Hudson* – Correspondence between Palmerston and James Hudson, secretary to the British Legation in Brazil (1845–50) and British minister to Brazil (1850–51), mainly relating to the suppression of the slave trade, 1845–51.

- *GC/LA/118–134 – Lavradio* – Letters from Francisco de Almeida Portugal Lavradio, the Portuguese minister to Britain, concerning Portugal's role in the suppression of the slave trade, 1851–64.

- *GC/OU/107–149 – Ouseley* – Letters from William Gore Ouseley, secretary and chargé d'affaires to the British Legation in Brazil (1833–45), including correspondence concerning the slave trade, mainly 1833, 1839–40.

SLT – Slave Trade
This very large category of documents (1806–65) includes correspondence, memoranda and notes relating to the slave trade and its abolition, especially in the Atlantic area, and reflecting Palmerston's activities.

SLT/18–34 – Slave Trade: Brazil
Material directly relating to Brazil mainly concerns the years from 1836. Papers include:

- Memorandum of vessels engaged in the slave trade at Rio de Janeiro, Oct 1836 to March 1837.

- Opinion of law officers on the British government's rights, powers and obligations under the treaty of 1826 with Brazil as regards Brazilian ships and subjects engaged in the slave trade.

- Confidential memorandum, a copy of the Brazil Slave Trade Bill of 1845 (a draft of the Aberdeen Act).

- Memorandum discussing attempts to persuade Portugal to declare the slave trade as 'piracy' and therefore illegal under international law.

- Letter describing Brazilian resentment over Britain's increasingly stringent measures to suppress the slave trade, March 1846.

- Foreign Office memorandum with estimates of number of African slaves imported into Brazil annually since 1817, Aug 1864.

Wellington Papers
English

The Wellington Papers relate to the life and military, political and diplomatic career of Arthur Wellesley, first Duke of Wellington (1769–1852). The online catalogue includes a summary of each item that dates from 1819. In addition to copies of out-going correspondence and letters received by Wellington, there are also copies, or originals, of letters between other correspondents. The correspondents include most of the key British political and diplomatic figures of the time, with material of Brazilian interest being of considerable importance. In terms of identifying manuscripts in this very extensive collection, for the time being the papers can best be divided into three cataloguing periods: 1790–1818, 1819–32 and 1833–52.

1790–1818

This period covers Wellington's military career, with the duke achieving the rank of field marshall in 1813, and early diplomatic activities. As the papers from this period have so far been catalogued only by date and with the description 'To the Duke' or 'From the Duke', it is impossible to estimate any Brazil-related content. However, as Wellington was in command of the British Army in Portugal in 1808, there may be some relevant material.

1819–32

These years include Wellington's first period as prime minister (1828–30). The correspondence has been well catalogued in the form of an electronic database and a considerable amount of material relating to Brazil can be identified. The following indicate the range of correspondents and subjects:

- Correspondence between Wellington and George Canning concerning the slave trade, 1820s.

- Correspondence regarding British mediation between Portugal and Brazil following Independence, 1820s.

- Correspondence discussing whether British officers should be permitted to join the Brazilian army, 1820s.

- Letters from Manuel de Sarratea (ambassador of the United Provinces of the Rio de la Plata, London) to George Canning (foreign secretary) regarding Britain as a mediator

> between Brazil and the United Provinces over Montevideo and the Banda Oriental, 1826.
>
> - Letters from Lord Aberdeen (foreign secretary) to Wellington regarding mediating a reconciliation between Dom Miguel of Portugal and Don Pedro of Brazil, 1828.
>
> - Letter from Lord Aberdeen to Wellington discussing Brazil and the abolition of the slave trade, 1828.
>
> - Letters from Wellington to Aberdeen concerning Dutch or German emigrants bound for Brazil but stranded in Falmouth, Cornwall, 1828.
>
> - Correspondence between Wellington and Portuguese diplomats regarding the transfer from Plymouth to Brazil of Portuguese refugees and soldiers, 1828.

1833–52

The catalogue makes identification of possible Brazil-related material extremely difficult (see p. 232, '1790–1818'). However, these decades include Wellington's second period (1834–35) as prime minister, when he also held the post of foreign secretary, and it is likely that some correspondence on Brazilian subjects survives. One can expect few mentions of Brazil amongst the 1840s correspondence, years that Wellington was mainly in India.

MS 45 – Mogg Papers
English

Southampton-born William Mogg (1796–1875) joined the Royal Navy as a volunteer in 1811, spending much of his career as a clerk in surveying expeditions, most notably with Edward Parry's second and third Arctic expeditions. The years 1821–33 were mainly spent in South American waters, including on the HMS *Beagle* (1827–30) with Charles Darwin.

Between 1811 and 1868 Mogg kept a private journal which he assembled during the 1860s into six volumes. In volume three [*MS 45/AO183/3*] Mogg largely relates his South American travels, especially Patagonia. Also featured, however, are short but colourful descriptions of Rio de Janeiro, Santos, São Paulo, Paranaguá (all 1826) and the island of Santa Catarina (1830).

STAFFORD

STAFFORDSHIRE RECORD OFFICE

County Buildings
Eastgate Street
Stafford ST16 2LZ

www.archives.staffordshire.gov.uk

Tel: (01785) 278379 • **Fax:** (01785) 278384
E-mail: staffordshire.record.office@staffordshire.gov.uk

Open: Mon, Tues, Thurs 9am–5pm, Wed 9am–8pm,
           Fri 9.30am–4.30pm, Sat 9am–12.30pm.
Closed: Public holidays.
Admission: Appointment required.

Introduction:

The Staffordshire Record Office documents the history of the county and people of Staffordshire. Material relating to foreign countries is usually held only if the creator of a manuscript has a link with Staffordshire.

Collections:

It appears that only two collections held by the Staffordshire Record Office feature Brazil-related items.

Papers of the Legge Family, Earls of Dartmouth: William, 2nd Earl of Dartmouth, First Lord of Trade, Secretary for the Colonies, 1772–75
English
These papers include an account [*DW1778/V/311*] from the early 1770s, sent to the earl, of tobacco exported by Portuguese traders from Brazil to Africa, and of duties paid by them to the Dutch authorities at the West African trading post of Elmina.

Business Interests of 3rd Earl of Lichfield, Viscount Anson
English
This collection includes a file [*D615/PB/1*] of printed and
manuscript papers relating to the Brazil Great Southern Railway
Co. Included are an engineer's report (1883); shareholders'
memorandum (1885); copy correspondence, directors' and
engineers' reports and accounts (1885–88); and correspondence
regarding the international bridge over the Quarahim River linking
Brazil with Uruguay (1885–88).

TRURO

CORNWALL RECORD OFFICE

Old County Hall
Truro
Cornwall TR1 3AY

Tel: (01872) 323 127 • **Fax:** (01872) 322 292
E-mail: cro@cornwall.gov.uk

Open: Tues–Fri, 9am–4.30pm.
Closed: Public holidays.
Admission: Proof of identity required.

Introduction:

The Cornwall Record Office documents the history of the country and people of Cornwall. Documents relating to other counties and countries are held if they relate in some way to Cornwall.

Collections:

Cornwall has a long history of copper tin mining, with Cornish miners and mining engineers travelling thoughout the world for employment opportunities. During the 19th and early 20th centuries, British mining companies operating in Latin America, especially Mexico and Brazil, recruited extensively in Cornwall. Despite these important connections, very few documents relating to Brazil appear to be held by the Cornwall Record Office. There are a number of isolated documents concerning investment holdings in Brazil and papers relating to Cornish individuals who died in the country, but only one reasonably substantial and relevant collection has been identified.

ADI 1730 – *Thomas Martin, Mine Captain, Brazil*
English (some in Portuguese)
Thomas Martin was born in 1799 in Gwennap, a copper mining district that was once referred to as the "richest square mile in the Old World". He later moved to Perranarworthal, the location of a tin smelting works, from where he joined the Imperial Brazilian Mining Association. In 1827, while working at the Gongo Soco gold mine (in Minas Gerais), Martin was made Head Captain and

Superintendent of Mines. He lived and worked in Brazil until 1860 or 1861 after which it appears that he settled in Wales where he died in Dolgellau in 1870.

The collection consists of 68 documents from between 1827 and 1862, mostly letters written to Thomas Martin. The letters are significant for detailing the maintenance of financial and family connections between Cornwall and Brazil.

WARWICK

WARWICKSHIRE COUNTY RECORD OFFICE

Priory Park
Cape Road
Warwick CV34 4JS

**www.warwickshire.gov.uk/
countyrecordoffice**

Tel: (01926) 412735 • **Fax:** (01926) 412509
E-mail: recordoffice@warwickshire.gov.uk

Open: Tues–Thurs 9am–5.30pm, Fri 9am–5pm, Sat 9am–12.30pm.
Closed: Public holidays.
Admission: No appointment is necessary; proof of identity and
address required.

Introduction:

The Warwickshire County Record Office documents the history of the
county and people of Warwickshire. Material relating to foreign countries is usually held only if the creator of a manuscript has a link with
Warwickshire.

Collections:

Very few Brazil-related items have been identified as being held by the
Warwickshire County Record Office.

CR136/A/296 – *Diary of A.L. Newdigate*
English
The diary of A.L. Newdigate, a civil engineer from Arbury, records
a voyage from England to Rio de Janeiro and onwards to South
Africa between October 1867 and February 1868 and details
impressions of both places.

CR114A/421 – *Sir George Francis Seymour Papers*
English
These are accounts and notes (1845–48) made by Sir George Francis
Seymour while commanding the Royal Navy's Pacific Station.
Although the centre of operations was the west coast of South America,
included are descriptions of visits to Rio de Janeiro.

WOLVERHAMPTON

WOLVERHAMPTON ARCHIVES

42–50 Snow Hill
Wolverhampton WV2 4AG

www.wolverhampton.gov.uk/
archives

Tel: (01902) 552480 • **Fax:** (01902) 552481
E-mail: wolverhamptonarchives@dial.pipex.com

Open: Mon–Tues and Fri 10am–5pm, Wed 10am–7pm,
             Sat 10am–5pm (1st and 3rd of month only).
Closed: Public holidays.
Admission: Proof of identity required.

Introduction:

The archives collect material relating to Wolverhampton, including local government records and the records of businesses associated with the town. Documents concerning other parts of England or other countries are held only if the creator has an association with Wolverhampton.

Collections:

Only one item, within the large business history collection of the Records of Goodyear Tyre and Rubber Company (Great Britain) Ltd, has been identified as featuring some Brazil-related content.

DB–20/G/6 – Lady Wickham's Diary
English
Lady Wickham's diary throws additional light on the starting of the rubber plantation industry in Malaya and the activities of her husband, Sir Henry Wickham, in collecting rubber seeds in the Amazon and smuggling them out of Brazil in the 1870s for propagation at Kew Gardens. (See also Royal Botanic Gardens, Kew, p. 186.)

APPENDIX 1:
Secretaries of State for Foreign Affairs
(1782 to 1945)

U ntil well into the 20th century, ministerial correspondence was considered the postholder's personal property. As a result, not all secretary of state papers have survived and, where they have, they are not always complete. Duplicate correspondence to and from the secretaries of state for foreign affairs is, however, often found within Foreign Office files that are held by the Public Record Office, Kew.

The list of British secretaries of state for foreign affairs includes reference to relevant entries within the guide. Where no such page references are given, Brazil-related material within collections has not been identified. To locate holdings of such secretaries of state, readers should consult the National Register of Archives' website (see p. 251).

March–July 1782
Fox, Charles James

July 1782–April 1783
Grantham, 2nd Lord, Thomas Robinson

April–Dec 1783
Fox, Charles James

19–22 Dec 1783
Temple, 3rd Earl, George Nugent Temple Grenville, later 1st Marquess of Buckingham

23 Dec 1783–April 1791
Carmarthen, Marquess of, later 5th Duke of Leeds, Francis Godolphin Osborne

April 1791–Feb 1801
Grenville, Lord, William Wyndham Grenville
(See British Library, pp. 107–8)

Feb 1801–May 1804
Hawkesbury, Lord, later 2nd Earl of Liverpool, Robert Banks Jenkinson

May–Dec 1804
Harrowby, 2nd Lord, later 1st Earl of Harrowby, Dudley Ryder

Jan 1805–Feb 1806
Mulgrave, 3rd Lord, later 1st Earl of Mulgrave, Henry Phipps

Feb–Sept 1806
Fox, Charles James

(continued overleaf)

Sept 1806–March 1807
Howick, Lord, later 2nd Earl Grey, Charles Grey

March 1807–Oct 1809
Canning, George
*(See British Library, p. 109; Hartley Library, Southampton, p. 232;
India Office Library, pp. 124–25; Leeds District Archive, pp. 78–79)*

Oct–Dec 1809
Bathurst, 3rd Earl, Henry Bathurst

Dec 1809–Jan 1812
Wellesley, 1st Marquess, Richard Colley
(See British Library, p. 111; Hartley Library, Southampton, p. 229)

Feb 1812–Sept 1822
**Viscount Castlereagh, later 2nd Marquess of Londonderry,
Robert Stewart**
(See Public Record Office of Northern Ireland, p. 7)

Sept 1822–April 1827
Canning, George
*(See British Library, p. 109; Hartley Library, Southampton, p. 232;
India Office Library, pp. 124–25; Leeds District Archive, pp. 78–79)*

April 1827–May 1828
Dudley and Ward, 4th Viscount, later Earl of Dudley, John William Ward
(See British Library, p. 109)

May 1828–Nov 1830
Aberdeen, 4th Earl of, George Hamilton-Gordon
(See British Library, pp. 103–5; Hartley Library, Southampton, p. 233)

Nov 1830–Nov 1834
Palmerston, 3rd Viscount, Henry John Temple
(See Leeds District Archive, p. 78; Hartley Library, Southampton, pp. 229–31)

Nov 1834–April 1835
Wellington, 1st Duke of, Arthur Wellesley
(See Hartley Library, Southampton, pp. 232–33)

April 1835–Aug 1841
Palmerston, 3rd Viscount, Henry John Temple
(See Hartley Library, Southampton, pp. 208–10)

Sept 1841–July 1846
Aberdeen, 4th Earl of, George Hamilton-Gordon
(See British Library, pp. 103–5; Hartley Library, Southampton, p. 233)

July 1846–Dec 1851
Palmerston, 3rd Viscount, Henry John Temple
(See Hartley Library, Southampton, p. 208)

Dec 1851–Feb 1852
Granville, 2nd Earl, George Leveson Gower

Feb–Dec 1852
Malmesbury, 3rd Earl of, James

Dec 1852–Feb 1853
Russell, Lord John, later 1st Earl
(See National Archives, p. 153)

Feb 1853–Feb 1858
Clarendon, 4th Earl of, George Villiers
(See Bodleian Library, p. 213; National Archives, p. 151)

Feb 1858–June 1859
Malmesbury, 3rd Earl of, James Harris

June 1859–Oct 1865
Russell, Lord John, later 1st Earl
(See National Archives, p. 153)

Nov 1865–July 1866
Clarendon, 4th Earl of, George Villiers
(See Bodleian Library, p. 213; National Archives, p. 151)

July 1866–Dec 1868
Stanley, Lord, Edward Henry, later 15th Earl of Derby
(See Liverpool Record Office, p. 68)

Dec 1868–July 1870
Clarendon, 4th Earl of, George Villiers
(See Bodleian Library, p. 213; National Archives, p. 151)

July 1870–Feb 1874
Granville, 2nd Earl, George Leveson Gower

Feb 1874–April 1878
Stanley, Lord, Edward Henry, later 15th Earl of Derby
(See Liverpool Record Office, p. 85)

April 1878–April 1880
Salisbury, 3rd Marquess of, Robert Cecil
(See Hatfield House, pp. 72–73)

April 1880–June 1885
Granville, 2nd Earl, George Leveson Gower

June 1885–Feb 1886
Salisbury, 3rd Marquess of, Robert Cecil
(See Hatfield House, pp. 72–73)

Feb–July 1886
Rosebery, 5th Earl of, Archibald Primrose

Aug 1886–Jan 1887
Iddesleigh, 1st Earl of, Stafford Northcote

(continued overleaf)

Jan 1887–Aug 1892
Salisbury, 3rd Marquess of, Robert Cecil
(See Hatfield House, pp. 72–73)

Aug 1892–March 1894
Rosebery, 5th Earl of, Archibald Primrose

March 1894–June 1895
Kimberley, 1st Earl of, John Wodehouse
(See Bodleian Library, p. 214)

June 1895–Nov 1900
Salisbury, 3rd Marquess of, Robert Cecil
(See Hatfield House, pp. 72–73)

Nov 1900–Dec 1905
Lansdowne, 5th Marquess of, Henry Petty-Fitzmaurice

Dec 1905–Dec 1916
Grey, Sir Edward, later Viscount Grey of Fallodon

Dec 1916–Oct 1919
Balfour, Arthur James, later 1st Earl of Balfour

Oct 1919–Jan 1924
Curzon, Earl, later 1st Marquess of Kedleston

Jan–Nov 1924
MacDonald, James Ramsay

Nov 1924–June 1929
Chamberlain, Sir Austen

June 1929–Aug 1931
Henderson, Arthur

16 Aug–Nov 1931
Reading, 1st Marquess of, Rufus Isaacs

Nov 1931–June 1935
Simon, Sir John, later 1st Viscount

June–Dec 1935
Hoare, Sir Samuel, later 1st Viscount Templewood

Dec 1935–Feb 1938
Eden, Anthony, later Sir Anthony Eden (1954) and 1st Earl of Avon
(See National Archives, p. 152; University of Birmingham Library, p. 11)

March 1938–Dec 1940
Halifax, 3rd Viscount, later 1st Earl

Dec 1940–July 1945
Eden, Anthony, later Sir Anthony Eden (1954) and 1st Earl of Avon
(See National Archives, p. 152; University of Birmingham Library, p. 11)

APPENDIX 2:
British Diplomats and Brazil

Most surviving correspondence of British diplomats is found within general Foreign Office files held by the Public Record Office (PRO). There are also collections of private papers of diplomats that have been deposited at the PRO or in other British or Irish archival repositories. Brazil-related private papers of the diplomats listed here have been identified, with the dates corresponding to the years they held positions in Brazil and for which Brazil-related material has been identified. Where diplomatic postings were in other countries, the years relate to the period of correspondence of Brazilian interest.

Viscount Strangford (1807–10 and 1828–30) – *(See British Library, p. 103; Leeds District Archive, p. 78)*

Henry Chamberlain (1816–18) – *(See British Library, p. 111; Royal Naval Museum, p. 224)*

Edward Thornton, Sr (1819–24) – *(See Leeds District Archive, p. 79; National Archives, p. 153)*

Richard Pitt Amherst (1823) – *(See India Office Library, pp. 124–25)*

William A'Court (1824–28) – *(See Leeds District Archive, p. 62; British Library, p. 92)*

Charles Richard Vaughan (1825–26) – *(See All Souls College, pp. 211–12)*

Robert Gordon (1826–28) – *(See British Library, pp. 104 and 108–9; Durham University Library, p. 48; Leeds District Archive, p. 79)*

John Ponsonby (1826–29) – *(See British Library, pp. 103 and 108–9; Durham University Library, pp. 47–48)*

Arthur Aston (1826–33) – *(See National Archives, p. 152)*

Woodbine Parish (1828) – *(See National Archives, p. 152)*

Robert Belgrave Hoppner (1831–33) – *(Hartley Library, Southampton, p. 230)*

George Jackson (1832–41) – *(See National Archives, p. 152)*

(continued overleaf)

Henry Stephen Fox (1833–36) – *(Hartley Library, Southampton, p. 230)*

William Gore Ouseley (1833–45) – *(Hartley Library, Southampton, p. 231)*

John Hobart Caradoc (1841–48) – *(See British Library, p. 104)*

Henry Ellis (1842–43) – *(See British Library, pp. 104 and 105)*

Charles James Hamilton (1842–46) – *(See British Library, p. 104)*

James Hudson (1845–51) – *(See Hartley Library, Southampton, p. 230)*

William Christie (1863) – *(See British Library, p. 110; National Archives, p. 153)*

Edward Thornton, Jr (1865–67) – *(See National Archives, p. 153)*

George Buckley Mathew (1867–79) – *(See Glamorgan Record Office, p. 26; Liverpool Record Office, pp. 84 and 85)*

Richard Burton (1868) – *(See Royal Geographic Society, p. 194; Wiltshire and Swindon Record Office, p. 32)*

Hugh Guion Macdonell (1885–88) – *See British Library, p. 111)*

Henry Beaumont (1897–99) – *(See Imperial War Museum, p. 120)*

Roger Casement (1906–13) – *(See National Archives, p. 165; National Library of Ireland, p. 39)*

Daniel O'Sullivan (1907–21) – *(See Trinity College Dublin, p. 41)*

Harold Beresford Hope (1914) – *(See Imperial War Museum, p. 120)*

Maurice De Bunsen (1919) – *(See Bodleian Library, p. 214)*

Leslie Fry (1963–66) – *(See India Office Library, p. 125)*

APPENDIX 3:
British-owned or -financed Railways in Brazil

Archival holdings relating to British-owned or -financed railways in Brazil are, with few exceptions, disappointing. Companies were amalgamated or liquidated, their records often destroyed, disappearing into the vaults of solicitors' offices or simply lost. For some companies, however, fragmentary construction, operational or financial records have survived. For technical material – not specific to Brazil but concerning the development of locomotives and rolling stock – the archival collections of the National Railway Museum in York [www.nrm.org.uk] may be worth consulting.

Bahia and San Francisco Railway – *(See Institution of Mechanical Engineers, p. 126; Rothschild Archive, p. 183; University College London, p. 197)*

Bahia & Timbo Railway – *(See Rothschild Archive, p. 183)*

Brazil Great Southern Railway – *(See Staffordshire Record Office, p. 235)*

Brazil Railway Company – *(See Bank of England, p. 94; National Archives, p. 162)*

Brazil Victoria Minas Railway – *(See Baring Archive, p. 97; Rothschild Archive, p. 185)*

Ceará, railways in – *(See Royal Geographic Society, p. 193)*

Central Bahia Railway – *(See Guildhall Library, p. 116)*

Great Northern Railway of Brazil – *(See National Archives, p. 139)*

Hunslet Engine Co. Ltd – *(See Leeds District Archive, p. 79)*

Leopoldina Railway – *(See National Archives, p. 140)*

Madeira-Mamoré Railway – *(See National Archives, p. 145; National Library of Ireland, p. 39; Royal Geographic Society, p. 192)*

Manaus to Boa Vista railway concession – *(See National Archives, p. 141 and p. 155)*

Mogyana Railway Company – *(See Lloyds TSB Group Archives, p. 130)*

Northern Mato Grosso Railway – *(See National Library of Scotland, p. 57)*

Porto Alegre and New Hamburg Railway – *(See National Archives, p. 146)*

São Paulo Railway – *(See National Archives, p. 158 and p. 162; Rothschild Archive, p. 183)*

Triangulo Mineiro Railway – *(See National Library of Scotland, p. 57)*

União Mineira Railway – *(See Institution of Mechanical Engineers, p. 126)*

Victoria e Natividade Railway – *(See National Library of Scotland, pp. 56–57)*

APPENDIX 4:
Natural History

There are many natural history collections described in the guide featuring manuscripts relating to exploration, ethnography and economic botany. Many such items are found in the Royal Geographic Society Archives (pp. 190–94). Readers should also direct their attention towards the papers of the following explorers, collectors and scientists:

Elizabeth Agassiz – *(See Natural History Museum, p. 178)*

David Angus – *(See National Library of Scotland, pp. 56–57)*

Joseph Banks – *(See British Library, p. 112)*

Henry Walter Bates – *(See British Library, p. 113; Natural History Museum, p. 178)*

William Burchell – *(See Royal Botanic Gardens, Kew, pp. 187–88)*

Charles Carlisle – *(See Royal Botanic Gardens, Kew, p. 188)*

Robert Cunningham – *(See Royal Botanic Gardens, Kew, p. 188)*

Charles Darwin – *(See University of Cambridge Library, pp. 19–20)*

Robert FitzRoy – *(See University of Cambridge Library, p. 20)*

George Gardner – *(See Royal Botanic Gardens, Kew, p. 188)*

Victor Gärtner – *(See Royal Botanic Gardens, Kew, p. 188)*

Rupert Gordon – *(See University of Liverpool Library, p. 90)*

William Hooker – *(See Royal Botanic Gardens, Kew, pp. 187–88)*

John Miers – *(See Natural History Museum, p. 178–79)*

Fritz Müller – *(See Royal Botanic Gardens, Kew, p. 188)*

David Charles Solander – *(See British Library, p. 112)*

Richard Spruce – *(See Royal Botanic Gardens, Kew, p. 188)*

Wolferston Thomas – *(See University of Liverpool Library, p. 89)*

H.M. Tomlinson – *(See National Library of Scotland, pp. 57–58)*

James W.H. Trail – *(See University of Aberdeen Library, p. 1)*

Alfred Russell Wallace – *(See Natural History Museum, p. 179)*

Henry Wickham – *(See Royal Botanic Gardens, Kew, p. 188; Wolverhampton Archives, p. 239)*

‎Additional Resources

The following printed and web resources are invaluable tools to help identify Brazil-related holdings of manuscripts, books and pictures in Britain and Ireland and the fast-developing electronic catalogues accessible on the internet.

Printed guides:

- Biggins, Alan, and Valerie Cooper (2002), *Latin American and Caribbean Library Resources in the British Isles* (London: Institute of Latin American Studies)

Over two hundred library collections in Britain and Ireland are listed and described. The country index allows the user to identify holdings relating to Brazil and their general strengths, such as books, newspapers and periodicals, manuscripts or photographs.

- Bloomfield, B.C. (1997), *A Directory of Rare Book and Special Collections in the UK and Republic of Ireland* (London: Library Association)

A useful guide to antiquarian and other rare books and especially helpful in understanding the British Library's collections, which are rich in Braziliana.

- Bridson, Gavin D.R., Valerie Phillips and Anthony Harvey (1980), *Natural History Manuscript Resources in the British Isles* (London: Mansell)

Archival holdings relating to natural history are described with an attempt to list individual manuscripts. The index permits the identification of items of Brazilian or general South American interest.

- Foster, Janet, and Julia Sheppard (2002), *British Archives: A Guide to Archive Resources in the United Kingdom* (Basingstoke: Palgrave)

Outlines the main areas of specialisation and contact details for several hundred national, regional and local archives in the United Kingdom.

- Helferty, Seamus, and Raymond Refaussé (1999),
Directory of Irish Archives (Dublin: Four Courts Press)

Outlines the main areas of specialisation and contact details
of some 249 archives in Ireland. Although the index does not
provide any direct help in identifying material of Brazilian interest,
it lists personal, business and organisational names which may
be helpful.

- Orbell, John, and Alison Turton (2001), *British Banking:
A Guide to Historical Records* (Aldershot: Ashgate)

General descriptions are provided of manuscript holdings in British
archival repositories relating to British banks. The volume is
especially useful for identifying the locations of papers relating to
smaller, amalgamated or otherwise defunct banks and for the histories
of the individual banks that are listed.

- Walne, Peter, ed. (1973), *A Guide to Manuscript Sources for the
History of Latin America and the Caribbean in the British Isles*
(London: Oxford University Press)

Although largely researched in the 1960s, this archive-by-archive
attempt at an inventory of manuscripts remains a useful tool for
historians of the region. Some important entries are dated, however,
due to holdings having been transferred, added to or lost.

Web resources:

- **A2A: Access to Archives**
www.a2a.pro.gov.uk

A2A: Access to Archives is a database enabling one to search across
detailed catalogues from over 130 archival repositories beyond the
National Archives (Public Record Office). Archives linked to the
database include a steadily increasing number of local record offices,
museums, university libraries, and national and specialist institutions
across England. For some of these repositories catalogues listing entire
collections may be searched, but for many others the link with *A2A* is
in an earlier stage of development.

- **Archives Hub**

  www.archiveshub.ac.uk

The *Archives Hub* provides a single point of access to descriptions of archives held by United Kingdom universities and colleges. There is a facility to enable users to search archives' electronic catalogues that make up this resource.

- **Archives Network Wales**

  www.archivesnetworkwales.info

Archives Network Wales is a web resource project allowing easy *online* searching of the key collections of documents held by county record offices, universities, museums and libraries in Wales, so that users are able to identify which repositories hold information relevant to their research or interest. Searches on 'Brazil' and 'Rio de Janeiro' reveal documents that do not also appear via general British electronic databases.

- **British Association of Picture Libraries and Agencies**

  www.bapla.org.uk

The British Association of Picture Libraries and Agencies (BAPLA) is a trade association for picture libraries, representing over four hundred companies. BAPLA's website has a search facility to enable the user to identify picture libraries likely to hold images on the general field being sort (for example, 'social history'). By following the links it is possible to access to members' websites. Many of the collections – including, for example, those of the National Maritime Museum (p. 172) and the Mary Evans Picture Library – have online catalogues.

- **Exeter Local Maritime Archives Project (ELMAP)**

  www.centres.ex.ac.uk/cmhs/ELMAP

This is a searchable *online* database of references to records with maritime and naval signicance that are held in local record offices and other archives across England and Wales. Searches on 'Brazil' and 'Rio de Janeiro' reveal documents that do not also appear via other more general electronic databases.

- **The National Register of Archives**

  www.hmc.gov.uk/nra

The *National Register of Archives (NRA)* has been created by the Historical Manuscripts Commission (HMC), the United Kingdom's central advisory body on archives and manuscripts. Established in 1869, the HMC is the principal source of information on the nature and location of records in the United Kingdom.

The indexes of the *NRA* may be searched on the web by name of individual, family or organisation to identify a repository and the collection's HMC number. Although catalogues of individual collections are not online, these are all available for consultation on open shelves in the search room of the HMC. The value of the catalogues varies enormously, ranging from detailed inventories of holdings to very general descriptions.

• Scottish Archive Network
www.scan.org.uk

The *Scottish Archive Network* was established in 1999 to create an electronic network and search room linking the catalogues of over fifty Scottish archives. The catalogues will be available via the internet, probably from 2003.

Index

Names of repositories are printed in capitals. Named archival series are printed in bold – in some cases two collections share the same name. Page references in italics indicate material found in other collections that is related to named archival series. The subjects of appendices are printed in bold italics.

see also under 'Azores', 'Madeira', 'independence', 'Royal Family, Portuguese' and 'slaves and slave trade'
postal services: 113–14
Powis Papers: Robert Clive: 3
Presbyterians: 19, 51
Prestes, Olga: see under 'Benario, Olga'
Priaulx & Le Quesne: 70
PRIAULX LIBRARY: 69–70
Priaulx, Tupper & Co.: 68
Price, David: 48
Public Record Office see under 'National Archives, Kew'
PUBLIC RECORD OFFICE OF NORTHERN IRELAND: 6–8
railways: see 'Appendix 3', 247
Ramsay, George, 12th Earl of Dalhousie: 21
Ransome & Co. Ltd, A: 209
Rawlinson Papers: 214
Recife: see under 'Pernambuco'
Recife and San Francisco (Pernambuco) Railway Company: 182
Recife Drainage Company Ltd: 130
Reckitt & Sons Ltd: 74
RECKITT'S HERITAGE: 74
Reed, Rev. G.V.: 5
Reed Family Papers: 5
refugees in Brazil: see under 'immigrants'
Reis, Alfredo: 168
Republic Ship Co.: 17
RHODES HOUSE LIBRARY: 216–20
rice: 123
Rice (Willian McPerson) Papers: 193
Richards, Dr Joan: 3–4
Rio de Janeiro: 17th and 18th-century descriptions, 54, 112, 175–76; 19th-century descriptions, 5, 20, 27, 28, 31, 35, 55, 76, 80, 115, 177, 233, 238; 20th-century descriptions, 41, 175; banks, 128–29, 198–200; British consulate, 149; fire brigade, 115; mercenaries, 38–39; merchants and trade, 6, 8, 35, 49, 62–63, 67, 68, 97, 116, 117, 122; missionaries, 19, 51; slavery, 230, 231
Rio de Janeiro City Improvements Co. Ltd: 149

Rio de Janeiro Flour Mills and Granaries Ltd: xiii
Rio de Janeiro Harbour & Dock Co. Ltd: 184
Rio de Janeiro Lighterage Co.: 117
Rio Doce Company: 31
Rio Flour: xiii
Rio Grande (Rio Grande do Sul): 115, 128
Rio Grande do Sul: iv, 3, 4, 69, 89, 115, 128, 146, 149, 184, 185, 199, 200, 206
rivers: Amazon, 90, 102, 107, 178, 179, 214; Branco, 106, 155; Madeira, 57, 192; Negro, 106, 179, 192, 193; Paraná, 21, 115; Quarahim, 235; Tacutú, 106; Tocantins, 105; see also under 'Amazon basin' and 'Booth Steamship Co. Ltd'
Robertson, Capt. William: 209
Roraima: see under 'Boa Vista' and 'British Guiana/Guyana-Brazil frontier'
Rothschild (N.M.) & Sons 93, 94, 181–86
ROTHSCHILD ARCHIVE: 181–86
Rover Co. Ltd: 34
ROYAL BOTANIC GARDENS, KEW: 186–90
Royal Family, Portuguese: court life (1810s), 57; transfer to Brazil, 7, 21, 67, 78, 138, 159, 232
ROYAL GEOGRAPHIC ARCHIVES: 190–94
Royal Mail: 113–14
Royal Mail Line: 174–75
Royal Mail Steam Packet Company: 174–75
ROYAL NAVAL MUSEUM: 223–24
Royal Navy: see under 'Admiralty', 'shipping', 'ships' names' and 'slaves and slavery'
rubber: 39, 82, 90, 123, 163, 165, 188–90, 193, 239
Rubber Corporation of Brazil Ltd: 163
Russell (Lord John) Papers: 153
Russia: 146, 227–28
sails: 45
Saco-Lowell: see under 'Platt Saco Lowell'

St Andrew's Society (Rio de Janeiro): 125
St Helena, island: 75, 103, 111, 143, 154
St John d'El Rey Mining Company: xiv, 162
St Paul's School (São Paulo): 171
St Peter Port: see under 'Island Archives, The' and 'Greffe, The'
Salisbury Papers: 1st Marquess: 71–72
Salisbury Papers: 3rd Marquess, 72–73
Salvador: see under 'Bahia'
Samuel, Phillips & Co.: 186
Santa Catarina: 9, 20, 28, 53, 81, 108, 174, 188, 233
Santa Cruz (Rio de Janeiro): 28
Santa Isabel de Paraguassa (Bahia): 192
Santarém: 54
Santo André (São Paulo): 74
Santos (São Paulo): 20, 32, 39, 115, 129, 131, 150, 194, 197, 233
Santos–Jundaí Railway: 158
São Paulo: 19th-century descriptions, 20, 115, 233; agriculture, xvi, 165; banks and finance 97, 129, 199, 200; Bienal 171; British consulate, 120, 150; coffee, 14–15, 97, 123, 197; fire brigades, 115; immigration, 14–15, 123–24, 165, 202; industry, 44, 74; railways, 124, 130, 158, 162, 181, 183; St Paul's School, 171; trade, 12, 43, 228; Sociedade Paulista de Cultura Anglo Brasileira, 171; water company, 162; see also under 'Olympia', 'Santo André', 'Santos' and 'Taubaté'
São Paulo Bienal: 171
São Paulo e Goyaz Railway: 124
São Paulo Railway Company: 158, 162, 181, 183
São Paulo Water Services: 162
Saracen Foundry: xiii
Sauvarin, Pierre: 67
sawmill engineers: 209
Schomburgk, Sir Robert H.: 11, 106, 192
Scott, Col. J.: 214
Scottish and Mercantile Investment Co. Ltd: 115
SCHOOL OF ORIENTAL AND AFRICAN STUDIES LIBRARY: 194–96
Security Services: 168

Seixas, Isabel Bezarra de: 57
Seixas Brothers & Co.: 26
Seychelles, islands: 123–24
Seymour, Sir George Francis, Papers: 238
SHETLAND ARCHIVES: 81
Shetland Islands: 81, 174
ship passenger lists: 162–63
shipping: xv, 65–67, 69–70, 80, 94, 99, 103–4, 113–17, 178, 200, 206, 207; see also under 'Admiralty' and 'ships' names'
ships' names:
Achilles, HMS, 206
Alert, 175
Argyle, 209
Beagle, HMS, 19–20, 233
Beeswing, 16–17
Brecon, HMS, 176
Bristol, HMS, 120
Briton, HMS, 263
Cadmus, HMS, 176
Canada, 153
Canopus, HMS, 120
Centaur, HMS, 30
Columbine, HMS, 174
Conway, HMS, 176
Cornwall, HMS, 120
Crown, 84
Cyclops, HMS, 30
Devastation, HMS, 75
Dryad, HMS, 176
Eclair, HMS, 65
Endeavour, HMS, 112
Europa, 123
Kelbergen, 120
Gorgon, HMS, 75
Margaret Richardson, 54
Marlborough, HMS, 21
Minas Gerais, 173
Minho, 228
Narcissus, HMS, 21, 176
Quito, 5
Reindeer, HMS, 139
Republic, 17
Rio de Janeiro, 173
Sapphire, HMS, 193
Sirena, 30
Spartan, HMS, 6
Spiteful, HMS, 176

122, 154, 156–7; see also under 'banks and banking', 'coffee', 'merchants and merchant houses', 'shipping' and 'slaves and slavery'
Trail, James W.H: 1
trams: 117
Treasury (British government): 161–62
Triangulo Mineiro Railway: 57
Trinidade, island: 72, 164, 223
TRINITY COLLEGE LIBRARY, DUBLIN: 40–41
Triple Alliance, War of: see under 'Paraguayan War'
Turnball, Peter Evan: 60
Tweedales & Smalley Ltd.: 226
umbrellas: 204
União Mineira Railway: 126
United Commission of Arbitration: 2
United Kingdom Atomic Energy Authority: 169–70
United Provinces of the Rio de la Plata: see Argentina
United States: 86, 110, 153, 175, 210–11, 221
United States Naval Mission in Brazil: 175
UNIVERSITY COLLEGE LONDON LIBRARY: 196–200
UNIVERSITY OF ABERDEEN LIBRARY: 1
UNIVERSITY OF BIRMINGHAM LIBRARY: 10–11
UNIVERSITY OF DUNDEE ARCHIVES: 45–46
UNIVERSITY OF HULL: 75–76
UNIVERSITY OF LIVERPOOL LIBRARY: 87–90
UNIVERSITY OF NOTTINGHAM: 208–9
UNIVERSITY OF SOUTHAMPTON: 228–33
UNIVERSITY OF WARWICK LIBRARY: 33–34
urban layout: 115
Uruguay: 28, 139, 147, 150, 152, 230, 235
U.S. & Brazil Mail Steamship Company: 195–96
utility companies: see under 'electricity', 'gas', 'trams', etc.

valorisation, coffee: 94, 97, 182
Vaughan (Sir Charles Richard) Papers: 210–11
Venezuela: 141, 157
Vereker, Commander F.C.P.: 193
Vernon (Captain George) Narrative: 175
Vestey Group: xvi
Vickers Archive: 21–22
Victoria e Natividade Railway: 56–57
Vieira, Father Antonio: 106
Villiers, George: 151
Villiers, John Charles: 78
Vitória: see under 'Espírito Santo'
Wallace, Alfred Russel: *178*, 179
War Office: 167
Ward, John William, Viscount Dudley: 109
WARWICKSHIRE COUNTY RECORD OFFICE: 238
water: 62, 115, 137, 162, 163
Waurá: 3
Webb, Henry Bellamy: 96
Wednesbury: 9
Weerdenbuch, Col. Gen.: 134
Weil, Bruno: 201
Wellesley (Richard Colley, 1st Marquess) Papers: 111
Wellesley, Capt. W.: 193
Wellington (Arthur Wellesley, 1st Duke) Papers: 232–33
Welsh in South America: 4
WEST SUSSEX RECORD OFFICE: 29–30
West Yorkshire Archive Service: see under 'Bradford District Archive' and 'Leeds District Archive'
Western Telegraph Co. Ltd: 197–98, *221–22*
whaling: 53, 81, 153, 174
wheat: 184
Whitehead, J.J.: 193
Wickham, Lady, Diary: 239
Wickham, Sir Henry Alexander: 188, *239*
WIENER LIBRARY, THE: 200–1
WIGAN ARCHIVE SERVICE: 80
Wilberforce, William: 217
Wilson (General Sir Robert Thomas) Journals: 112

Lightning Source UK Ltd.
Milton Keynes UK
UKOW04f0917140714

235079UK00001B/106/P